LESSONS FROM PRIVATIZATION

LESSONS
FROM
PRIVATIZATION

LABOUR ISSUES IN DEVELOPING
AND TRANSITIONAL COUNTRIES

edited by Rolph Van der Hoeven
and Gyorgy Sziraczki

INTERNATIONAL LABOUR OFFICE   GENEVA

Van der Hoeven, R.; Sziraczki, G.
Lessons from privatization: Labour issues in developing and transitional countries
Geneva, International Labour Office, 1997

/Case study/, /privatization/, /employment/, /Labour relations/, /trend/, /Bulgaria/, /Czech Republic/, /East/, /Germany/, /Hungary/, /India/, /Korea R/, /Mexico/. 03.04.6
ISBN 92-2-109452-9

ILO Cataloguing in Publication Data

Printed by the International Labour Office, Geneva, Switzerland

Preface

The process of privatization has increased rapidly since the second half of the 1980s. In developing countries privatization often took place in the general climate of stabilization, adjustment and debt reduction, while in countries in transition the systemic changes included several waves of privatization. The present volume looks especially at the employment and labour market consequences of privatization. Based upon more than 20 case studies, the chapters consider the effects of privatization on productivity and the level and structure of employment in general. For two countries, Hungary and Mexico, the privatization of telecommunications, one of the sectors of the economy currently being widely privatized, is looked into in more detail. The evolving patterns of industrial relations in privatized firms and the subsequent changes in wage systems and non-wage benefits are also examined.

Despite the wide range in levels of economic development and in the social and economic systems of the countries where privatization took place, the volume still distils a number of common lessons. One of the principal lessons is that privatization should not be an end in itself. In cases where it was regarded as such, it often failed. For privatization to be successful for the new owners of enterprises, for workers in the enterprises and for the economy as a whole, the various case studies show clearly that it should be part of a medium-term policy and a logical component of a healthy private sector with well-functioning goods, capital and labour markets in a system of democratic control. Absence of one or more of these conditions is often bound to lead to insurmountable opposition to privatization or to the creation of monopolies, which don't produce efficiently and in which industrial relations deteriorate. The first chapter of this volume therefore discusses the conditions under which employment opportunities and efficiency gains are possible under various forms of privatization.

This volume is a product of the Interdepartmental Project on Employment and Structural Adjustment which was managed by Rolph van der Hoeven in cooperation with the Employment Department, where Gyorgy Sziraczki was responsible for work on privatization.

Werner Sengenberger
Director
Employment Department

Acknowledgements

The work for this volume was undertaken as part of the ILO's Interdepartmental Project on Structural Adjustment in cooperation with the Employment Department. Many people were associated with this project and have provided us with valuable advice and assistance. We would like first and foremost to thank Jack Martin, former Assistant Director-General of the ILO, who initiated the interdepartmental activities and who gave us support throughout. Special thanks go to Rashid Amjad, Jacques Gaude, Rafael Gijon von Kleist, Max Iacono, Eddy Lee, Andrès Marinakis, João Oliveira, Hedva Sarfati, Michael Sebastian, Werner Sengenberger and Zafar Shaheed. Susan Porter, from the beginning of the project, and Margaret Roberts, later on, have been helpful in the production while Caroline Hartnell edited the manuscript with great skill. John McLin and Andrès Marinakis of the ILO and Colin Kirkpatrick of Bradford University provided useful advice at the end stage of the activities.

Contents

List of tables

1. Privatization and labour issues

Rolph van der Hoeven and Gyorgy Sziraczki*

Transferring the formal political and economic rules of successful Western market economies to third world and Eastern European economies is not a sufficient condition for good economic performance. Privatization is not a panacea for solving poor economic performance. [1]

Many countries have launched privatization schemes, often as part of a public sector reform or a structural adjustment programme. Privatization usually involves restructuring and changes in management and enterprise behaviour, all with far-reaching effects on employment and labour relations. This book assesses some of the labour market consequences of recent privatization schemes in a number of developing countries and transition economies, involving about 20 case studies. Some of the case studies in this book deal with completed or nearly completed privatization exercises (such as those in the Republic of Korea, Chapter 2; former Eastern Germany, Chapter 6; Czech Republic, Chapter 7; and the telecommunications sector in Hungary, Chapter 8; and Mexico, Chapter 4) with a view to drawing lessons for labour issues from these. Others describe ongoing processes of privatization (such as in India, Chapter 3; and Bulgaria, Chapter 5) emphasizing the consequences for labour through these processes. Among the issues considered is the effect of privatization on productivity and on the level and structure of employment, including changes in employment and job security, employment practices and forms of employment contracting. The evolving patterns of industrial relations in privatized firms and the subsequent changes in wages, remuneration systems and non-wage benefits are also examined. This chapter provides a general discussion and highlights some of the findings of the country studies.

1. The objectives and scope of privatization

Privatization has different meanings to different people. Three distinct kinds of activities which can be privatized may be distinguished. First are those performed by public enterprises which operate in a competitive market (e.g. plants producing consumer goods or capital goods). Second are those activities performed by public enterprises which operate in a monopoly situation, and can be subdivided into "natural" monopolies (electricity, gas, water) and "artificial" monopolies created by limiting the ability of other enterprises, either

---

* International Labour Office.

foreign or domestic, to enter the market (car factories are often a case in point). A third kind of activity involves the contracting out of public services, such as garbage collection and the prison service. In contrast to other types of privatization, there are no individual products or services sold to individuals; rather, the State enters into lump-sum or piecemeal contracts to pay for services. Although this form of privatization is often controversial and gaining in importance, especially in the United States and certain parts of Europe, case studies in this volume concentrate mainly on privatization of enterprises which sell products or services to the public. As to the process of privatization itself one can distinguish various forms of privatization (Kikeri et al. 1992). Kühl (Chapter 6) distinguishes three basic forms of privatization, i.e. *political privatization* where all citizens are provided with shares or vouchers of state enterprises regardless of their economic viability, their capital stock and their management, *fiscal privatization* where firms are sold to the highest bidder in order to increase public revenues; and *economic privatization*, in which the government or a government agency manages the restructuring and negotiates clauses on employment, social benefits, training and redundancies with potential private entrepreneurs. Political privatization has been, and still is, applied in various countries in transition, while fiscal and economic privatization is applied in both transition and developing economies.

In order to assess privatization properly it might be relevant to recollect briefly the reasons why public enterprises were created in the first place. One reason for establishing public enterprises has been *national security*: public defence industries and public transport enterprises have often been created for this reason. Another reason has been to ease *revenue raising*: product procurement and marketing boards have often served this end, especially in cases where tax collection would be difficult or impossible. *Economic control and self-reliance* have been another important motive behind the creation of public enterprises. Another has been provided by the infant industry argument, with protection extending into ownership. *The lack of private investment* for undertaking large-scale activities has been a powerful incentive for the creation of public enterprises, especially in poorer developing countries. *Equity considerations* have frequently played a role in the establishment of public enterprises, or in the taking over by the public sector of private enterprises which are not functioning profitably any more. Finally, *the fear of a private monopoly situation* has often resulted in the establishment of public enterprises, which it was assumed would use the monopoly revenues in the public interest.

Privatization of public enterprises is often advocated in cases where the original reasons for establishing such enterprises are not seen to be relevant any more (for example, where well-functioning capital markets have emerged which were absent earlier) or where the management of public enterprises, because of multiple demands, has been inefficient (or corrupt in certain cases), thus diminishing the profit to the State or increasing the losses the State is incurring. In most cases, however, privatization is a political act, undertaken as part of a broader structural adjustment or economic transformation programme. The very act of privatization is often used as a signal to domestic and international markets that a new economic climate is about to be established. As we will discuss later, some of the more far-reaching privatization programmes in Latin America have been in effect the outcome of "debt for equity" swaps as part of a debt reduction strategy, with the implicit expectation of not only reducing public sector debts but also of gaining access to international capital markets in order to obtain fresh funds to replace technologically obsolete capital. They have also induced foreign investors to bring in new money: in the early 1990s one-third to over half of all foreign and domestic investment in Latin America and Eastern Europe has been for privatization (Sader, 1995).

The fact that privatization is often undertaken in tandem with other economic reforms makes it difficult to evaluate its effects separately. The success or failure of privatization is often closely related to the success or failure of the whole economic reform process. Frequently, lay-offs and retrenchments in government itself dominate the political discussion around privatization of public sector enterprises. It is therefore difficult, and often impossible, to develop a counter-factual relating to what would have happened in the absence of privatization, other things being equal. For this reason, in this book we have followed the more modest approach of discussing the results of privatization along the lines of a number of case studies.

A further complication in assessing the effects of privatization is that economic theory is generally agnostic about ownership. According to Killick and Commander (1988), "while mainstream economic theory does point to preferability of competition it is actually silent on the ownership issue." Adam et al. (1992) therefore advance the notion of principal-agent behaviour. The principal is the owner of the enterprise and the agent is the manager. These two do not necessarily have the same objectives. The objectives of the public sector as owner may be different from those of a private person as owner, while the manager, too, will have his or her own preference function. The complex question then becomes: to what extent does ownership influence management? Added to the interaction between owner and manager is another factor, namely that the freedom of the manager (or agent) is determined not only by the owner of the enterprise but also by the whole gamut of regulations which govern product and factor markets. If, for example, competition is seen as the best vehicle to increase efficiency, a change in ownership in the absence of changes in regulations to allow for competition will not result in increased efficiency but in rents being transferred from public sector entrepreneurs (or bureaucrats in the public sector cashing in on these rents) to private sector entrepreneurs, who would be more than willing to pay a high price for a protected enterprise allowing them to cash in on rents. Yet privatization often is recommended on the implicit premise that the process in itself will create less protection and more competition.

One reason for privatization that is often advanced is that it generates revenue for the government. However, a study for the International Monetary Fund (IMF) argues that, in theory, the fiscal advantages are the same, over the long run, under private or public ownership (Hemming and Mansoor, 1988). The reasons for this are easy to understand. Where there are perfect markets and perfect discounting, the (asset) price of the enterprise is determined by the expected discounted future flow of revenues, and in a competitive market the enterprise will be sold for that price — this is the assumption made in many privatization programmes. Hence, all that is involved is a portfolio shift between public and private sector, in which the public sector exchanges an asset with a future stream of revenue for instant payment. The proceeds of privatization could be invested in bonds in order to ensure a future stream of income or used to reduce public debt, thus lowering future debt payments. Although many developing and industrialized countries alike have advocated privatization in order to obtain current financing, an evaluation of privatization practices in Latin America shows that revenue from privatization sales has done little to reduce fiscal deficits (Pinheiro and Schneider, 1994), although in some cases it helped to reduce future government subsidies to loss-making public enterprises.

2. An overview of privatization activities

The considerations advanced in the previous section led to the establishment of many state-owned enterprises in developing countries, following independence. By the early 1980s state-owned enterprises accounted for 17 per cent of GDP in Africa and 12 per cent in Latin America, but only 3 per cent in Asia (excluding China, India and Myanmar) (Kikeri et al, 1992). On average 45 per cent of domestic capital formation in developing countries was effected by state-owned enterprises (Pfeffermann and Madarassy, 1992). In Eastern Europe state-owned enterprises were responsible for up to 90 per cent of total domestic production. Privatization has increased rapidly since the second half of the 1980s for two distinct reasons. For many developing countries, in the general climate of stabilization and adjustment policies and programmes to decrease the debt burden, privatization was seen as an omnibus policy which could *reduce the budget deficit* by forgoing subsidies to public enterprises, *reduce debt* by writing down the proceeds received from the sale of public enterprises, *stimulate private sector investment* and thus lower public sector investment, *signal a new political climate* and *increase the efficiency of former state-owned enterprises.* While these privatization programmes started to take place in developing countries, the systemic changes in Eastern Europe also induced several waves of privatization. The motive here was to change from a command economy to a market economy rather than budgetary objectives.

A third factor which has certainly contributed to privatization in developing countries is the imitation of privatization efforts in industrialized countries, which came into vogue in the early 1980s. Since privatization in industrialized countries often involves large entities, the number of sales in industrialized countries is far lower than that in developing and Eastern European countries, but the proceeds of sales were superior until very recently. In 1992, however, the total volume of sales in developing countries was for the first time larger than that in industrialized countries (US$23 billion versus US$17 billion). In 1993 the picture was again reversed (Sader, 1995).

Privatization in developing countries has often taken place in sectors which had a monopoly or were very labour-intensive, attributes which made them candidates for public sector ownership at an early stage. Privatization was often popularized by pointing to the poor quality of products and services delivered by many state-owned enterprises. Over the period 1988-93 privatization sales amounted to US$96 billion, of which: US$32 billion came from sales in infrastructure sectors, including electricity, transportation and telecommunications; US$25.7 billion from sales of manufacturing enterprises, especially chemicals; and US$20 billion from sales of financial institutions.

However, these global distribution figures represent a differing regional pattern. Given that Latin American privatization revenues represent two-thirds of all privatization in developing countries, its overall sectoral distribution has a great influence on the total picture. The Latin American picture is in turn heavily dominated by privatization in Argentina, Mexico and Venezuela. Privatization in East Asia is dominated by infrastructural projects, while in South Asia sales of manufacturing enterprises amounted to almost 50 per cent of total sales (see table 1.1).

The picture in Eastern Europe is rather different. Privatization of infrastructure was of limited importance between 1988 and 1993, the period when Eastern European countries

Table 1.1. Sectoral distribution of privatization by region, 1988-93
(percentage unless otherwise indicated)

Sector/region	Primary sector	Industry	Infra-structure	Financial services	Other	Total amount in US$ billion
Latin America	15	18	41	24	2	55.2
Europe and Central Asia	8	50	11	21	10	17.9
East Asia and Pacific	6	29	45	10	10	16.1
South Asia	22	44	4	24	6	6.0
Sub-Saharan Africa	25	7	1	4	63	2.4
North Africa and Middle East	7	39	8	34	12	0.7

Source: Sader, 1995.

started their move from a planned economy to the market system. Reforms started with "small" privatization, through which governments divested themselves of such small assets in the service sector as restaurants, shops, retail units and service workshops. Progress was also made in agriculture, the urban housing stock and the restitution of property confiscated by previous regimes. All this was followed, within a short period of time, by the second wave of privatization, which involved the commercialization of medium and large-scale industrial enterprises and their transfer into private hands. Some countries are progressing slowly, while others, especially Germany, the Czech Republic and to some extent Hungary, had almost completed this task by the mid-1990s. Since then, the focus of privatization has shifted to the infrastructure.

The various case studies in this book confirm this general picture. In *developing regions* the key issues have become the ways in which efficiency can be increased and public deficits reduced through privatization. In *Mexico*, growing foreign debt and fiscal crises induced the Government to launch a privatization programme in 1982. Since then almost 900 state-owned enterprises have been privatized, including Telmex (Teléfonos de México), the third largest company in the country. Revenues from privatization have been used to reduce internal debts and to finance an increase in social expenditures.

In the *Republic of Korea*, privatization has been one component of the Government's economic liberalization policy. The latest privatization scheme started in 1987, when the Privatization Proceeding Committee decided on a partial or total divestment of 11 public companies. By selling shares, the Government expected to ease its financial burden, generate revenues for social development and give a boost to the stock market.

India has taken a cautious approach to privatization. This is due to the country's employment situation, the Government's fear of large-scale job losses and a fierce opposition to privatization, mainly from trade unions. Privatization has been, perhaps as a deliberate strategy, decentralized and diluted to take the route of deregulation and partial divestment. The emphasis is on reducing support to loss-making firms, increasing the autonomy of public enterprises, easing entry barriers for private firms, expanding private sector involvement in the management of partially privatized enterprises, and encouraging competition in the economy.

In *Central and Eastern Europe*, where the national economies were state-managed until the end of the 1980s, privatization has been a fundamental element in the process of creating a competitive market environment. The speed of reforms, however, varies greatly among the different countries. *Germany* has pursued a policy of rapid reorganization and privatization of all state-owned enterprises of the former German Democratic Republic (GDR). It was implemented by the Treuhandanstalt (THA), a public institution set up in July 1990. As owner of the bulk of state-owned companies, the THA initially controlled thousands of firms with a total workforce of 4.1 million, about half the total workforce in the GDR in 1989. Privatization of these firms was based on a managed economic process, which the German authorities preferred above that of political privatization by providing all citizens with shares or vouchers, or in the form of fiscal privatization by selling firms to the highest bidders irrespective of economic effects. Between mid-1990 and mid-1993, 12,360 firms were partially or wholly privatized. The remaining 1,900 THA-owned firms had been transferred, with a few exceptions, to private owners or to local authorities by the end of 1994, thus completing the privatization process in eastern Germany.

Some Central and Eastern European countries have managed, within a short period of time, to establish the basic conditions for private sector development, including the adoption of laws and regulations related to private ownership, and the creation of product and labour markets. In *Hungary* new small-scale private firms are mushrooming, and the privatization of small-scale service and retail units is complete; the demonopolization and commercialization of state firms, through the creation of a string of limited liability companies and joint stock companies out of the old conglomerates in the state sector has also been completed. Since mid-1995, the Government's privatization policy has focused its attention on public utilities (power stations, energy distribution systems and telecommunications) and on the remaining national companies in a monopoly position (oil refineries, gas stations, pipelines, etc.). *Bulgaria* embarked on market-oriented reforms somewhat later than Hungary. However, since the Bulgarian Parliament adopted the Transformation and Privatization Law in the spring of 1992, the process of denationalization has accelerated. By 1995, the private sector's contribution to the GDP had reached 45 per cent. (The same figure for Hungary and the Czech Republic was 60 per cent and 70 per cent, respectively.)

The Government of the *Czech Republic* has pursued a policy of rapid privatization. The restitution of property, "small" privatizations and the encouragement of entrepreneurship had created thousands of small businesses employing more than 600,000 workers by mid-1994, while most large enterprises have been transferred to new owners through the voucher scheme. The first round of voucher privatization took place in 1992 and 1993, and involved 1,500 enterprises. Through the scheme about 8.5 million citizens gained ownership rights in the former state-owned firms. The second round started in autumn 1993 and came to an end in 1995. The Government has thus implemented a speedy and radical privatization programme, leaving the uneasy task of restructuring enterprises and shedding labour to the new owners.

3. Will privatization increase efficiency and employment?

3.1 Efficiency effects

Privatization is widely expected to promote productivity and efficiency. However, this largely depends on whether an environment exists in which privatized firms can operate efficiently and, even if it does exist, on how efficiently individual firms operate. The case studies show a rather varied picture. The performance of 15 firms in the Republic of Korea, privatized in the early 1980s, suggests that not all firms benefited equally from the change in ownership. While six firms showed increases in efficiency, two actually declined in efficiency after privatization. For the other seven firms, the effects were not significant. Five companies privatized since the late 1980s also display mixed performances. In two firms productivity has improved, while in the others it has remained unchanged (see Chapter 2). Whether the improvements are as a direct result of privatization, or the result of an economy-wide reorganization of production is, for reasons explained earlier, difficult to say. Incomplete market structures, continued government regulation and interference in enterprise-level decision-making, and neglected human resources management have been suggested as causes of the failure of some enterprises to improve their operation.

The experience of India is also instructive. Industrial malaise is pervasive not only among public enterprises but also in the private sector, owing to bureaucratic controls and firms' soft budget constraints; privatization by itself has not increased efficiency. Deregulation and the creation of a market environment conducive to technological, product and process innovation, which would provide a firm basis for the growth of productivity and the long-term viability of enterprises, stand out as issues still to be tackled in many countries.

Cook and Kirkpatrick (1995) argue that there has been comparatively little attention given in privatization programmes outside the OECD to monopoly regulation. Legislative controls and the development of institutions to prevent collusion, price fixing and predatory pricing practices have long attained a degree of maturity in the OECD economies but this is in marked contrast to the situation in developing countries where few had restrictive business practice legislation. The lack of development towards competition policy in developing countries can in part be explained by the high demands it places on administrative capacity that is already known to be weak and subject to manipulation by influential interest groups.

In Central and Eastern Europe, cuts in subsidies, the collapse of the CMEA market and trade liberalization have left most firms in a hopelessly uncompetitive situation because of their obsolete technology and the poor quality of their products. The success of privatization depends largely on whether it is accompanied by a restructuring and modernization of enterprises. In eastern Germany, a survey of industrial firms revealed that productivity has increased much faster in privatized firms than in those waiting to be privatized (see Chapter 6). Workforce reductions apart, the most important sources of productivity gains are innovations both in products and production processes and in firm-specific training programmes. Modernization of capital equipment, adequate supplies of materials, smaller production units and a more efficient organization of production have also contributed to increased productivity. Whereas many old firms produce a considerable range of goods and services, the privatized firms tend to concentrate their production on a very limited range. This picture from eastern Germany is confirmed by evidence from Bulgaria and Hungary showing that those firms that cannot gain access to resources and modern technology through privatization are rapidly disappearing.

3.2 Employment effects

What are the employment effects of privatization? This question, which is often raised, is difficult to answer in the abstract. The first thing to be clarified is whether we are talking about the effects on workers in the enterprises to be privatized or the effects on workers in the rest of the economy. It is also important to be clear whether employment is being looked at from a static, short-term point of view or from a dynamic, long-term one. Usually privatization will involve immediate job losses since the introduction of more capital-intensive techniques in a period of slow growth — a characteristic of the general setting in which many privatization exercises take place — will lead to less demand for labour. In these cases, the direct employment effects depend on the bargaining power of the workers in the privatized enterprise (Edgren, 1990). The employment effects for workers in the rest of the economy are limited. Growth in employment in privatized enterprises can be expected over the longer run, stemming from a supposed increase in their profitability which might result in more investment and greater labour demand. Another positive effect can be expected from greater forward and backward linkages of the privatized industry.

The magnitude of the employment effect of privatization is determined by the relative share of public enterprise employment in total employment, the number of lay-offs expected just before or after privatization, and the potential of the economy to generate employment for those who have been laid off both immediately and in the longer run. Many of these factors are not dependent on the privatization process *per se* but on general economic and social policies, some of which are linked to the process of privatization but many of which are not.

The share of public enterprise employment in total employment varies widely among developing and developed countries alike. Heller and Tait (1983) give an overview of the situation in the early 1980s for the various regions of the world. If public enterprise employment is represented as a share in non-agricultural employment, then the employment share in developing countries is more than three times as large as for the developed countries, with the lowest share in Latin America and the highest in Africa and Asia (the latter due to the high share of India and China). However, if public enterprise employment is represented as a share in total population (as a rough proxy for total labour force) then the situation for industrialized countries and developing countries becomes fairly similar, with Africa and Latin America having a lower share and Asia a higher share than the industrialized market economies.

Marinakis (1992) has investigated changes in public enterprise employment over time. Despite the increased attention given to privatization, amazingly little analysis has been made of employment issues. Marinakis looked at various data sets and compared general government employment growth and total public sector growth (the latter being the sum of general government employment and public enterprise employment), and found

Table 1.2. Public sector employment growth, 1980-85 (percentage growth rate)

Africa		General government employment	Total public sector employment
Africa	1975-80	6.4	3.8
	1980-85	4.9	3.9
	1985-latest	3.7	−0.8
Asia	1975-80	4.1	6.8
	1980-85	4.3	2.6
	1985-latest	4.1	3.6
Latin America	1975-80	2.1	3.9
	1980-85	4.1	2.9
	1985-latest	0.4	1.2

Source: Marinakis (1992), table 5.

that the growth of total public sector employment had been much slower or even negative, especially during the second half of the 1980s (table 1.2). The possible exception was Latin America, where general government employment was seriously compressed because of the debt crisis and where in the 1980s some of the general government activities were transferred to public enterprises. What emerges is that the percentage share in employment of public enterprises in most developing countries is relatively small and that employment growth in public enterprises was often modest or negative even before privatization took place. The effect of privatization on total employment in developing countries can therefore be deemed to be small.

This does not, of course, mean that the issue of employment can be neglected, as is all too often the case, but it does point to a situation where measures to deal with the immediate effects of privatization should be taken in the realm of labour market policies — negotiated severance pay, retraining programmes, support for the establishment of small and medium-sized enterprises, etc. — as would be applicable in normal restructuring processes.

Several of the case studies support the general picture sketched above. In the Republic of Korea hardly any employees have been laid off because of privatization. This can be attributed to the performance of the economy and the enterprises concerned, and to the guarantee of both employment and of job protection in the privatized firms. In the few cases where the level of employment was reduced after privatization, this was achieved by freezing recruitment and offering generous retirement schemes.

The picture just described for most of the developing countries is not, however, correct for countries in Eastern Europe. There, public enterprises were the backbone of the economy and responsible for a large share of total output; rather than being single production units they provided social infrastructure for a large part of the population (table 1.3). In addition, enterprises under soft budget constraints tended to hoard much more labour than they actually needed to meet production targets. This was "rational" behaviour in a centrally planned economy because the larger a firm was in terms of employment, the more

Table 1.3. Employment share of the private sector in some Central and Eastern European countries (as a percentage)

	1989	1994
Czech Republic	1.0[b]	57.4[a]
Eastern Germany	2.1[d]	78.4[e]
Hungary	21.6[f]	57.0[a]
Poland	33.3[c]	55.1
Slovakia	0.7[b]	28.3[a]

[a] Including employment in mixed ownership and in institutions such as civic associations, churches etc. Source: National Labour Force Surveys: Czech Republic, Winter 93/94; Hungary, 3rd quarter 1994; Poland, August 1994; Slovakia, 3rd quarter 1994. [b] Yearly average figures. Source: *National Statistical Yearbook*, 1990. [c] Source: *National Statistical Yearbook*, 1991. [d] Self-employment including helping family members. Source: *Statistical Yearbook of the German Democratic Republic*, 1989. [e] Source: data provided by the German Federal Statistical Office, 1995. [f] Including employment in private business, members of cooperatives, self-employed and unpaid family workers. Source: Hungarian Statistical Yearbook, 1989.

bargaining power its management had in securing subsidies, preferences and special treatment from the planners (Kornai, 1980). Because of the sheer size of public enterprises and the high level of labour surpluses, it is intuitively clear that the employment effects of privatization cannot be dealt with in the realm of normal or additional labour market policies. Its direct and indirect effects have to be part of a larger social, economic and political calculus which takes into account not only the immediate effects but also the second- and higher-order effects of privatization.

In most Eastern European countries, privatization — accompanied by redundancies and the introduction of hard budget constraints on enterprises — has resulted in large-scale job losses. This has created a pool of unemployed workers which often cannot be absorbed by other privatized firms or new firms (Jackman, 1994). Furthermore, as has been demonstrated clearly in the case of the former USSR, many workers never appear in the unemployment statistics because, either before or after the privatization process, they are sent on leave without pay or with very much reduced pay (Standing, 1994, 1995; Windell et al., 1995). It is therefore not surprising that in many Eastern European countries the speed of privatization has been slowed because of the fear of its social and political consequences.

In the case of telecommunications, an industry that involves rapid technological changes, slight gradual reductions in employment have been observed. However, the reduction in employment took place in both public and privatized enterprises and has often been the consequence of technological development rather than of privatization *per se*. The restructuring of the various Hungarian telecommunications companies provides a good example of this. In Mexico, the April 1989 labour contract, which paved the way for the privatization of Telmex, not only provided employment protection but also introduced a flexible labour relations framework to accommodate new technologies and rationalization. Thus, while employment was secured, management obtained greater flexibility to redeploy workers within the company. Ultimately the combination of employment security and job flexibility (agreed in management-union negotiations) benefited both parties. Some argue, however, that the win-win situation for workers and management was partly due to a favourable set of regulations and generous concessions for price increases (Galal et al., 1994).

It is easy to provide safeguards in profitable and expanding companies but hardly possible in contracting and unviable firms. In Pakistan, where many public enterprises are grossly overstaffed, the privatization of manufacturing firms has sometimes led to substantial job losses. But most of the job losses in Pakistan's public sector are the consequence of restrictions in the government sector itself. The number of job losses in privatized industries is relatively small and often voluntary (Kemal, 1993). In Central and Eastern Europe, redundancies have occurred on a massive scale in the wake of economic reform, privatization and the resultant restructuring. For example, an ILO survey carried out in 1992 has shown that between December 1989 and December 1991 industrial employment in Bulgaria fell by 31.3 per cent, with no significant difference between state-owned and commercialized companies (Standing et al., 1993). In eastern Germany, privatized firms employed about 1 million workers in October 1995, which was about one-quarter of the number employed in the THA controlled firms at the beginning of the privatization process four years before. In total, about 3 million jobs were destroyed owing to restructuring and privatization.

The case studies demonstrate that any attempt to assess the impact of privatization on employment is confronted by the same difficulties as those encountered when assessing the effect of privatization on efficiency. One needs to separate the impact of the privatization measures from other policy changes that occurred at the same time. This is particularly problematic when privatization forms part of a more general process of economic reform — not to mention changes in product markets and the impact of enterprise restructuring.

In addition, it would be desirable to consider the effects that emerge over the longer term. Ideally, this requires a data set that enables one to assess the significance of the various factors associated with privatization measures. Unfortunately, the comprehensive database required for this kind of analysis is not available. Only tentative conclusions may therefore be drawn from country reports and case studies, with many questions concerning the impact of privatization on efficiency and employment remaining unanswered.

It seems that in the short term the employment effect will be either negative or to preserve the status quo. (In many cases privatization *per se* does not seem to be the main cause of employment reduction.) But what is likely to happen in the longer run is less clear from the available studies. Some argue that privatization will increase the capacity of the economy to create employment by generating more resources for investment and growth (Vuylsteke, 1988; World Bank, 1995). Others disagree: while private industry has demonstrated a higher capacity for generating productive employment through a more efficient use of both capital and labour, this does not mean that privatizing existing public enterprises will generate more employment in the long run (Edgren, 1990). Without an improved database for systematic analysis, the question of whether or not the employment-generating potential of the economy will be increased by a transfer of ownership remains difficult to answer.

4. Privatization and labour retrenchment: Employment policy responses

In many cases privatization results in labour retrenchment. Privatization can be very difficult unless special measures are implemented to help cushion the negative impact on employment. The country studies point to three major groups of possible policy measures.

The first group actually consists of measures to delay employment reduction or spread it over a longer period after privatization. In many cases, privatization includes arrangements to protect employment in a privatized enterprise for a specific period after the change in ownership. Subsidized short-time working, widely used in eastern Germany, is another measure used. Such arrangements have helped to smooth the implementation of a privatization process, and a more favourable macroeconomic environment may have emerged by the time the employment protection arrangements have expired. The main disadvantages of such measures are obviously that they tend to slow down employment adjustment and might involve a financial burden on the State and the employers concerned. On the other hand, increased unemployment benefits are avoided. The debate should thus be carried on at a broader level than that of the enterprise. Freezing of recruitment and early retirement have also been used to minimize the number of redundancies and ease the transition.

A second group of policy measures relates to severance payment regulations and a system of early warning for mass lay-offs. Such measures have been implemented in a number of countries. Payments to laid-off employees have varied from the minimum legally required severance pay to more generous ad hoc compensation (Kemal, 1993). But some Eastern European case studies have noted that these measures have sometimes been circumvented by unfair managerial practices (Sziraczki, 1988). Employers have, for example, laid off workers in small numbers, thus evading the necessity of observing the stricter regulations relating to mass redundancies. Furthermore, where a large company has been split into small firms, collective agreements and employment contracts have sometimes been modified in such a way that the workers have lost their seniority rights and severance pay entitlement (see Chapter 8).

Another form of compensatory measure involves bonuses for employees who resign voluntarily instead of severance pay for retrenched workers. To secure political support for privatization and the cooperation of the unions, the governments in Pakistan and the Republic of Korea have offered generous termination payments for employees who voluntarily leave overstaffed companies after privatization. In Pakistan, for example, out of the almost 17,000 workers employed in the newly privatized industrial enterprises in the early 1990s, 43 per cent left with a "golden handshake". As a consequence, a massive employment reduction was achieved without any involuntary retrenchment. But the scheme entailed considerable costs to the Government, and it also backfired on the enterprises. The "golden handshake" provision encouraged the most productive workers to quit, leaving relatively less productive workers with the firm (Kemal, 1993).

The third group of policy measures aims to facilitate the reintegration of laid-off workers into other forms of employment. Such measures have included job search and mobility assistance, retraining or vocational training, and job creation schemes. The development of business advisory services and credit facilities linked to enterprise restructuring or privatization projects has enhanced the mobility of some groups of laid-off employees, while public works programmes have provided temporary employment opportunities for those threatened by long-term unemployment. Counselling and support mechanisms for the general promotion of entrepreneurship, the enhancement of productivity growth and the development of micro, small and medium-sized enterprises have also played an important role in generating new jobs. Evidence about the relative magnitude and effectiveness of these programmes is still scattered, however, and it remains unclear how many workers have found new jobs through these special measures and how many additional jobs have been created. Oliveira (1993), for example, cautions against too much expectation from special vocational training programmes for workers made redundant as a consequence of privatization. Based upon various case studies in Hungary, the Czech Republic and Slovakia, he observes a marked decrease in training activities undertaken by enterprises and public training institutions. However, even if training programmes were to be increased, Oliveira argues that training plays an important but limited role in helping people to find jobs. Newly established enterprises prefer to train their employees and selection is often more based on attitudes and general skills than specifically acquired skills in training programmes for unemployed workers.

Some countries (eastern Germany, Hungary, the Czech Republic and, to a lesser degree, Bulgaria) have introduced a comprehensive system of compensatory and proactive measures to deal with labour dislocation. In other countries (Pakistan and India), where social safety net and labour market policies are underdeveloped or largely lacking, there is a greater emphasis on *privatization-induced social protection measures*, focusing on the regions, the companies and the workers affected by the transfer of ownership. However, these measures have often been taken after the privatization process has taken place. A number of the measures to deal with retrenchment follow logically from the ILO Termination of Employment Convention, 1982 (No. 158). The main reason for such termination is the economic, technological and structural position of the enterprise. Convention No. 158 (which has been ratified by 25 countries) calls for various measures, including two types of social protection — severance payments and benefits from unemployment insurance and other forms of social security — as well as placing an obligation on employers to consult workers.

5. Privatization and labour relations

The employees of state-owned enterprises often oppose privatization because they fear a loss of job security and social protection as well as a deterioration in the industrial relations system. In many countries, though certainly not all, employees in state-owned enterprises have conditions of service equal to or resembling those of civil servants, both in terms of job security and social protection and in terms of regulations relating to union membership and collective bargaining. Workers often belong to public service unions, which are in many countries the largest union. Fear of insecurity and of being marginalized in terms of collective bargaining often makes public enterprise or public sector unions opposed to privatization schemes, especially when the unions have not been involved in initial discussions on privatization (thus augmenting the fear that one of the intentions of the privatization exercise is to marginalize the unions). Often because of close links between certain parts of the trade union movement and political opposition parties, something which started as a union-government dispute may develop into a political dispute, thus blocking privatization exercises or making them extremely difficult to implement.

However, privatization does not always mean a threat to collective bargaining and workers' involvement. As Schregle (1992) has pointed out, there may already be constraints on public sector enterprises in the sense that the management of these enterprises, in its negotiations with the unions, is bound by a limited bargaining margin or by bargaining guidelines dictated by budget limitations and imposed by government. Furthermore, in certain cases labour legislation imposes constraints on state-owned enterprises in the form of limitations on full collective bargaining and restrictions on the right to strike.

A shift from civil service to private employment is therefore not always negatively perceived. For example, when the Korea Tobacco and Ginseng Corporation changed its status (from government authority to autonomous public enterprise) in the 1980s its employees also changed status from public servants to civilian employees. Those who did not want to lose their public servant status were given the option of transferring to another government authority. In fact, not many workers took advantage of this possibility, because wages and fringe benefits were higher in autonomous public enterprises than in government authorities. Furthermore, a special provision was made to guarantee the same pension benefits they had enjoyed as public servants. With the privatization of the Korea Stock Exchange, the employees lost their lifelong employment security, which had been guaranteed under public ownership, but their wages and welfare benefits increased and their promotion prospects improved. These examples indicate that the impact of privatization on employment conditions is not necessarily straightforward: there may be some trade-off between the different effects. But it is hard to say whether the overall balance has been positive or negative, particularly in the long term.

In Pakistan, the 1991 decision of the Government to divest public enterprises aroused great dissatisfaction amongst workers. Prior to privatization, the Government therefore entered into an agreement with the trade unions operating in the public sector. The agreement contained a set of provisions: employment protection for a year after privatization; generous termination payments for voluntary leavers; retraining and unemployment benefits or credits to become self-employed for laid-off workers (Kemal, 1993). In a similar move, the Indian Government set up a National Renewal Fund in 1992 to cope with the social consequences of public sector reform and privatization. The Fund provides assistance to firms to cover the costs of retraining and redeployment of redundant workers, to provide compensation to employees affected by restructuring and closure, and to support job creation. Currently six regions, where industrial malaise is rampant, have been selected to implement the programme on a pilot basis. However, the National Renewal Fund has been designed by the Government; it is not the outcome of a collective bargaining process, and most unions do not regard it as their programme (see Chapter 3).

While retrenched workers are given severance pay, the remaining workers are often offered stock options as part of the privatization package. The aim is to help forge a new firm-based identity among workers and to give them an incentive to increase productivity. Our case studies suggest, however, that the level of financial participation by workers in most of these schemes is low; moreover workers are often excluded from decision-making. In Mexico, the Government guaranteed a low-interest loan to the telephone workers' union to acquire 4.4 per cent of Telmex's public shares. Unionized workers bought 3 per cent as individuals, and 1.4 per cent was purchased by the union's retirement fund. Non-unionized employees were also authorized to purchase a certain number of shares through an additional fund established by the Government. The union did not acquire a seat on the company's board, but it was agreed that workers would be allowed to continue purchasing shares, and when they reached 10 per cent of all shares they would be entitled to a seat. However, the union leadership's goal of participating on Telmex's board appears difficult to achieve. Control of 10 per cent of the company has remained elusive, as many workers cash in their shares and others choose to exert direct control over their shares rather than hand them over to the union's share fund management (see Chapter 4). The lessons learnt from the privatization of the Hungarian telecommunications sector are similar in many respects: the workers' share generally remains negligible, much less than would be needed to secure participation in decision-making, or to provide a real incentive to increase productivity (see Chapter 8).

In Bulgaria, the 1992 Privatization Law grants employees in commercialized state-owned enterprises the right to buy shares in their own enterprise at a reduced price, but with no voting rights for three years. A survey of 4,600 employees in manufacturing revealed that workers are rather cautious about purchasing shares in their own establishment. Only 10-15 per cent are willing to risk more than a quarter of a year's income to buy shares. Employees are uncertain about future ownership of their enterprise, and generally feel that they have little influence on the process of privatization and the future of the firm (see Chapter 5).

6. Labour flexibility

In Bulgaria, Hungary and India efforts have been made to reform the labour laws in order to ease labour adjustment and increase labour flexibility after privatization. At the same time, there is a tendency to move away from regular employment towards increasing use of temporary, casual and contract labour. Enterprises have shifted to the use of more flexible forms of labour relations, in part to enable them to adjust more quickly and without cost to fluctuating demand for their products, in part to reduce their fixed labour costs, and in part to respond to the increasing technological options. For the workers, this trend usually implies less employment security, though the level of wages is sometimes higher than with regular jobs.

An apparent feature of the growth of external flexibility in Mexico is the increasing use of non-unionized contract labour. In Pakistan, contract workers may constitute as much as 32 per cent of the workforce in the large-scale manufacturing sector. In Bulgaria, more and more employers are putting newly recruited workers on so-called civil contracts, which give no security of employment and from which workers can be released either without notice or with less than the normal notice and severance pay. In addition, employers are not obliged to pay social contributions for civil contract labour; consequently workers are not entitled to unemployment compensation if they lose their jobs (see Chapter 5).

The growing use of non-regular forms of employment raises the issue of what safeguards should be put in place to ensure that the benefits to enterprises of having flexible labour relations are not coupled with a general deterioration in wages, benefits and working conditions. For both employers and workers, the benefits of flexibility have to be balanced by a careful consideration of equitable conditions of employment to ensure that those employed in relatively precarious work relations are not penalized by comparison with those in regular employment. This is important not only for countries where privatization is taking place but also for other countries adjusting to globalization. As US Labor Secretary Reich has stated, "Unless people have the security they need to adapt to the future, I believe they will seek security by trying to preserve the past" (Reich, 1993).

7. Conclusions

Despite the fact that the cases of privatization discussed in this book have taken place in countries at various levels of economic development, with a wide range of social and economic systems, and in which there were different reactions to balance of payments problems and budget deficits, a number of lessons can be inferred from the experiences so far. Perhaps the most important lesson is that privatization is not an end in itself. In cases where it was regarded as such it often failed, either because supporting structures had not been put in place, or because it led to insurmountable opposition from various interest groups.

For privatization to be successful — for the new owners of enterprises, for workers in the enterprises and for consumers buying the products of the enterprises — privatization should be seen as part and parcel of a medium-term policy and a logical component of a set of well-defined long-term policies, which includes development of a healthy private sector with well-functioning goods, capital and labour markets in a system of widely respected democratic control. In many cases, it has been found that it is the exposure to competitive forces rather than the nature of ownership by itself that creates the greatest pressure for improved efficiency. The absence of one or more of these factors may produce various side-effects which often result from privatization programmes, such as declining consumer surplus because of the continuation of monopolies, the development of crony capitalism through favouring ownership of political clients, and the concentration of capital markets on exploitation of workers.

Political support for privatization is greatest if it is seen as part of a wider process of increasing human concerns and participation in the society and as part of a democratic process of deciding whether the State should subsidize loss-making enterprises or invest more in health and education, which would benefit a greater part of the population. Such considerations can be part of a nationwide dialogue on new development directions.

The experiences of the countries examined in this volume suggest that when privatization has been combined with thorough reforms, both within the enterprise and in its policy environment, it has produced substantial positive results. But it remains to be debated whether these results could not have been achieved without privatization, with the same type of internal and external reforms. The evidence gathered so far on the privatization of public enterprises does not allow us to answer the question of whether a change in ownership *per se* will increase efficiency. It is difficult to separate the impact of different factors on the performance of an enterprise. In addition, no systematic studies have been carried out to monitor the efficiency of the divested enterprises over a longer period, and to compare this with projections made on the assumption that they had remained in the public sector.

What has also become clear is that there must be a recognition of the costs of privatization and of the uses to which the resulting revenues can be put. In many countries privatization has entailed higher costs than anticipated (Kühl, Chapter 6) and it has rarely played (although it was supposed to do so) a significant role in stabilization programmes. Governments aiming to achieve internal and external equilibrium and to privatize at the same time have found this to be difficult and often impossible because the accompanying structures and regulatory measures take time to be put in place.

Furthermore, the question of who should bear the social cost of privatization, including the accompanying retrenchment programmes and other measures affecting social security, is often a highly political one which is difficult to answer in an economy which is undergoing a stabilization programme. It is much easier to settle such questions at times when the economy is growing and the government is not caught in a strait-jacket by its need to stabilize the economy.

Fear of privatization is often great among workers and in many cases it is justified. Especially in Central and Eastern European countries, but also in some developing countries with far-reaching privatization programmes, workers face a great risk of being marginalized, either through worsening employment conditions or through being made redundant and having to accept more vulnerable employment conditions in other enterprises or no job at all, particularly in the immediate future.

The establishment of proper social security programmes, income maintenance measures and social safety nets, as well as training, placement and other labour market programmes, is becoming an essential part of the process of privatization. This often places a heavy financial and organizational burden on the government. Two problems regarding social safety nets must be mentioned. First, social safety nets should be part of a larger process of structural change and not organized in an ad hoc way. Second, they are not an alternative to job creation and wider participation in decision-making. Several of our country studies have shown that hasty programmes, introduced under the pressure of high levels of unemployment, are not the right way to address the social consequences of privatization and broader structural change.

Workers' fears of privatization can be responded to by proper government policies, but that is not sufficient. Management, too, must make all possible efforts to consult workers and alleviate unjustified fears. Consultation and negotiation can address the merits and rationale of privatization and the union's concerns. Where severe employment problems are expected to arise, a productive dialogue on possible measures to lessen the adverse consequences for employees is of crucial importance. It is essential to address employee concern as early as possible when initiating and implementing a privatization programme. The weight placed on human factors and workers' involvement through consultation and negotiation will determine the degree of employee confidence in, and support for, the privatization process. The experience of the most successful programmes has been that genuine consultation and involvement in the privatization process, from start to finish, not only ease the process but also, by mobilizing the cooperation of the workforce, enhance the prospects of a good outcome.

References

Adam, C.; Cavendish, W.; Mistry, P. 1992. *Adjusting privatization: Case studies from developing countries.* London, James Currey.

Cook, P.; Kirkpatrick, C. (ed.) 1995. *Privatization policy and performance: International perspectives,* Hemel Hempstead, Harvester, Wheatsheaf.

Edgren, G. 1990. *Privatization, efficiency and employment.* IILS, ILO Discussion Paper No. 23, Geneva.

Galal, A.; Jones L.; Tandon, P.; Vogelsang, I. 1994. *Welfare consequences of selling public enterprises.* Oxford, Oxford University Press.

Heller, P.; Tait, A. 1983. *Government employment and pay: Some international comparisons.* IMF Occasional Paper 24. Washington, DC, IMF.

Hemming, R.; Mansoor, A. M. 1988. *Privatization and public enterprises.* IMF Occasional Paper 56. Washington, DC, IMF.

Jackman, R. 1994. "Economic policy and employment in the transition economies of Central and Eastern Europe. What have we learned?", in *International Labour Review,* Vol. 133, No. 3.

Kemal, A. R. 1993. *Retrenchment policies and labour shedding in Pakistan,* Interdepartmental Project on Structural Adjustment, Occasional paper No. 17, Geneva, ILO.

Kikeri, S.; Nellis, J.; Shirley, M. 1992. *Privatization: The lessons of experience.* Washington, DC, World Bank.

Killick, T.; Commander, S. 1988. "Privatization in developing countries: A survey of issues", in P. Cook and C. Kirkpatrick. 1988. *Privatization in less developed countries.* Hemel Hempstead, Harvester, Wheatsheaf.

Kornai, J. 1980. *Economics of shortage.* Amsterdam, North Holland.

Marinakis, A. (1992) *Public sector employment in developing countries: An overview of past and present trends.* Interdepartmental Project on Structural Adjustment, Occasional Paper No. 3. Geneva, ILO.

North, D. 1994. "Economic performance through time", in *American Economic Review,* Vol. 84, No. 3, June 1994.

Oliveira, J. 1993. *Training and privatization in Eastern European Countries: Suggestions for an operational agenda.* Interdepartmental Project on Structural Adjustment, Occasional Paper No. 13, Geneva, ILO.

Pfeffermann, G. and Madarassy, A. 1992. *Trends in private investment in developing countries 1993.* Washington, DC, International Finance Corporation.

Pinheiro, A.; Schneider, B. 1994. *The fiscal impact of privatization in Latin America.* Princeton, Princeton University; mimeo.

Reich, R. 1993. Address to the Employment Week organized by the European Commission, Brussels; mimeo.

Sader, F. 1995. *Privatization, public enterprises and foreign investment in developing countries 1988-93.* Foreign Investment Advisory Service, Occasional Paper No. 5, Washington, DC, World Bank.

Schregle, J. 1992. *Privatization and industrial relations: General perspectives.* Paper presented at Top Management Forum on Labour Management Cooperation, Privatization and Industrial Relations, Tokyo, 21-26 Sep. 1992, Geneva, ILO; mimeo.

Standing, G. 1994. "Labour market implications of 'privatization' in Russian industry in 1992", in *World Development,* Vol. 22, No. 2.

————. 1995. "Enterprise restructuring in Russian industry and mass unemployment", in *Labour Market Papers*, No. 1, Geneva, ILO.

Standing, G.; Sziraczki, G.; Windell, J. 1993. *Employment dynamics in Bulgarian industry.* Labour Market Analysis and Employment Policies Working Paper No. 63. Geneva, ILO, Aug.

Sziraczki, G. 1988. "Redundancy and unemployment in a North Hungarian steel valley", in *Labour and Society*, Vol. 13, No. 4.

Vuylsteke, V. 1988. *Techniques of privatization of state-owned enterprises,* Vol. I. World Bank Technical Paper No. 88. Washington, DC, World Bank.

Windell, J.; Anker, R.; Sziraczki, G. 1995. *Kyrgyzstan: Enterprise restructuring and labour shedding in a free-fall economy.* Labour Market Papers No. 4. Geneva, ILO.

World Bank 1995. *Bureaucrats in Business. The economics and politics of government ownership*, Washington DC, World Bank.

Note

[1] Douglas North: "Economic performance through time", acceptance lecture, 1993 Alfred Nobel Memorial Prize in Economic Sciences (North, 1994).

2. Privatization and employment in the Republic of Korea

Young-Bum Park*

1. Introduction

The public sector has played a crucial role in the Republic of Korea's rapid economic development since the 1960s, particularly in the provision of social infrastructure such as hydroelectric power plants, gas, roads, public housing and so forth. The proportion of value added generated by public enterprises amounted to 9.4 per cent of GDP in 1990.

Since the Republic of Korea implemented its first economic and social development plan in 1962, privatization has been suggested as a way of improving the efficiency of public sector operations. Two large-scale privatization schemes were implemented in the 1980s: one in the early part of the decade with the birth of the Fifth Republic and one starting in 1987. This paper looks at the Republic of Korea's experience of privatization in the 1980s with a view to drawing some lessons from its labour market consequences.

In the Republic of Korea, privatization broadly follows three patterns: transformation of a government authority into a public authority; partial privatization, which means that a certain proportion of government shares in a public enterprise are sold to the private sector, with the Government remaining the major shareholder; and total privatization.

Five public enterprises which were partially or totally privatized in the 1980s have been selected for detailed study: Korea Telecom and the Korea Tobacco and Ginseng Corp., which belong to the first privatization category; the Korea Electric Power Corp. and the Pohang Steel and Iron Co., which belong to the second category; and the Korea Stock Exchange, which can be considered a total privatization. In each case, the level and structure of employment, labour productivity, labour flexibility, job security, industrial relations, and wages before and after privatization are examined. Finally, there is an overview of past experiences of privatization and their labour market implications.

* Korea Labour Institute.

2. The history of privatization in the Republic of Korea

2.1 The public sector and the economy

In 1991, the public sector in the Republic of Korea employed 1,253,000 workers, mainly in non-manual occupations, which represented 6.7 per cent of total employment, as shown in table 2.1. The public sector can be divided into two parts. First are *government authorities* (GAs), in which the employment relationship is regulated by the Public Servant Act. GA employees can be classified into six occupational groupings: general public administration; police and fire departments; education; technicians; general clerical duties; and judges, attorneys and foreign servicemen. Government authorities include government enterprises such as Korea National Railroad because of the legal status of the employees. Second are *public authorities* (PAs), in which the Labour Standard Act, which also sets basic labour standards for the private sector, regulates the employment relationship. The PAs can be further classified into three groups: public enterprises, government-financed authorities (GFAs), and government-subsidized authorities (GSAs).

Public enterprises include: government-invested enterprises (GIEs), in which at least 50 per cent of the equity is owned by the central government; government-backed enterprises (GBEs), in which less than 50 per cent of the equity is owned by the central government (but the central government is still a major shareholder); subsidiary companies of the GIEs, in which the largest shareholders are the GIEs; and the local public enterprises (LPEs), in which more than 49 per cent of the equity is owned by the local government. GFAs, whose financing comes mostly from the Government, are supposed to be independent, but most of them work closely with their affiliated government ministries. GSAs have a proportion of their expenses financed by the Government.

Public enterprises have played a crucial role in the national economy. The value added of all public enterprises in 1990 was 12,367 billion won (US$1,545 billion), which comprised 9.4 per cent of GDP. This share had increased from 9.0 per cent in 1986 (Song and Song, 1992). Public enterprises are very capital-intensive. For example, depreciation constituted 37.3 per cent of the GIEs' total expenses in 1987 as compared to 18.8 per cent for the manufacturing sector as a whole (Park, 1988). The capital formation of all public enterprises, which comprised about 30 per cent of gross domestic capital formation from 1963 to 1981, still comprised 8.9 per cent of new capital investment in 1990. The budget of all public enterprises was 6,200 billion won (US$775 million) in 1990, 40 per cent larger than the general account of the Government.

Until very recently, the business activities of firms in the Republic of Korea, including privatized enterprises, were heavily regulated by the Government, reflecting the leading role played by the Government in the process of economic development. Regulation applied particularly to large enterprises.

Government regulation of private sector business activities has taken place in several ways. First, as new enterprises have sprung up, the Government has controlled their entry into new markets. Second, most of the domestic capital markets have been, and still are, owned and controlled by the Government. The import of foreign capital has also been regulated by the Government. Third, the prices set by most large firms have been controlled by the Government, as part of their strategy for the efficient management of the country's

Table 2.1. Public sector employment and union membership, Republic of Korea
(000s)

Type of organization	Public sector employment			Union membership		
	1980	1987	1991	1980	1987	1991
Government authorities	596	705	854	n.a.	—	—
Public servants	—	—	—	—	44	50
Non-public servants	—	—	—	—	13	19
Public enterprises	n.a.	n.a.	308	n.a.	116	184
Government-invested enterprises (GIEs)	—	—	213	—	107	137
Government-backed enterprises	—	—	39	—	7	9
Subsidiary companies of GIEs	—	—	39	—	2	27
Local public enterprises	—	—	17	—	0	11
Government-financed authorities	n.a.	n.a.	41	n.a.	1	18
Government-subsidized authorities	n.a.	n.a.	50	n.a.	0	25
Total public sector	n.a.	n.a.	1 253	n.a.	174	296
Total labour force	13 707	16 354	18 756	945	1 050	1 803

n.a. = not available.

macroeconomy. Moreover, where public enterprises are partially privatized, the Government has maintained its control over their activities, particularly their personnel policies, through additional measures, including participation on the boards of the privatized enterprises.

Most of this government regulation is to some extent maintained. Since the mid-1980s, however, lessening government involvement in private sector activities has emerged as one urgent agenda item to improve the efficiency of the economy. The current privatization scheme, introduced in 1987, aimed to decrease the Government's direct involvement in the national economy. The Seventh Republic, which started in 1993, has also promised less government involvement in private sector activities, but no detailed plans have yet been revealed.

2.2 Past experiences of privatization

Before the current privatization programme, two large-scale privatization schemes had been implemented in the Republic of Korea, one from 1968 to 1973 and one in the early 1980s.

Under the first scheme, 18 public enterprises were reorganized and eight were sold to private firms and financial institutions. The scheme was carried out under the country's second five-year plan, which started in 1967 and can be considered the first real plan, in the sense that it was drawn up on the assumption that it formed part of a development planning process that would last some considerable time. The major objectives of the plan included creating a base for the country's industrial upgrading, especially through the development of the steel, chemical and machinery industries.

Most public enterprises existing in the 1960s were established under Japanese colonial rule and were nationalized with the liberation of Korea from Japan. Quite a few of these public enterprises needed to be reshaped to enable them to play a leading role in the export-oriented, outward-looking development strategy adopted with the birth of the Third Republic in the early 1960s.

The enterprises that were privatized included the Korea Express Co., the Korea Line Corp., the Korea Shipbuilding and Engineering Corp., Korea Air Lines, the Korea Mining Promotion Corp., the Korea Salt Co., the Commercial Bank of Korea, and the Korea Marine Industry Development Corp. Most of the privatized enterprises still held a monopoly in their product markets even after privatization. However, their activities were subject to heavy government regulation, as were those of most large private sector firms. The workers' reaction to privatization is not well documented. Considering that the country did not reach its Lewis-type turning point in migration at that time, it can be assumed that most workers affected by privatization were quite content as long as their jobs were protected, as they were.

The second privatization programme was implemented in the early 1980s as one component of a general policy of liberalization adopted by the Government in 1980 with the birth of the Fifth Republic. Negative GNP growth rates were recorded consecutively in 1980 and 1981 for the first time since development planning started in the 1960s. It was concluded that the financial sector was less developed than the real sector, and that this was causing serious problems for the country's sustained economic development. Four major banks were sold to private firms and investors through an asset sale method. The privatized banks were Hanil Bank, Korea First Bank, Bank of Seoul and Trust Company, and Cho-hung Bank.

The Government has in fact managed to retain control over most of the activities of the privatized banks, since there was a share limit for both private firms and individual investors. For example, the Government still appoints board members as well as presidents of the banks. Some argue, therefore, that the objectives of privatization have not been realized mainly because the Government continues to control the privatized banks (Kang, 1988).

In the first half of the 1980s, two government enterprises were also changed to government-invested enterprises (GIEs) within the Government's overall privatization framework: the Korea Telecommunications Authority (later renamed Korea Telecom) and the Korea Tobacco and Ginseng Authority (later renamed the Korea Tobacco and Ginseng Corp.). In 1982, public servants in the Ministry of Postal Service who worked in telecommunications were transferred to the Korea Telecommunications Authority. The same thing happened with public servants in the Office of Monopoly, which became the Korea Tobacco and Ginseng Authority in 1987. The transfer of these public servants to GIEs was significant in labour terms because labour regulations are different for government authorities and public authorities, as already mentioned. Some manufacturing firms were also privatized under the second privatization programme.

Workers' views were not considered by policy-makers during the process of privatization in the early 1980s, workers' rights being at a particularly low ebb since the birth of the Fifth Republic, which seized power through a military coup in 1980.[1] However, workers' jobs were well protected in the newly privatized enterprises, as will be elaborated below in the cases of Korea Telecom and the Korea Tobacco and Ginseng Corp.

Calculations of indicators such as total profit and average rates of return and sales per employee for 15 firms privatized under the first and second privatization programmes (Kang, 1988) suggest that not all firms benefited equally from privatization. While six firms showed increases in efficiency, two actually experienced drops in efficiency after privatization. For the other seven firms, the effects were not significant. The market structure of some firms and the continued government regulation (particularly of banks) have been suggested as causes of the failure of some firms to improve their performance.

2.3 The current privatization scheme

In April 1987, the Privatization Proceeding Committee, chaired by the Vice-Minister of the Economic Planning Board, was formed with a view to privatizing selected public enterprises. Since then, 11 government-invested enterprises and government-backed enterprises have been selected for total or partial privatization, as shown in table 2.2.

The Korea Stock Exchange, the Korea Appraisal Board, the National Textbook Co., the Korea Technology Development Corp. and the Foreign Exchange Bank were chosen for total privatization. The government shares in the Korea Stock Exchange were sold to the member firms of the Korea Stock Exchange in 1988.

The Citizen National Bank, the Small and Medium Industry Bank of Korea, the Korea Electric Power Corp., Korea Telecom, the Korea Tobacco and Ginseng Corp. and the Pohang Steel and Iron Co. were chosen for partial privatization. Under the plan, some proportion of the government holding in these six enterprises was to be sold, but the Government was still to remain the major shareholder. The government shares in these six firms and in the Foreign Exchange Bank were expected to be sold mainly through the People's Share Programme announced in November 1987. The Government planned to sell 5,000 billion won (US$7.1 billion) worth of government-held shares in public enterprises over the period 1988-92. Under this programme, 75 per cent of the government shares were set aside for low-income buyers,[2] 20 per cent for the employees of the privatized enterprises, and 5 per cent for the general public. As the purchase price of the shares was below market price, low-income buyers and public enterprise employees were expected to make some capital gains. In April 1988, the Pohang Steel and Iron Co. was partially privatized through the People's Share Programme; about 3.2 million people participated. The share price was set at 15,000 won (US$20.6) per share. The starting price of the shares, when traded in the stock market in June 1988, was 43,000 won (US$59).[3]

The Privatization Proceeding Committee also decided that the functions of the other seven public enterprises should be adjusted to the new economic environment. Some selected public banks would be reorganized in line with future plans for restructuring the

Table 2.2. Current privatization schedule, 1990

	Enterprise	Government holding (%)		Date of privatization
		Before privatization	After privatization	
Total privatization	Korea Stock Exchange	68.1	0.0	1988
	Korea Appraisal Board	49.4	20.4	1990
	National Textbook Co.	96.5[1]	0.0	46.5%: 1990; 50.0%: after 1991
	Korea Technology Development Corp.	22.1	0.0	15.1%: 1990; 7.0%: after 1991
	Foreign Exchange Bank	100.0[2]	0.0	1990
Partial privatization	Citizen National Bank	72.6	51.0[3]	1990
	Small and Medium Industry Bank of Korea	99.9	51.03	10%: 1990; 38.9%: after 1991
	Korea Electric Power Corp.	100.0	68.0	21%: 1989; 11%: 1990
	Korea Telecom	100.0	51.0	25%: 1990; 24%: after 1991
	Korea Tobacco and Ginseng Corp.	100.0	51.0	1991
	Pohang Steel and Iron Co.	69.1[1]	35.01	1988

[1] The share of the Korea Development Bank is included.   [2] The share of the Bank of Korea is included.
[3] Total privatization will be considered in the near future.

whole banking industry. The GIEs have also been encouraged to privatize their subsidiary companies as part of the Government's privatization plan.

When the current privatization scheme was introduced, the Government stated the following objectives. First, the role of the Government in the national economy would be reduced. The Government has initiated and led the country's economic development, but it is now generally accepted that its role should be adjusted, given the enormous economic growth achieved during the last three decades. In this context, the role of public enterprises in the national economy should be reconsidered. By privatizing major public enterprises, the role of the Government was expected to decrease and that of the private sector to increase.

Second, expanding private sector involvement in the management of the partially privatized public enterprises was expected to enhance their economic efficiency. Massive government subsidies were given and excessive price increases allowed to compensate for the mismanagement of public enterprises (Park, 1988).

Third, the financial burden on the Government would be reduced. From 1976 to 1989, for example, financial support from the Government to the GIEs amounted to 14,600 billion won (US$27.7 million). At the same time, by selling the government shares, the Government was expected to earn revenue of 5,000 billion won (US$7.1 billion) over the five-year period, which would be used for social development, including social welfare.

Finally, the stock market would be boosted by the choice of the People's Share Programme as the privatization method. The ratio of the market value of the total stocks traded on the Korea Stock Exchange to GNP increased from 6.9 per cent in 1980 to 57.8 per cent in 1988. Before the total liberalization of the capital market, which was then planned for 1992, the Government aimed to give a boost, in both quantitative and qualitative terms, to the country's capital market and to bring it close to the level of that in industrialized countries. The People's Share Programme was to contribute to the development of the Republic of Korea's capital market.

However, the current privatization scheme through the People's Share Programme has been completely suspended since 1990. The Government, which was afraid of inflicting further damage on the country's troubled stock market by selling a large volume of new stock, announced in May 1990 that the People's Share Programme would be suspended until the stock market stabilized. Since then, the stock market has not recovered, but has deteriorated further. No steps have been taken to privatize the subsidiary companies of the GIEs. On the contrary, the number of subsidiaries increased from 68 in 1988 to 90 in 1991.

3. Privatization and social and labour protection

3.1 Government authorities

Most public servants do not have the legal right to join trade unions. Low-ranking public servants in the Ministry of Communications, the Korea National Railroad and the National Medical Centre are entitled to join trade unions and discuss employment terms with their employers because they had trade unions prior to their inclusion as government branches. As of 1991, 6.1 per cent of all public servants have the legal right to become union members. On the other hand, daily workers (temporary and/or casual workers) employed in the government authorities have the same labour rights as workers in the private sector.

The Ministry of Government Administration is responsible for all personnel matters relating to public servants, including determination of the distribution of various categories of occupations and grades for each government authority. It also determines wage levels for public servants in collaboration with the Economic Planning Board, which sets the budget for the public sector. Even the wages of unionized public servants are in practice often determined unilaterally by the Government, since workers do not have the right to strike. There is a commission to advise the Minister of Government Administration on appropriate public sector wages, but it has not been called on at all during the last few years.

Table 2.3. Wage differentials among government authorities, public enterprises and all enterprises (government estimates), **1988** (in thousand won)

General administration

Grade	Government authorities (A)	Occupation	Public enterprises (B)	All enterprises (C)	(B/A) x 100	(C/A) x 100
G2S8	1 268	Managing Director	2 331	2 682	183.8	211.5
G4S8	983	Manager	1 947	1 592	198.0	162.1
G6S9	735	Deputy Chief	1 032	883	140.4	120.2
G7S1	358	University graduate (no experience)	583	548	162.9	153.1
G9S1	290	High school graduate (no experience)	454	403	156.5	138.9
Average differential					157.2	141.2

Source: Unpublished data from the Ministry of Government Administration.

Public servants' wages (table 2.3) are generally believed to be lower than those of equivalent workers in the private sector.[4] In recent years public servants' wages have increased substantially in certain sectors because public servants have not been affected by the Government's low-wage policy since the late 1980s.

Public servants do not come under the Labour Standard Act. Even minimum legal labour standards, such as overtime premiums, are not guaranteed. However, public servants benefit from a very good pension scheme. Since a national pension scheme covering the non-GA sector began a few years ago, an employee leaving a job either in a public authority or in the private sector is entitled to a severance payment, which should be at least one month's wages for each year of service. Table 2.4 compares the lump-sum severance

Table 2.4. Severance payment schedule, 1991 (proportion of one month's wages)

Employer	Years of tenure						
	1	5	10	15	20	25	30
Government authorities[1]	1.5	7.5	15.5	24.0	33.0	42.5	52.5
Public authorities	1.0	6.8	14.8	21.2	28.9	34.8	41.8
Private sector	1.0	5.5	11.7	17.1	23.1	28.4	34.1

[1] Pension is converted to lump-sum payment schedule.

Source: Park, forthcoming.

payment given under the government pension scheme with that available in the other sectors. The government pension scheme offers the best terms, and the scheme for PAs the next best. Public servants also enjoy a good medical insurance system,[5] which existed long before a national medical insurance system was introduced for the private sector.

3.2 Public authorities

Before 1987, Korean trade unions did not properly represent workers' interests in the process of wage-fixing. In the public sector, few establishments were even organized: only 32 public authorities (PAs) were unionized as of June 1987. In practice, therefore, the wages of public sector employees were determined unilaterally by the Government until 1987.

With the amendment of the Trade Union Act in 1987, labour rights equal to those enjoyed in the private sector were given to public sector employees. Central government is not officially involved in wage-fixing. However, its role in public sector collective bargaining is still more critical than it might appear. Despite the fact that 83.6 per cent of the public authorities were organized as of the end of 1991, the budgets of all government-financed authorities (GFAs) and government-subsidized authorities (GSAs) are examined by the affiliated ministries as well as by the Economic Planning Board, and annual wage increments are determined in advance before wage bargaining begins. Since most local public enterprises depend on the Government for finance, their budgets are closely examined both by their affiliated ministries and by the Economic Planning Board. Even government-invested enterprises (GIEs), which have the most autonomy under the Government Invested Enterprise Regulation Act, must follow the Government's wage policy. Government limits on public sector budgets have sometimes led to strikes. In 1988, for example, the trade unions of many government-financed research institutes (which come into the GFA category) held a joint strike to oppose the predetermined 3 per cent wage increase in their 1989 budgets.

Employment in the PAs is regulated by the Labour Standard Act, in the same way as private sector employment. Only small employers are excluded from its coverage. Benefits to which workers are entitled under the Act include overtime pay (one and a half times the normal hourly wage rate), paid leave and holidays, severance pay (an employee's average monthly wage over the last three months for every year of service) and minimum wages. In the case of industrial accidents and illness, most workers receive compensation under the Industrial Accident and Compensation Act.

PAs are supposed to determine their own levels of employment as well as the distribution of their employees among the various grades and occupations. However, a PA must obtain approval from its governing board, of which one member must by law be a government official from an affiliated government ministry, before finalizing any major personnel management decision. The usual result is that employment levels and distribution of employees among grades and occupations are greatly influenced by the affiliated ministry.

Workers in such essential services as public transport, water, electricity, gas, oil refineries, public health, medical services, banks, broadcasting and communications — whether or not in the public sector — are subject to emergency mediation and/or compulsory arbitration in the case of severe strikes. Employees of some public enterprises, including the Korea Broadcasting System, Korea Telecom, the Korea Gas Corp. and the Korea Electric Power Corp., are considered to be essential service providers.

Wages in the PAs are on average higher than those in the private sector, even after skill differences in the two sectors have been controlled for (see table 2.3). This reflects the fact that most PAs have a monopoly position in their product market and/or the agent costs incurred in the public sector (Park and Lee, 1989). Fringe benefits in the PAs include paid leave, severance pay and other welfare benefits and are considered to be better than those in the private sector. The schedule for severance pay is higher than the legal minimum. (In the early 1980s, with the birth of the Fifth Republic, the Government forcibly reduced the level of severance payments in some public enterprises.) All workers are entitled to overtime pay of at least one and a half times their basic pay, except those in the government authorities. Most PAs now pay the legally required overtime premium owing to pressures from the union movement since the mid-1980s. Since 1988, all employees who work in an establishment with more than nine employees (four employees since 1991) have benefited from a national pension scheme. The pension premium is paid half by the employer and half by the employee under the national pension scheme, which applied equally to PAs and the private sector.

3.3 Social protection and privatization

Public employees' labour and social rights are protected by a different legal framework depending on whether they belong to a government authority or a public authority.

When a GA is changed to a PA, which is considered to be a form of privatization, the rights of GA employees are for the most part respected. For example, when the Korea Telecommunications Authority and the Korea Tobacco and Ginseng Corp. were established in accordance with the Government's privatization plans, in 1982 and 1987 respectively, schemes for the two PAs were implemented to reduce the need for compulsory redundancies in unskilled or outdated occupations. These schemes were carried out without difficulty because displaced workers were given early retirement benefits, called a privileged retirement plan. Workers were also given the option of being transferred to another GA instead of working for the PA. Very few public servants availed themselves of this option. As a GA is changed to a PA, the wages of former GA employees usually increase substantially, reflecting the big wage differential between GAs and PAs.

However, when a GA (a rare case) or PA is privatized totally, there is no guarantee that employees' labour and social rights will be protected, even though the same Labour Standard Act regulates the employment relationship in both PAs and the private sector. Because the private sector principle of profit maximization would reduce the agent cost which occurs because of public ownership, it would bring a retrenchment scheme for redundant workers. The law also gives employers the right to dismiss workers for purposes of business restructuring, which usually takes place when the ownership of an establishment changes. On the other hand, what is remarkable is that no major retrenchment schemes have ever been enforced in the public sector, which reflects the performance of the national economy over the last 30 years.

4. Case studies

Five public enterprises, which were privatized partially or totally in the 1980s, have been selected for study: the Korea Tobacco and Ginseng Corp., Korea Telecom, the Korea Stock Exchange, the Pohang Steel and Iron Co. and the Korea Electric Power Corp. KTG and Korea Telecom both changed from government enterprises to government-invested enterprises, POSCO and KEPCO were partially privatized through the People's Share Programme in the late 1980s, while the Korea Stock Exchange was totally privatized.

4.1 Privatization of government enterprises into government-invested enterprises

Korea Tobacco and Ginseng Corp. (KTG)

KTG is a government-invested enterprise (GIE) whose operations include both the production and the sale of tobacco and ginseng. Ginseng is a health and nutrition product, and Korean ginseng is considered to be the best in the world. The share of the ginseng business in the corporation's total turnover for 1991 was 3.4 per cent. Its annual turnover, net profit and public profit for 1991 were 2,525 billion won (US$3,319 million), 271 billion won (US$355 million) and 2,108 billion won (US$2,771 million) respectively.[6] Its total number of employees as of the end of 1991 was about 8,600.

KTG was established as a government bureau under the Ministry of Finance in 1948 with the birth of the Republic of Korea: it was then called the Bureau of Monopoly. It became an independent government agency in 1952, and was renamed the Office of Monopoly. In 1987 it was transformed from a government enterprise to a GIE as part of the overall government privatization scheme. From its establishment until its transformation to a GIE, KTG's revenue was one of the Government's major sources of income, particularly in the 1950s and 1960s when the national economy was still relatively undeveloped.

KTG's privatization is considered a successful one. The Republic of Korea opened up its tobacco market in 1988, but the share of foreign tobacco companies in the market was still below 5 per cent at the end of 1991. In Japan and Taiwan, China, by contrast, foreign firms had taken shares of 14.5 per cent and 22 per cent respectively by the end of 1989. In the annual performance evaluation conducted by the Government Invested Enterprise Performance Evaluation Commission, KTG was ranked fairly high. It was ranked ninth out of 23 GIEs in 1987, eighth in 1988, sixth in 1989 and 1990. The process of privatization involved no major management-union conflicts. Nor have there been any labour disputes since 1987 despite the country's generally disturbed industrial relations.

A trade union was established in KTG (then the Office of Monopoly) as early as 1954, just one year after the enactment of the Trade Union Act. Since then the union has played an important role in the country's labour movement, particularly in the 1950s and 1960s when the labour movement had not yet evolved in the private sector. The number of union members was 8,000 at the end of 1990, with an organization rate of almost 100 per cent.

Labour productivity

Table 2.5 shows changes in a number of productivity indices before and after the privatization of KTG. Public profit, net profit, turnover and value added have continued to increase since privatization both in per employee and in absolute terms. KTG's turnover increased at an average annual rate of 4.3 per cent in the three years before privatization, while it has increased by 10.9 per cent annually since privatization. The increase in turnover is even greater in per employee terms since KTG has made substantial reductions in its workforce since privatization. Turnover per employee increased at an average annual rate of 7.7 per cent in the three years before privatization, while the annual rate of increase since privatization has been 17.1 per cent. This outstanding performance is also evident in terms of value added and profits, as shown in table 2.5.

The number of cigarettes produced per employee-hour increased at an annual rate of 5.8 per cent in the three years before privatization, while since privatization it has risen by 11.7 per cent annually. The volume of ginseng produced per employee-day has also increased greatly since privatization.

The increases in labour productivity were particularly remarkable in the first year of privatization. In 1988 public profit, turnover and value added per employee grew by 40.2 per cent, 31.7 per cent and 32.9 per cent, respectively. In the same year, the number of cigarettes produced per employee-hour increased by 19.4 per cent, while the volume of ginseng produced per employee-day rose by 39.9 per cent. There was also a substantial increase in capital productivity, with the ratio of public profits to fixed capital increasing by 25.0 per cent in 1988.

The good performance of KTG since privatization is attributed to the fact that it has implemented a successful retrenchment scheme and that its sales have increased substantially, despite the opening of the Republic of Korea's tobacco market to foreign firms. The size of the workforce was reduced by 10.6 per cent and 7.2 per cent in 1988 and 1989 respectively. The boost in sales was due to enhanced marketing activities and to a growing preference among Korean consumers for more expensive brands of cigarette. The share of high quality cigarettes in KTG's sales increased from 63 per cent in 1985 to 72 per cent in 1987 and 77 per cent in 1988.

Wages and working conditions

In the Republic of Korea pay in the government authorities is generally lower than in the public authorities or the private sector. After the change in status of KTG employees from public servants to civilians employed in a public enterprise, the wages of KTG employees increased very substantially. Table 2.5 shows that KTG's labour cost per employee increased by 67.6 per cent in 1987, the first year of privatization. Since the Government has pursued a low-wage policy for the public authorities since the late 1980s, the wage increases for 1990 and 1991 were fairly moderate. Highly ranked government officials experienced larger wage increases right after the privatization, while wage increases were higher for low-ranking workers in the following years.

Provisions for paid holidays and compensation for industrial accidents also changed with privatization. The maximum amount of paid annual leave for a public servant is 25 days, with one extra day for every two years of tenure. Under the Labour Standard Act,

Table 2.5. Selected labour productivity indicators, Korea Tobacco and Ginseng Corp.

Indicator	1983	1984	1985	1986	1987	1988	1989	1990	1991
Turnover (million won) (A)	1 343 676	1 412 087 (5.1)	1 470 919 (4.2)	1 523 405 (3.6)	1 669 128 (9.6)	1 964 993 (17.7)	2 159 304 (9.9)	2 360 973 (9.3)	2 524 759 (6.9)
Value added (million won) (B)	971 333	1 065 980 (9.7)	1 116 567 (4.7)	1 136 714 (1.8)	1 215 922 (7.0)	1 444 207 (18.8)	1 605 566 (11.2)	1 790 101 (11.5)	1 948 808 (8.9)
Public profit (million won, in 1983 constant prices) (C)	1 092 891	1 134 873 (3.8)	1 126 097 (−0.8)	1 184 922 (5.2)	1 290 019 (8.9)	1 616 236 (25.3)	1 740 594 (7.7)	1 995 569 (14.6)	2 108 474 (5.7)
Net profit (million won) (D)	n.a.	n.a.	n.a.	n.a.	n.a.	54 720	126 070 (130.4)	198 955 (57.8)	270 900 (36.1)
Wage and welfare costs (million won) (E)	96 884	99 405 (2.6)	104 546 (5.2)	107 362 (2.7)	168 770 (57.2)	188 850 (11.9)	193 671 (2.6)	207 907 (7.4)	222 471 (7.1)
Number of employees (F)	12 656	12 288 (−2.9)	11 916 (−3.0)	11 472 (−3.7)	10 758 (−6.2)	9 616 (−10.6)	8 927 (−7.2)	8 745 (−2.0)	8 646 (−1.1)
A/F	106.17	114.2 (8.2)	123.44 (7.4)	132.79 (7.6)	155.15 (16.8)	204.35 (31.7)	241.89 (18.4)	269.98 (11.6)	292.02 (8.2)
B/F	76.75	86.75 (13.0)	93.70 (8.0)	99.07 (5.7)	113.01 (14.1)	150.19 (32.9)	179.86 (19.8)	204.70 (13.8)	225.40 (10.1)
C/F	86.35	92.36 (7.0)	94.50 (2.3)	103.29 (9.3)	119.91 (16.1)	168.08 (40.2)	194.98 (16.0)	228.20 (17.0)	243.87 (6.9)
D/F	n.a.	n.a.	n.a.	n.a.	n.a.	35.69	14.12 (148.1)	22.85 (61.1)	31.33 (37.7)
E/F	7.66	8.89 (16.1)	8.77 (−1.3)	9.36 (6.7)	15.69 (67.6)	19.64 (25.2)	21.70 (10.5)	23.77 (9.6)	25.73 (8.2)
Public profit/fixed capital	2.29	2.30 (0.5)	2.16 (−6.1)	2.21 (2.1)	2.36 (7.0)	2.95 (25.0)	3.18 (7.9)	3.60 (12.9)	3.71 (3.1)
Number of cigarettes produced per employee hour	n.a.	4.20	4.37 (3.9)	4.70 (7.6)	5.63 (19.7)	6.72 (19.4)	7.65 (13.8)	8.46 (10.5)	9.17 (8.5)
Ginseng production per employee day (kg)	n.a.	1.48	1.49 (1.2)	1.68 (12.4)	1.85 (10.0)	2.59 (39.9)	2.83 (9.2)	2.91 (2.3)	3.10 (6.5)
Overall economy: Rate of wage change (%)	11.0	8.7	9.2	8.2	10.1	15.5	21.1	18.8	17.5
Inflation rate (%)	3.4	2.3	2.5	2.8	3.0	7.1	5.7	8.6	9.7

Numbers in parentheses are the percentage change with respect to the previous year.   n.a. = not available.

which applies to public authorities, the maximum is 34 days. Most of the benefits KTG employees had as public servants were retained even after privatization. A special provision was made so that they would not lose the pension benefits they had enjoyed as public servants, since a national pension scheme had not yet been introduced at the time of privatization. But overtime provisions are much more favourable in the public authorities and KTG employees have come to enjoy these too.

Employment security

When KTG was privatized, the employment security of most workers was well protected. First, any low-ranking workers who did not want to lose their public servant status were given the option of transferring to another government authority. Second, the privileged retirement plan was introduced in order to reduce the size of the workforce. Third, new hiring was limited for the first few years of privatization.

Under the privileged retirement plan, workers were given, in addition to the ordinary severance payment, a lump-sum payment equivalent to their current monthly wages multiplied by half of their remaining years until the compulsory retirement age. In 1987 and 1988, a total of 1,153 workers took advantage of the plan. As a result, the share in the workforce of the over-50 age cohort decreased from 36.6 per cent in 1986 to 30.5 per cent in 1989. New hiring was also limited: only 35 workers were hired in 1987, with 251 and 175 hired in 1988 and 1989, respectively.

Workers in KTG enjoy full employment protection. Unless they commit a criminal offence, or are given a penalty according to the company's regulations, workers are entitled not to be temporarily laid off, or demoted, or displaced against their will. Nor can workers be assigned to another job within one year of being assigned to a job except under special circumstances. Finally, management must give due consideration to where workers live when they are assigned to jobs. These regulations are set out in the collective agreement between the workers and management of KTG. It can therefore be assumed that they have been reasonably observed, considering that trade union activity in the Republic of Korea has expanded since 1987 when KTG was privatized.

Human resources management

KTG has put great efforts into transforming itself from a bureaucratic government authority into a concern run on private business lines, despite its legal status as a government-invested enterprise. These efforts have been reflected in its human resources management practices.

With privatization a preliminary job analysis was begun in order to forecast long-term staffing needs. When KTG was a government authority, there used to be a specified number of posts available for each grade. In general, the specified posts were more than needed. At the end of 1986, for example, KTG could fill only 11,465 out of the 13,082 posts available. With long-term planning, its management of posts has become more satisfactory. The difference between the number of specified posts and the actual number of employees decreased from 1,617 in 1986 to 796 in 1987 and 249 in 1989.

Post management has also become more flexible. KTG used to need to obtain prior approval from its board in order to increase the number of posts for a grade in a section.

Under the new system adopted in 1988, the number of posts for a grade in a section can be changed without prior approval, and the board considers the matter afterwards.

Criteria for job rotation, promotion and performance evaluation were also reviewed. An incentive system was introduced in the first year of privatization, as required by the Government Invested Enterprises Management Act. Under this system, individual employees' bonuses are partly determined by the results of KTG's performance evaluation by the Government Invested Enterprise Performance Evaluation Commission and partly by their own performance. A Management Information System was also introduced in 1988 for more systematic personnel management.

Industrial relations

With privatization and the amendment of the Trade Union Act, the employees of KTG have come to enjoy full labour rights. However, there have been no major disputes at KTG since its privatization. Management and union cooperated throughout the process of privatization, and almost no one was forced to leave KTG against their will. The wages and working conditions of employees who remained after privatization have improved substantially. Labour costs per employee increased by almost 70 per cent in 1987, as mentioned above, and overtime pay started to be given.

Industrial relations at KTG have to some extent improved since privatization: in addition to the union, another forum now exists for workers and management to discuss matters of mutual concern, the Labour and Management Council. Under the Labour and Management Act, in any establishment with 50 or more permanent employees, apart from a government authority, a Labour and Management Council (LMC) must be set up and meet quarterly.[7] Through the Council, KTG's labour and management have been able to settle their differences over major issues peacefully.

Korea Telecom

Korea Telecom was established as a GIE in 1982 when its telecommunications business was removed from the Ministry of Postal Service as telecommunications became an increasingly crucial part of the infrastructure needed for the country's sustained economic development. Most of the employees who worked in the telecommunications sector of the Ministry of Postal Service were transferred to the Korea Telecommunications Authority, which was renamed Korea Telecom in 1990.

Korea Telecom's annual turnover and net profit in 1991 were 4,120 billion won (US$5,415 million) and 476 billion won (US$626 million), respectively; it employed 58,000 workers. Korea Telecom is considered one of the most popular sources of employment for new university graduates, mainly because telecommunications is seen as a key sector in the next century and Korea Telecom enjoys a monopoly position.

Korea Telecom's privatization is also considered successful. A primary task for the newly privatized industry was to build a circuit facility at a cost of 2,000 billion won (US$2,855 million). This was successfully completed as an investment project under the country's fifth five-year economic and social development plan. From 1981 to 1986, the total number of circuits increased by 140 per cent to 8,903,000, with an additional circuit supply of 6,143,000. This resulted in an increase in the diffusion rate from 8.9 to 19 per

100 over the same period. Moreover, the automation rate increased from 14.1 per cent (88.0 per cent) in 1981 to 65.3 per cent (99.2 per cent) in 1986. The quality of telecommunications services also improved substantially. The average length of time a telephone is out of order dropped from 120.68 minutes per year in 1981 to 28.28 minutes in 1986, and the "completion rate" of city calls increased from 58.3 per cent to 76.4 per cent during the same period. Performance evaluations by the Government Invested Enterprise Performance Evaluation Commission were good: Korea Telecom was ranked first in the 1986 evaluation.

The Korea Telecom trade union was organized in 1982 at the time of privatization: its members had previously belonged to the Postal Service Union. It has played a leading role in the Federation of Postal Service and Telecommunications Unions (until 1988) and the Federation of the Telecommunications Unions. At the end of 1990, its membership stood at about 48,000.

Labour productivity

Many of the selected productivity indicators, in particular those relating to finance, did not change much after privatization, as shown in table 2.6. The rate of increase of some indicators such as turnover actually fell, mainly because the industry was already very profitable even before privatization. A comparison of productivity before and after privatization per employee cannot be made since the number of employees who worked purely in the telecommunications sector under the Ministry of Postal Service cannot be identified.

However, other labour productivity indicators did increase substantially. The number of subscribers per employee, for example, rose from 92.6 in 1982 to 114.4 in 1984 and 144.8 in 1986. This was possible partly because Korea Telecom maintained reasonable control over increases in the size of its workforce. After privatization, Korea Telecom's workforce increased by only 32.4 per cent in five years, while its annual turnover grew by 90.1 per cent over the same period. Korea Telecom also put a great deal of effort into meeting customers' needs. In 1984, for example, it conducted 159 customer satisfaction surveys involving a total of 83,420 customers.

Wages and working conditions

The wages of Korea Telecom employees increased substantially with privatization by an average of 60.2 per cent in the first year, according to Park and Lee (1989), and by 25.6 per cent in the second year, which was high, considering that the national average wage increase for the same year was just 11.0 per cent. Korea Telecom employees also came to enjoy benefits under the Labour Standard Act and labour rights under the Trade Union Act as a result of the change of status from public servants to civilians. However, their right to take collective action was limited until the Trade Union Act amendment of 1987 gave employees of public enterprises the right to strike.

Employment security

This was not a problem for most employees when Korea Telecom was privatized. The telecommunications business was booming, so Korea Telecom had no need to cut its

Table 2.6. Selected labour productivity indicators, Korea Telecom

Indicator	1979	1980	1981	1982	1983	1984	1985	1986
Turnover (million won) (A)	310 924	488 832 (57.2)	647 253 (32.4)	962 463 (48.7)	1 141 787 (18.6)	1 388 145 (21.6)	1 605 662 (15.7)	1 839 053 (14.5)
Public profit (million won, in 1982 constant prices) (B)	350 317	428 642 (22.4)	473 432 (10.4)	475 215 (0.4)	593 820 (25.0)	800 668 (34.8)	973 560 (21.6)	1 298 669 (33.4)
Net profit (million won) (C)	n.a.	n.a.	n.a.	132 570	106 278 (–20.0)	132 228 (24.4)	65 232 (–51.7)	233 043 (257.3)
Wage and welfare costs (million won) (D)	91 650	126 122 (38.1)	160 229 (27.1)	228 570 (42.7)	325 053 (42.1)	382 156 (17.6)	422 544 (10.6)	458 611 (8.5)
Number of employees (E)	n.a.	n.a.	n.a.	35 876	40 641 (13.3)	42 602 (4.8)	44 877 (5.3)	47 512 (5.9)
Public profit/fixed capital	0.16	0.16	0.15 (–5.6)	0.13 (–17.0)	0.13 (1.6)	0.15 (14.0)	0.15 (3.4)	0.18 (15.1)
A/E	n.a.	n.a.	n.a.	26.83	28.09 (4.7)	32.58 (16.0)	35.78 (9.8)	38.71 (8.2)
B/E	n.a.	n.a.	n.a.	13.24	14.61 (10.4)	18.79 (28.6)	21.69 (15.4)	27.33 (26.0)
C/E	n.a.	n.a.	n.a.	3.70	2.62 (–29.2)	3.10 (18.3)	1.45 (–53.3)	4.9 (217.2)
D/E	n.a.	n.a.	n.a.	6.37	8.00 (25.6)	9.09 (13.6)	9.42 (3.6)	9.65 (2.4)
Time out of order per subscriber (minutes)	58.42	73.34 (25.5)	120.68 (64.5)	85.26 (–29.4)	69.38 (–18.6)	51.60 (–25.6)	35.21 (–31.8)	28.28 (–19.7)
Number of subscribers per employee	n.a.	n.a.	n.a.	92.57	102.85 (11.1)	114.40 (11.2)	128.45 (12.3)	144.76 (12.7)
Overall economy: Rate of wage change (%)	28.3	23.4	20.7	15.8	11.0	8.7	9.2	8.2
Inflation rate (%)	18.3	28.7	21.6	7.1	3.4	2.3	2.5	2.8

n.a. = not available.

workforce. In the first five years of privatization, the number of employees in fact rose by 32.4 per cent. Retraining was provided to some redundant workers including telephone operators. An early retirement plan has also been on offer since 1986. However, not many employees have taken advantage of this compared to KTG employees, despite the fact that the two firms' schemes are almost identical. This is mainly because telecommunications is considered such a growth industry in the Republic of Korea.

Korea Telecom employees are well protected. First, a worker cannot be assigned to another job within one year of being assigned to a job unless there are special circumstances. Second, only in the case of a criminal offence or a decision of the disciplinary committee can a worker be displaced.

Human resources management

Human resources management practices at Korea Telecom have changed a lot since privatization, partly because the structure of employment has changed substantially with the large number of new entrants. The proportion of workers with two years in college or higher education, for example, increased from 10.2 per cent in 1982 to 20.0 per cent in 1986.

A series of extensive job analyses was conducted, and a new payment system introduced.[8] More responsibilities have been given to middle management. Long-term manpower forecasting has also begun. A Total Quality Circle was introduced in 1987. Criteria for job rotation, promotion and performance evaluation are now made public. An incentive system has also been introduced, as required by the Government Invested Enterprises Management Act.

Industrial relations

When Korea Telecom was privatized in 1982, the labour rights of most workers in the Republic of Korea were limited. As a result, the views of the trade union were not seriously considered during the process of privatization, nor was the union offered much opportunity to participate in the process. It should, however, be noted that most union members were in favour of privatization because of the substantial improvements in wages.

4.2 Privatization through the People's Share Programme

Korea Electrical Power Corp. and Pohang Steel and Iron Co.

The People's Share Programme was originally intended to sell 5,000 billion won (US$7.1 billion) worth of government-held shares in six selected public enterprises over the period 1988-92. In April 1988, 34.1 per cent of the shares in the Pohang Steel and Iron Co. (POSCO) were sold to the public under the programme and in May 1989 the Korea Electric Power Corp. (KEPCO) was partially privatized. However, the programme has not been implemented further mainly because of the troubled state of the country's stock market.

POSCO, which was established in the early 1960s, has become one of the biggest steel firms in the world. Its success within a short period of time is well known worldwide.

In 1991 its annual turnover and net profit were 5,827 billion won (US$7,659 million) and 146 billion won (US$192 million), respectively. The number of employees at the end of 1991 was 25,000. KEPCO, which was established in 1943, is the only power company in the country. It employed 35,000 workers at the end of 1991. Its annual turnover and net profit for 1991 were 5,702 billion won (US$7,495 million) and 719 billion won (US$945 million), respectively.

The Government claims that one of the benefits which employees of the public enterprises privatized under the People's Share Programme can enjoy is capital gain through participating in the programme, as a proportion of the shares are set aside for employees. POSCO employees were offered, on average, 313 shares each, while KEPCO employees were offered around 1,000 shares each. Employees who did not sell their shares for three years were supposed to benefit from some capital gain because the purchase price of the shares was set much below the market price as well as below the price offered to the general public.

However, the capital gains for employees have turned out to be small. Song and Song (1992) estimated that the profit rates for the shares in the two public enterprises have decreased substantially since the implementation of the programme. For POSCO employees, the estimated profit rate decreased from 294.3 per cent in June 1988 to 78.2 per cent in December 1989, 32.9 per cent in December 1990 and 22.1 per cent in December 1991, as shown in table 2.7. The estimated profit rate for KEPCO employees also decreased from 152.7 per cent in August 1989 to 37.9 per cent in December 1990 and 23.9 per cent in December 1991. Considering that the interest rate for an ordinary savings account is about 15 per cent in the Republic of Korea, the capital gains for employees seem to be much smaller than expected. Members of the general public who sold their stocks after 1990 actually experienced some capital losses. The poor profit rates are attributed mainly to the troubled state of the stock market, which is described in the next section.

In introducing the People's Share Programme as a means of privatization, the Government claimed that the efficiency of the privatizing public enterprises would be increased by having a substantial number of shareholders involved in the decision-making

Table 2.7. Estimated profit rates for shares in the Korea Electric Power Corp. and the Pohang Steel and Iron Co.

	Type of purchase	Aug. 1989	Dec. 1989	Dec. 1990	Dec. 1991
Korea Electric Power Corp.	Ordinary purchase	0.769	0.735	0.154	0.103
	Discounted purchase	1.527	1.478	0.379	0.239

	Type of purchase	June 1988	Dec. 1988	Dec. 1989	Dec. 1990	Dec. 1991
Pohang Steel and Iron Co.	Ordinary purchase	1.760	1.573	0.491	0.180	0.117
	Discounted purchase	2.943	2.676	0.782	0.329	0.221

Source: Song and Song, 1992.

Table 2.8. Selected labour productivity indicators, Korea Electric Power Corp.

Indicator	1985	1986	1987	1988	1989	1990	1991
Assets (million won) (A)	12 249 179	12 569 776 (2.6)	12 566 492 (−0.03)	12 584 035 (0.1)	13 021 769 (3.5)	13 843 516 (6.3)	15 969 315 (15.4)
Turnover (million won) (B)	3 425 340	3 649 170 (6.5)	4 006 401 (9.8)	4 421 233 (10.4)	4 568 253 (3.3)	5 031 742 (10.1)	5 702 157 (13.3)
Net profit (million won) (C)	253 280	322 871 (27.5)	481 114 (49.0)	891 433 (85.3)	766 117 (−14.1)	605 831 (−20.9)	719 049 (18.7)
Wage and welfare costs (million won) (D)	n.a.	226 330	258 956 (14.4)	314 176 (21.3)	387 200 (23.2)	452 224 (16.8)	530 434 (17.3)
Number of employees (E)	22 770	23 696 (4.1)	25 212 (6.4)	25 999 (3.1)	26 147 (0.6)	27 337 (4.6)	28 278 (3.4)
A/E	538.0	530.5 (−1.4)	498.4 (−6.1)	484.0 (−2.9)	498.0 (2.9)	506.4 (1.7)	564.7 (11.5)
B/E	150.4	154.0 (2.4)	159.0 (3.2)	170.1 (7.0)	174.7 (2.7)	184.1 (5.4)	201.6 (9.5)
C/E	11.1	13.6 (22.5)	19.1 (40.4)	34.3 (79.6)	29.3 (−14.6)	22.2 (−24.2)	25.4 (14.4)
D/E	n.a.	9.6	10.3 (7.3)	12.1 (17.5)	14.8 (22.3)	16.5 (11.5)	18.8 (13.9)
Overall economy:							
Rate of wage change (%)	9.2	8.2	10.1	15.5	21.1	18.8	17.5
Inflation rate (%)	2.5	2.8	3.0	7.1	5.7	8.6	9.7

n.a. = not available.

Table 2.9. Selected labour productivity indicators, Pohang Steel and Iron Co.

Indicator	1985	1986	1987	1988	1989	1990	1991
Assets (million won) (A)	3 327 309	4 479 527 (34.6)	5 139 175 (14.7)	55 625 195 (8.2)	89 440 049 (3.5)	98 748 226 (10.4)	10 646 231 (7.8)
Turnover (million won) (B)	2 047 252	2 241 622 (9.5)	2 919 369 (30.2)	3 701 118 (26.8)	4 364 288 (17.9)	4 805 023 (10.1)	5 827 412 (21.2)
Net profit (million won) (C)	61 729	62 010 (0.5)	70 331 (13.4)	134 357 (91.0)	114 511 (−14.8)	79 025 (−31.0)	145 680 (84.3)
Wage and welfare costs (million won) (D)	101 421	114 307 (12.7)	162 483 (42.1)	182 912 (12.6)	256 014 (40.0)	311 480 (21.7)	402 462 (29.2)
Number of employees (E)	15 000	16 500 (10.0)	19 094 (15.7)	19 353 (1.4)	20 402 (5.4)	22 537 (10.5)	25 074 (11.3)
A/E	221.8	271.5 (22.4)	269.2 (−8.5)	287.4 (6.8)	438.4 (52.5)	438.2 (−0.04)	424.6 (−3.1)
B/E	136.5	176.9 (29.6)	152.9 (−13.6)	191.2 (25.0)	213.9 (11.9)	213.2 (−0.3)	232.4 (8.9)
C/E	4.1	3.8 (−7.3)	3.7 (−9.8)	6.9 (86.5)	5.6 (−18.8)	3.5 (−37.5)	5.84 (65.7)
D/E	6.8	6.9 (1.5)	8.5 (23.2)	9.5 (31.6)	12.5 (31.6)	13.8 (10.4)	16.1 (16.7)
Overall economy:							
Rate of wage change (%)	9.2	8.2	10.1	15.5	21.1	18.8	17.5
Inflation rate (%)	2.5	2.8	3.0	7.1	5.7	8.6	9.7

process. However, this expectation has not been realized for either POSCO or KEPCO, mainly because the Government has remained the major shareholder in both enterprises. The Government still holds 35 per cent of POSCO's shares and 79 per cent of KEPCO's.

The impact of partial privatization on the two public enterprises does not seem to have been great, as shown in tables 2.8 and 2.9. Some of the productivity indicators have actually declined since privatization, mainly because of the relatively poor performance of the national economy since the late 1980s. The GNP growth rate dropped from 12.4 per cent in 1988 to 6.7 per cent in 1989; it increased to 9 per cent in 1990, but this was still below the GNP growth rates of over 12 per cent experienced in 1986-88.

Human resources management practices have not changed much at either POSCO or KEPCO as a result of the partial privatization. However, industrial relations in the two firms have changed substantially along with the overall changes in the national industrial relations scene. The POSCO trade union was organized in 1988. Most of the differences between university graduates and high school graduates as regards wages, promotion, job rotation, etc., were abolished and a skill payment system was introduced in 1990.[9] This change in the payment system meant that the average wages of POSCO employees increased by more than 20 per cent in that year. KEPCO has a long history of unionization, but there have been some recent changes in industrial relations. For example, the union played a key role in organizing a campaign to restore the severance payment schedule, whose benefits were reduced in the early 1980s by the military government. However, these changes in industrial relations at the two firms are considered to have little to do with privatization itself.

4.3 Total privatization

The Korea Stock Exchange

The Korea Stock Exchange was established in 1956 with joint contributions from banks, insurance companies and securities firms. With the enactment of the Securities and Exchange Act, the Exchange was reorganized into a joint stock corporation in 1962. In 1983, with the amendment of the Securities and Exchange Act, the Exchange was again reorganized into a non-profit, government-owned corporation; it came to be included as one of the GIEs with the enactment of the Government Invested Enterprises Management Act in 1984. In 1988, the Exchange was totally privatized into a membership corporation as the Government sold its two-thirds shareholding to the member firms.

The privatization of the Korea Stock Exchange took place as part of the mid-term plan for internationalization of the Republic of Korea's capital market during the period 1989-92. However, its overall relationship with the Government, including the Ministry of Finance, has not changed much since privatization. Under the Securities and Exchange Act most of the Exchange's business activities are still regulated by the Ministry of Finance, and the Chairman of the Exchange is still appointed by the Minister.

Table 2.10 shows that the labour productivity indicators for the Exchange have declined since privatization. This is due to the overall decline of the country's stock market since 1988. The Korean Composite Stock Price Index (KCSPI) decreased from 1,007.77 on 1 April 1989 to 909.72 on 31 December 1989 to 696.11 on 31 December 1990 and finally to 610.92 on 31 December 1991.

Table 2.10. Selected labour productivity indicators, Korea Stock Exchange

Indicator	1984	1985	1986	1987	1988	1989	1990	1991
Turnover (million won) (A)	5 792	6 774 (17.0)	11 237 (65.9)	20 674 (84.0)	31 419 (52.0)	18 044 (–42.6)	13 148 (–27.1)	18 840 (43.3)
Net profit (million won) (B)	583	1 572 (169.6)	5 534 (252.0)	13 593 (145.6)	20 942 (54.1)	6 260 (–70.1)	1 104 (–82.4)	625 (–43.4)
Wage and welfare costs (million won) (C)	2 894	3 338 (15.3)	3 488 (4.5)	3 946 (13.1)	5 682 (44.0)	7 244 (27.5)	8 235 (13.7)	9 752 (18.4)
Number of employees (D)	307	296 (–3.6)	284 (–4.1)	307 (8.1)	365 (18.9)	401 (9.9)	418 (4.2)	463 (10.8)
A/D	18.9	22.9 (21.2)	39.6 (72.9)	67.3 (69.9)	86.1 (27.9)	45.0 (–47.7)	31.5 (–30.0)	40.7 (29.2)
B/D	1.9	5.3 (178.9)	19.5 (267.9)	44.3 (127.2)	57.4 (29.6)	15.6 (–72.8)	2.6 (–83.3)	1.3 (–50.0)
C/D	9.4	11.3 (20.2)	12.3 (8.8)	12.8 (4.1)	15.6 (21.9)	18.1 (16.0)	19.7 (8.8)	21.1 (7.1)
Overall economy: Rate of wage change (%)	8.7	9.2	8.2	10.1	15.5	21.1	18.8	17.5
Inflation rate (%)	2.3	2.5	2.8	3.0	7.1	5.7	8.6	9.7

Human resources management practices and industrial relations at the Korea Stock Exchange have remained more or less unchanged. However, employees' wages and working conditions have to some extent improved since the Government began to interfere less with internal matters such as wages, employee numbers and the structure of the organization. The costs of wages and welfare benefits per employee increased by 21.9 per cent and the number of employees rose by 18.9 per cent in 1988. New job titles were created in the first year of privatization, which meant that more employees were promoted.

5. Conclusions

Case studies (see section 4) show that in the Republic of Korea, privatization has not meant workers losing benefits which they previously enjoyed. Even for employees of government authorities which have changed to public authorities, wages and working conditions have improved substantially with privatization. The employment security of employees in the privatizing organizations has been on the whole well protected: almost no one has been forced to leave an organization against their will.

This can be attributed to a number of factors. First, the privatized enterprises have remained part of the public sector or, like the Korea Stock Exchange, are seen as organizations which serve the public interest. Second, the performance of the national economy in the last three decades has been remarkable. This has meant that any major retrenchment schemes in the public sector would have been socially unacceptable. Finally, some of the privatized enterprises, including KTG, have done reasonably well in transforming themselves from bureaucratic government authorities to organizations run on private business lines.

Effects of privatization on other labour market outcomes such as labour productivity and human resources management practices have been mixed. In the newly created public authorities such as KTG and Korea Telecom, whose relationship with the Government has undergone a fundamental change, both labour productivity and human resources management have improved. In the other three organizations, including the Korea Stock Exchange, for which regulation from the Government remains virtually the same after privatization, little change has been observed, which was to be expected since the Government still remains in control of most of their activities.

Even when the current privatization scheme, which has been suspended since 1990, is re-implemented and completed, little improvement in efficiency is expected in most privatizing enterprises since the Government will still remain the major shareholder. The current privatization plan should therefore be reconsidered with a view to improving efficiency in the various operational aspects of public enterprises, including human resources management and industrial relations.

Real privatization within the context of a restructuring of the public sector, not just selling some portion of government shares to the public, would be the best way to increase efficiency as well as to achieve industrial peace in the public sector. Privatization should be introduced with proper regulations, including controls on prices of services and increased competition. On the other hand, another measure to reduce the agent cost should be found for the government-financed authorities and government-subsidized authorities, because the high agent cost is not only due to the non-profit nature of these organizations.

References

Bai, M. 1981. "Turning point in the Korean economy", in *The Developing Economies*, Vol. 19, No. 1.

Kang, Shin Il. 1988. *Korea's privatization plans and past experiences.* Seoul, Korea Development Institute.

Park, Young-Bum. 1988. *Study on investment efficiency in government-invested enterprises.* Seoul, Korea Institute for Economics and Technology.

———. 1992. *State regulation, the labor market and economic development in South Korea.* Paper presented at an International Workshop organized by the International Institute for Labour Studies, Bali, Indonesia.

———. Forthcoming. *Public sector pay in the Republic of Korea.* Geneva, ILO.

———; Lee, Sang-duck. 1989. *Public sector industrial relations in Korea.* Seoul, Korea Labor Institute.

Song, Dae-hi; Song, M. 1992. "Analysis of the economic effects of the public enterprise privatization through the People's Share Program", in *Public Enterprise Studies*, Vol. 4, No. 1.

Notes

[1] See Park, 1992, for details about the labour situation in the early 1980s.

[2] This means people whose incomes do not exceed a certain limit, not poor people.

[3] The actual distribution of shares in the Pohang Steel and Iron Co. followed the envisaged pattern. The average number of shares bought by employees was 9.7, while the figure for low-income buyers was 7.8.

[4] The wages of public servants are supposed to be determined by wage comparability with the private sector, based on a wage survey conducted by the Ministry of Government Administration. However, since neither the methodology nor the results of the survey are made public and no outside interests are involved in its conduct, its credibility as reliable information is very weak.

[5] The medical insurance system for public servants was introduced in the 1960s, while the national medicare insurance system for the private sector started in the early 1980s. The national medicare system includes many low-income earners since its coverage is more than 70 per cent of the total population. The financial base of the public servants' medical insurance system is therefore stronger and the benefits schedule more favourable.

[6] Public profit is defined as turnover minus the sum of intermediate inputs, employment costs, rental expenses and the opportunity cost of working capital. The concept of public profit is used because most of the figures needed to calculate net profit are not available for the period before KTG's privatization and because the concept of net profit does not fit well with the objectives of the enterprise.

[7] The LMC's main function is to discuss ways to improve productivity, promote employees' welfare, resolve workers' grievances, and plan the workers' training programmes. The collective agreement covers annual wage increases, severance allowances, bonuses, other wage issues, working hours, kinds of paid leave, holidays, other welfare benefits, compensation for industrial accidents and disease, safety and health, job classification, rules and procedures governing dismissals, job mobility, criteria for promotion, training, and union activities. As trade unions have recently expanded their activities, the scope of bargaining has widened. As bargaining has extended from wages to non-wage issues such as work hours and quality of work life, and even participation in management decision-making, the scope of bargaining has often become itself a cause of disputes. The Government has suggested that these issues should be dealt with in the LMCs.

[8] Based on the job analysis, the payment system changed from the public servant system to one which is more appropriate for Korea Telecom's needs.

[9] Individual workers' wages and/or promotion in the Republic of Korea mainly depend on their educational attainment, age and tenure. Under the skill payment system, which originates in Japanese wage practices, workers can be promoted (hence, their lifetime wages can be increased) if their skills meet certain requirements set by the company.

3. Adjustment and privatization in India

C. S. Venkata Ratnam*

The moves towards privatization in India are largely associated with sectoral adjustment loans (SALs). Unlike many other developing countries, India seems to take a cautious and selective approach, rather than going in for rapid privatization. The basic thrust of privatization in India is not so much to reduce the role of the public sector as to allow an increasing role for the private sector in national economic development.

1. Reasons for public sector enterprise activities in India

The rationale for public sector enterprises — or state-owned enterprises (SOEs), as referred to in this chapter hereafter — is not merely economic but also social. The Constitution of India, successive industrial policy resolutions and the five-year plan documents highlight the role of the public sector in the national economy. The public sector is envisaged as the engine of growth accelerating planned economic development of the country; it is also progressively assigned a dominant role not only in industries of strategic importance but also in areas where private sector initiative is not commensurate with the requirements of the day.

The Industrial Policy Resolution 1948 classified industries into three broad categories. The first covers arms and ammunition, atomic energy and railway transport; these areas were to be "the exclusive monopoly of the Central Government". The second category covers coal, iron and steel, aircraft, shipbuilding, telephone, telegraph and wireless apparatus (excluding radio receiving sets) and mineral oils; the State was to have exclusive responsibility for establishing new industries in these areas except when private cooperation was needed in the national interest. Other industries were "normally to be left to private enterprise" subject to the proviso that "the state will also progressively participate in this field" without hesitating to intervene "whenever the progress of an industry under private enterprise is unsatisfactory". Subsequent industrial policy resolutions and successive five-year plans broadly endorsed this policy thrust, giving primacy to the public sector until the middle of 1991.

* International Management Institute, New Delhi.

The Government has adopted a programme of heavy industrialization to create a modern, complex, composite and heterogeneous industrial base of a kind unparalleled in most developing countries. It has also effected a series of nationalizations:

(a)   to fill the vacuum created by the lack of adequate response from the private sector (particularly in the energy sector);

(b)   to fulfil social objectives (bank nationalizations);

(c)   to conserve natural resources and facilitate their orderly exploitation (nationalization of coal and non-coking coal companies);

(d)   to protect threatened jobs (nationalization of textile mills).

Encouragement of the public sector was not guided by communism but by the desire to create a socialist pattern of society and by pragmatic considerations about the need to build a mixed economy where the resources of the State could supplement private sector contributions and initiatives.

Despite this emphasis on the public sector, the private sector's share in India's GDP in 1980/81 was 80 per cent (table 3.1). Though it declined to 76 per cent over the next decade, a shift in policies may improve the private sector's share in GDP during the 1990s and beyond. Agriculture and manufacture have accounted for around 50 per cent of India's GDP throughout the post-independence era. The private sector accounts for the lion's share (90 per cent and above) in these two sectors. The public sector has a near monopoly in mining and quarrying, infrastructure and core industries — industrial raw materials, minerals, metals, electricity, gas and insurance — and a dominant presence in finance, transport, storage and communications. The public sector therefore has a significant impact on the performance of the private sector. The role of the public sector has to be seen not in terms of its share in the country's GDP but in terms of its ability to control the ownership and distribution of infrastructure and industrial inputs. It has played a major role in seeking balanced regional development by putting an emphasis on industrialization of backward areas and setting up specialized institutions to provide financial, technical and consultancy support. The public sector in India has also been seen as an instrument to direct the ownership and control of the material resources of the community and to ensure that they are distributed in such a way as to promote the common good and avoid undesirable concentrations of wealth. The public sector has contributed significantly both to broadening the entrepreneurial base and to helping the underprivileged. It has done this through affirmative action programmes in employment and by according the poorer sections of society preferential access to credit, usually at concessionary rates of interest, and through public financial institutions to enable them to participate in a variety of livelihood and employment generation programmes.

SOEs operate in India at the central, state and local municipality level, in wide-ranging spheres of economic activity. There are over 800 SOEs with an investment of over Rs.460 billion (US$1 = Rs.30 approximately) run by 25 state governments, prominent among which are the state electricity boards and state road transport corporations (Shankar et al., 1992). Central government has, as at 1 April 1992, 237 operating non-departmental industrial and commercial enterprises with an investment of Rs.11,850 million employing about 2.3 million people. These 237 enterprises do not include the departmental undertakings (e.g. railways, post and telecommunications), financial institutions (commercial

Table 3.1. Share of public and private sectors in GDP by various economic activities, India (1980/81 prices)

Sector	Year	Amount (Rs. million)	% share in GDP	Public sector		Private sector	
				Amount	% share to GDP	Amount	% share in GDP
Agriculture, forestry and fishing	1980/81	46 649	38.0	1 357	1.1	45 292	37.0
	1985/86	54 218	34.6	1 547	1.0	52 671	33.6
	1989/90	63 263	31.7	1 535	0.8	61 728	30.9
	1990/91	66 292	31.6	1 504	0.7	64 788	30.9
Mining and quarrying[1]	1980/81	1 887	1.5	1 715	1.4	172	0.1
	1985/86	2 623	1.7	n.a.	n.a.	n.a.	n.a.
	1989/90	3 802	1.9	n.a.	n.a.	n.a.	n.a.
	1990/91	3 990	1.9	n.a.	n.a.	n.a.	n.a.
Manufacturing	1980/81	21 644	17.7	2 883	2.3	18 761	15.4
	1985/86	30 320	19.4	3 457	2.2	26 863	17.2
	1989/90	41 063	20.6	5 473	2.7	35 590	17.9
	1990/91	44 131	21.6	6 246	3.0	37 885	17.9
Electricity, gas and water supply	1980/81	2 070	1.7	1 878	1.5	192	0.2
	1985/86	3 099	2.0	2 834	1.8	265	0.2
	1989/90	4 484	2.3	4 192	2.1	292	0.1
	1990/91	4 792	2.2	4 543	2.2	249	0.1
Construction	1980/81	6 114	5.0	993	0.8	5 121	4.2
	1985/86	7 183	4.6	1 475	0.9	5 708	3.7
	1989/90	8 890	4.5	1 797	0.9	7 093	3.6
	1990/91	9 326	4.4	1 895	0.9	7 431	3.5
Trade, hotels and restaurants	1980/81	14 713	12.0	824	0.7	13 889	11.3
	1985/86	19 649	12.5	1 086	0.7	18 563	11.7
	1989/90	24 310	12.2	862	0.4	23 448	11.8
	1990/91	25 745	12.3	885	0.4	24 860	11.9
Transport, storage and communications	1980/81	5 724	4.7	3 104	4.7	4 019	2.2
	1985/86	7 951	5.1	3 932	5.1	6 344	2.6
	1989/90	10 685	5.4	10 685	5.4	5 959	3.0
	1990/91	11 185	5.3	11 185	5.3	6 344	3.0
Financing, insurance, real estate and business services	1980/81	10 791	8.8	2 931	2.4	7 860	6.4
	1985/86	14 708	9.4	5 092	3.3	9 616	3.1
	1989/90	20 404	10.2	8 997	4.5	11 407	3.0
	1990/91	20 985	10.0	9 080	4.3	11 905	3.1
Community, social and personal services	1980/81	12 835	10.5	8 546	7.0	4 289	3.5
	1985/86	16 815	10.7	11 867	7.6	4 948	3.1
	1989/90	22 602	11.3	16 458	8.2	6 204	3.0
	1990/91	23 345	11.1	16 774	8.0	6 571	3.1

n.a. = not available. Rs.31.20 = US$1 (December 1994). [1] Most mining and quarrying is in the public sector. Source: CSO, 1993.

banks, development finance institutions, etc.), ordinance factories, etc. It is difficult to estimate how many SOEs operate at municipality level.

Until the mid-1980s the public sector showed scarcely any concern with profitability. The net profit on capital employed in the public sector was around 2 per cent throughout the 1980s. A deeper analysis of the profitability profile of the SOEs reveals that, oil companies apart, three out of four public sector companies were making losses. A variety of controls, cost-plus administered price strategies and multiple goals (including socio-political considerations) makes it difficult to assess the effectiveness of the public sector in India. Blurred accountability certainly bred a counterproductive enterprise culture and a system of using public assets for private gain which, together, compounded the problems of the public sector. Though the image of the private sector may not have been any better, the public expect more from the public sector. For this reason, if for no other, public sector performance became the focus of attention for the public and policy-makers alike. Governments at all levels were finding it increasingly beyond their means to sustain SOEs that were making losses. The external debt problem proved to be the last straw requiring the Government to swallow the bitter pill of public sector reform and the encouragement of private sector development.

2. Public sector enterprise reform

Improvements in efficiency have been leading to job losses in many parts of the world. This is happening even in "excellent" companies that once guaranteed jobs. In economies like that of India, where organized sector employment is already thin and unemployment problems loom large, it is natural for governments to be hesitant about announcing measures that would inevitably mean job losses. In the 1991 Census the total population of India was 847 million; 37 per cent of the total formed the workforce (314 million). Employment in the organized sector (26.4 million in 1992) accounted for less than 10 per cent of the workforce, but 71 per cent of total employment in the organized sector was in the public sector (18.8 million). While the central Government and the seven union territories accounted for around 50 per cent of total public sector employment, the rest (9.7 million) was accounted for by the 25 states. The SOEs owned and managed by the Government of India employed just over 2 million people. No estimate exists of the number employed in state-level public enterprises.

Preserving existing unproductive jobs may in fact damage the interests of new entrants into the labour market. The jobless may be fewer with reform than without. Further, the money that is used to protect unproductive jobs could be gainfully used to create several times more jobs. Notwithstanding such arguments, the social consequences of large-scale redundancies in the already sparsely organized sector made the Government excessively cautious in its approach to reform.

The 1980s saw an alarming rise in fiscal deficits, a near doubling in absolute terms of central government expenditure during 1985/86 to 1990/91, and a fivefold increase in subsidies over the decade (table 3.2); but it was the balance of payments crisis, exacerbated by the growing share of non-discretionary imports (particularly oil) and the stagnation or decline of exports, that precipitated the Indian economic crisis. An almost bankrupt economy will find it difficult to finance unviable public enterprises for ever. Economic

Table 3.2. Fiscal deficit, government expenditure and subsidies, 1980-93
(at current market prices)

Year	Gross fiscal deficit		Total central government expenditure		Subsidies (central government)	
	Amount (Rs. m)	% of GDP	Amount (Rs. m)	% of GDP	Amount (Rs. m)	% of GDP
1980/81	8 299	6.1	22 495	16.5	1 912	1.4
1985/86	21 855	8.3	53 112	20.2	4 796	1.8
1990/91	44 632	8.4	104 973	19.7	10 728	2.0
1991/92	36 325	5.9	112 731	18.3	10 326	1.7
1992/93	40 173	5.7	127 753	18.1	10 188	1.4

Sources: Government of India, 1994a; CMIE, 1993.

necessity outweighed considerations of political risk and paved the way for the long overdue reform of the Indian public sector.

The trade and industrial policy reforms have either reduced the sphere of operation of the State (such as in state trading) or exposed the SOEs to increased competition (in many core sectors such as steel and power). Unless government controls over the functioning of the SOEs are eased, these partial reforms may jeopardize the interests of the public sector. The SOEs need greater autonomy to take investment decisions and greater control over decisions concerning their input and output markets and other administrative matters even as their dependence on budgetary support is drastically curtailed or eliminated.

Throughout the 1980s, the Government of India set up one expert committee after another, headed by such heavyweights in public life as Mohd. Fazal (1980-82); L. K. Jha (1983-84) and Arjun Sengupta (1986), in addition to the Parliamentary Committee on Public Undertakings, all of which reviewed the performance of the public sector (SCOPE, 1989). The bulk of the current wave of changes seem to reflect the considered views of the Arjun Sengupta Committee, which in turn coincide with the current thinking of the World Bank and the IMF in regard to public sector reform.

2.1 Organizational reform and management changes

Since the mid-1980s there has been a good deal of rethinking about the structure and strategy of the SOEs. Departmental undertakings have been transformed into autonomous corporations or into public limited companies under the Companies Act. Such a change will free these enterprises from possibly excessive parliamentary control and allow them freedom to raise and use funds more freely than before. Until recently the growth of SOEs was often limited by governmental controls and the need for budgetary support for fresh investments. The transformed SOEs have far more freedom to tap the capital markets though, unlike in the past, such public issues and bond flotations would not be backed by government guarantees.

Since disinvestment is carried out to a limited extent only, the Government continues to be a majority shareholder. There has been little change in the composition of the boards or the management style of the companies (Hakeem, 1993), even though the system of Memoranda of Understanding (MOUs) was designed to increase autonomy and impart greater accountability for performance and results. The Eighth Plan document acknowledges that changes are needed in management practices at enterprise level to promote efficiency, dynamic leadership, resourcefulness and innovation. It further admits that the "State level public enterprises have serious problems: interference, lack of professionalism, ad-hoc investment and employment decisions . . . A major effort is called for, in collaboration with the State governments, to promote reforms in them" (Government of India, 1992). Several state-level SOEs did not even have their accounts audited for over a decade.

The Sick Industrial Companies (Special Provisions) Act 1985 was amended in 1992 to cover the public sector also. Consequently, 44 SOEs were identified on the basis of 1992/93 results, out of which 40 have already been registered by the Bureau for Industrial and Financial Reconstruction (BIFR), a quasi-judicial agency that has the powers to decide whether sick units should be revived or closed. The Special Tripartite Committee on Structural Adjustment decided to consider all cases of sickness in SOEs before they are referred to the BIFR. No sick SOE has yet been closed, however, owing to political compulsions, though several have been identified as candidates for closure.

2.2 Performance contracts

During the Seventh Plan, the system of performance contracts or Memoranda of Understanding (MOUs), by which managements are to be granted greater autonomy and held accountable for results, was introduced. Unlike in the past, in the 1990s 50 per cent weight is accorded to profitability in evaluations of the performance of SOEs. Considering the chequered background of some of the taken-over units, the varied market situations and the diversity of activities in which the public sector in India is engaged, giving such weight to profitability has been criticized.

The Government's ambivalence towards the idea of autonomy for SOEs has produced glaring contradictions. In steel, controls have been completely removed. In coal, on the other hand, while the Government is serious about progressive withdrawal of budgetary support, it still controls output prices and decisions on continuing to run unviable underground mining operations for reasons of employment protection. It also forces the public sector coal company to continue to supply coal to the state electricity boards even though the latter are chronic defaulters as regards payment of arrears. In the case of the public sector cable company, government departments/corporations are the major buyers. The Government forced the cable company to continue to supply in 1993 at rates 3 per cent lower than those prevailing in 1991, though the public sector company's quotation was already the lowest, and it no longer received budgetary support nor any government help in containing input prices. Such examples abound.

The performance contracts, though conceptually sound, are in practice limited in value. First, the contract is between unequal partners. The chief executive of an SOE signs the contract with a person who evaluates his/her performance and plays a part in recommending extension of tenure. Second, the Government not infrequently fails to fulfil its side of the bargain. Third, the sudden shift in emphasis towards profitability is considered unjust and inconsistent with the original rationale for the very existence of some SOEs.

2.3 Reduced budgetary support

Phasing out budgetary support to sick or potentially sick SOEs has been another major aspect of government policy since the mid-1980s. Budgetary support to the SOEs decreased progressively from about 47 per cent in 1986/87 to less than 14 per cent in 1993/94 (table 3.3).

Withdrawal of budgetary support to the public sector has forced many companies to try to improve their performance.[1] There is need for caution, though, in interpreting the results of the sudden U-turn towards performance and profitability orientation. With the gradual withdrawal of budgetary support from the Government, the SOEs raised Rs.207 billion by issue of bonds between 1 April 1986 and 31 March 1992. These large public issues by the SOEs did not find a ready market. The SOEs therefore made arrangements with banks whereby the banks subscribed for a significant part of the issues and in turn the

Table 3.3. Resources of public sector enterprises, 1986/87 to 1993/94 (Rs. million)

	1986/87	1990/91	1991/92	1992/93	1993/94 estimated
Budgetary support	77 920 (46.9)	75 950 (27.1)	69 200 (23.5)	65 760 (17.9)	65 400 (13.8)
Equity		51 180 (18.2)	41 850 (14.2)	41 730 (11.4)	36 800 (7.8)
Loans		24 770 (8.8)	27 350 (9.3)	24 030 (6.6)	28 600 (6.1)
Internal and extra-budgetary resources (IEBR)	88 330 (53.1)	204 590 (72.9)	225 010 (76.5)	300 850 (82.1)	406 950 (86.2)
Internal resources	53 680 (32.3)	107 210 (38.2)	120 070 (40.8)	161 290 (44.0)	190 620 (40.4)
Bonds/debentures	13 640 (8.2)	49 330 (17.6)	57 220 (19.4)	62 910 (17.2)	58 820 (14.6)
External commercial borrowing/suppliers' credit	11 440 (6.9)	25 530 (9.1)	18 540 (6.3)	37 460 (10.2)	51 770 (11.0)
Others, e.g. deposits and inter-corporate transfers	9 570 (5.8)	22 510 (8.0)	29 910 (9.9)	39 190 (10.7)	95 740 (20.3)
Total (budgetary support and IEBR)	166 250 (100.0)	280 540 (100.0)	294 210 (100.0)	366 610 (100.0)	472 350 (100.0)

Source: CMIE, 1993.

SOEs placed the funds raised by the issues with the banks who subscribed to the issues (Janakiraman Committee Report, 1993).

2.4 Divestment of SOE shares

During the 1980s, the Mohd. Fazal Committee (1980) and, more importantly, the Arjun Sengupta Committee (1986) suggested various reforms of the public sector. Interestingly, however, they did not favour the sale of SOE shares (SCOPE, 1989). Partial divestment of shares in SOEs, both to mobilize non-inflationary sources of finance and to provide wider public ownership of the SOE shares, has nevertheless become one of the elements of the new policy concerning the public sector.[2] The new Industrial Policy Statement and the budget speech of July 1991 refer to the Government's decision to mobilize additional resources and encourage wider public participation through divestment of up to 20 per cent of government equity in selected public enterprises. The shares were to be offered to mutual funds, financial/investment institutions, SOE employees and the general public. Between 5 and 20 per cent of the equity in 31 SOEs was divested in two phases in 1991/92. The 31 SOEs whose shares were selected for divestment were a mix of 8 very good, 12 good and 11 not so good companies, with a net asset value shares with Rs.10 face value worth Rs.50, between Rs.20 and Rs.50, and less than Rs.20, respectively. The shares were offered as randomly structured portfolios in bundles consisting of nine SOEs, each with a notional reserve price. The reserve price was an average of net asset value and profit-earning capacity value. The shares were offered to selected financial institutions and mutual funds. As elsewhere, there were problems with the pricing of shares when the first instalments of shares were offloaded to public and private mutual funds at apparently low prices, to be followed by almost instantaneous back-to-back buying and a sudden spurt in share prices.

The total number of shares divested during 1991/92 constituted only 8 per cent of the government holding in 31 public enterprises at a total value of Rs.30,380 million. A similar exercise was carried out in 1992/93, when about Rs.19,120 million were mobilized by divesting around 5 per cent of the government equity holding in 16 enterprises. In the first round during 1991/92 the reserve price was reduced, in some cases by as much as 64 per cent, and the total revenue from disinvestment exceeded the target by 20 per cent. Subsequently the Government did not reduce the reserve price. In 1993/94, the government effort to divest did not bear much fruit. In 1994/95, however, the Government netted Rs.40 billion through divesting 2 to 10 per cent of its holding in five companies, three in oil and one each in steel and fertilizers. Workers in the companies responded more favourably by subscribing to the shares allotted to them and in some cases fighting for a higher allocation and rights issue along with the original share issue. The divestment to workers was at less than the market price; other shares were sold through auction, which meant the shares of the same company being sold to different parties at different rates, with the highest bids getting top priority and any bids above reserve price being accepted.

The major criticisms in the first two years of divestment concerned the lack of a systematic approach and a proper mechanism for divestment. Experts were consulted when reserve prices were fixed but not when they were reduced. The Government's decision that mutual funds should be compelled to accept uniform reserve prices was also considered rather arbitrary in certain quarters (Mishra et al., 1993). It is little wonder, then, that the

Comptroller and Auditor General (CAG) came out with stringent criticism (CAG Report, 31 March 1993) and an estimate that the under-realization of money from the sale of public sector shares during 1991 and 1992 was Rs.34,417 million. But the trend in share prices over the next six months revealed that the CAG estimates were grossly exaggerated. A statement by the Minister of State for Industry in Lok Sabha on 25 August 1993 showed that the prices of shares in six SOEs were significantly lower in August 1993 than at the time of divestment.

The controversy over the pricing of SOE shares led the Government to appoint a committee on divestment of shares in SOEs, chaired by C. Rangarajan, Governor of the Reserve Bank of India. In June 1993 the committee recommended that:

Equity disinvestment, in general, should be under 49 per cent in industries reserved for public sector and over 74 per cent in other cases. The target level of government ownership at 51 per cent in respect of all units reserved for the public sector will enable control over management. There should be a set of specific reasons for continued government ownership of enterprises except those reserved for public sector.

According to the committee, rigid annual targets for divestment were not needed, but clear action plans should be evolved. Ten per cent of the proceeds of divestment could be considered to be set apart by the Government for lending to the SOEs on concessionary terms to meet their expansion or rationalization needs. Part of the proceeds of divestment could be considered for use in social sectors such as literacy, health and employment creation in rural areas.

The committee recommended that preparatory steps for divestment should include:

(a) conversion into company form where necessary;

(b) deciding the desirable level of equity, and restructuring the finances with a proper debt or equity gearing;

(c) assessing the ongoing investment plans of SOEs;

(d) examining the scope for issuing convertible bonds as a measure of resource mobilization for SOEs;

(e) establishing an independent regulatory commission for the sector concerned, if necessary.

Valuation of SOE equity is commonly based on one of three factors: net asset value, profit-earning capacity and discounted cash flow. The choice of method must depend upon special circumstances such as the past focus of SOEs on social responsibilities rather than pure commercial considerations, financial performance being conditioned by a regime of administered prices, and so on.

The committee also recommended that a scheme of preferential offers to employees in SOEs should be introduced, with an individual ceiling of 200 shares, making up a total reservation of 5 per cent of equity. In the case of SOEs engaged in certain non-manufacturing and skill-based sectors such as consultancy services, the ceiling could go up to 20 per cent. Offers of shares to non-resident Indians and foreign investors should be on the same terms as to resident Indians. SOE boards of directors should be reconstituted with suitable non-government representation.

Efforts are also being made to raise fresh equity for the SOEs from the market.[3] There are pressures on the Government to resort to more "strategic approaches" to the problem like outright sales of units and more attractive and flexible auction arrangements that allow foreign investors to participate. In July 1993, a committee (headed by O. Goswami), appointed by the Union Ministry of Finance to report on "Industrial Sickness and Corporate Restructuring", asked for just such liberalization of the relevant legislation to ensure participation by foreign investors for the turnaround of sick units.

Regardless of whatever has been said so far, shares in profit-making SOEs have already attracted the attention of institutional investors, including foreign ones, as well as of employees. The demand from the private sector and a section of the public sector is for divestment not just of 20 per cent but of 51 per cent, so that the SOEs can be freed from governmental control. The Indian bureaucracy, which is not used to the idea of control without ownership, is not yet prepared for that. Nor has it considered the idea of "golden" shares as a way of retaining effective control with a minority holding.

3. Policies to promote a mixed economy and private sector initiatives

3.1 Encouragement to a mixed economy and joint ventures

India chose the path of a mixed economy at the beginning of its planned economic development in the 1950s. The public and private sectors not only coexist but have also promoted joint ventures, sharing investment and management. Leading public enterprises like Air India and more recently Indian Airlines have had private industrialists as their part-time chairmen. Several joint ventures already exist between the public and private sectors in the engineering, petroleum and fertilizer industries. The shares in such joint venture companies have long been quoted on the stock exchange. Contracting out public works — particularly road construction, irrigation projects, electricity generation, housing, etc. — is not a new development (Sengupta, 1992).

A series of measures was recently announced to encourage private investment, particularly in the energy sector "where the country is vulnerable to external shocks (oil exploration and refining) and to domestic supply bottlenecks (power)" and where large-scale infusions of private foreign capital are most feasible (EIU, 1992, p. 6). To encourage foreign investment significant changes were made in the Foreign Exchange Regulation Act (FERA), and the Multilateral Investment Guarantee Agency (MIGA) Convention was signed in 1992.

More importantly, the new policy allows foreign holdings of 51 per cent of equity (as against 40 per cent earlier). As a result, Suzuki of Japan has already become the majority shareholder, with 50 per cent of the equity and a controlling interest, in the public sector four-wheeler auto plant, Maruti Udyog Ltd. The Government of India owns 49.4 per cent of the shares and the remaining 0.6 per cent is owned by company employees. In the private sector, over a dozen companies, including Asea Brown Boveri, Cadbury, Indian Oxygen, Pepsi and Procter & Gamble have taken advantage to acquire majority shareholdings. A spate of joint ventures with foreign participation have already been approved, including some in the energy (oil and power) sector.

3.2 A greater role for private sector initiatives

Privatization *per se* is not the policy (Kumar, 1991). But the New Industrial Policy (NIP) of July 1991 and the subsequent pronouncements brought major changes in public policy on SOEs. The list of industries reserved for the public sector has been scaled down from 29 (earlier 17 areas were exclusively reserved for the public sector while 12 other areas were to be progressively state-owned) to the following eight: arms and ammunition and allied items of defence equipment; defence aircraft and warships; atomic energy; coal and lignite; mineral oils; mining of iron ore, gypsum, sulphur, gold and diamonds; mining of copper, lead, zinc, tin, molybdenum and wolfram and minerals specified in the Schedule to the Atomic Energy (Control of Production) Order, 1953; and railway transport.

The NIP (1991) envisaged that the portfolio of public sector investments would be so reviewed as to focus the public sector role on strategic, high-tech and essential infrastructure-related activities. Industrial licensing was abolished in all but 18 industries which are related to the security, strategic, social and environmental concerns of the country. Private sector competition was introduced in the reserved areas, though selectively. The Government has also declared it has no plans for further nationalization. After a gap of almost two decades, majority foreign holdings are again allowed in 34 groups of industries, the system of capital issues control has been abolished, the import-export regime has been drastically simplified, rupee convertibility has been introduced on the trade account (Sengupta, 1992), and restrictions on expatriate employment and managerial remuneration have been eased considerably.

Though 99 per cent of the equity investment in the SOEs owned and run by the central Government covered in the DPE survey has come from central government, its share in the total borrowing of these enterprises dropped sharply from 50 per cent in 1979/80 to 33 per cent in 1989/90. As the Economic Intelligence Service (CMIE, 1991) notes, the share of foreign participation in the total borrowing of these SOEs increased sharply from 8 per cent to 19 per cent while that of domestic private participation — largely flotations and public deposits — rose from 9 per cent to 22 per cent. As is well known, the equity investment in the public sector yields paltry returns. Returns by way of interest payments are higher, but they too work out to about half those in the private sector (7.2 per cent for the public sector as against 13.1 per cent for large-scale private sector industrial enterprises, as per CMIE calculations). The general point that is usually missed out in discussions on the subject is that even before the adjustment reforms began, the central Government's stake in its SOEs — loan and equity investment taken together — had declined from 70 per cent in 1979/80 to 56 per cent in 1989/90. The Eighth Plan (1992-97) envisages restraints on the use of tax-free bonds for raising capital to "predetermined levels" to protect tax revenue and avoid distortions in interest rates. This may actually restrain the flow of debt capital into the SOEs from foreign and domestic private sources.

4. Problems of privatization

By and large, the privatization programme in India has been decentralized and diluted, taking the route of deregulation and disinvestment. Several countries have set up separate administrative units — variously referred to as the Privatization Commission, Asset Privatization Trust, etc. — for carrying out government policies, recommending actions for cabinet approval and overseeing the privatization process. In India, however, several ministries (Finance, Industry and administrative ministries) and agencies (Planning Commission, Prime Minister's Office, Department of Public Enterprises, etc.) continue to have diffused responsibility. The absence of a principal agency with direct responsibility may affect the coordination of related activities. But it should perhaps be seen as part of a deliberate strategy of low-profile, decentralized privatization, the aim being to diffuse focus and attention and to ease the pressure of opposition from multiple pressure groups.

4.1 Privatization cannot take place in isolation

India has an ailing economy suffering from an overdose of bureaucratic control and from lavish, imprudent, and unproductive government spending. An insulated economy that was built under sheltered, sellers' market conditions with a heavy emphasis on import substitution and self-reliance, it is now finding itself unable to mobilize enough foreign exchange to finance its critical imports. Simultaneous efforts to liberalize and open up the economy seem to have accentuated the sickness in both public and private sectors, particularly because several firms in both sectors were heavily dependent upon trade with Central and Eastern Europe, now in transition, and with the former USSR, which is itself undergoing severe financial, economic and political crises. The reduction in trade with the former USSR and decanalization (lifting the state monopolization of procurement and channelling of trade) severely affected public sector trading companies.[4] This made the apex chambers of commerce re-examine their responses to the reforms, and they now seem to be saying that the Government should have liberalized first and opened up the economy later. Some chambers have even begun to argue that some measure of protection should be restored.

None the less, the private sector initiative seems to have been substantially influenced by disaffection with public sector performance and structural adjustment pressures. What is needed is a positive effort to create an enabling environment in which enterprises and economy can flourish without undue fetters. The familiar argument in India concerns the need to free, or privatize, the private sector first. Given the domination of public sector banking and financial institutions, it is little wonder that in most large and medium-sized private sector enterprises the private entrepreneurs' stake is nominal. Government policies on conversion of debt into equity, the role of the directors who are the nominees of the public sector financial institutions, and the general climate of an ailing economy with excessive controls, have together resulted in a stifling of enterprise in both private and public sectors. As a result, ownership by itself is not seen to make much difference. The liberalization and attendant changes in macroeconomic policy were supposed to be directed at freeing private enterprise and initiative. However, easing the regulations is not enough. A deregulated economy can do with a downsized bureaucracy if the reform process is to be taken to its logical conclusion. The climate should be congenial for risk-taking. Employers are therefore asking for easing not only of entry but also of exit. It is the latter which creates vexing problems.

In India, though private investment has been deregulated through delicensing in many cases, there are a variety of ways in which government can determine the viability of private investment. Tariff barriers, price and distribution controls, and the need for prior approval for closure, lay-offs and retrenchments are all considered to inhibit private investment. The attitudes of private investors also need to change. Average pre-tax profits in Indian private sector companies are around 20 per cent as against a mere 4 per cent in the Republic of Korea. Labour productivity lagged behind in the 1950s and the 1960s, but by the 1980s, while labour productivity had picked up, capital productivity had begun to lag behind. Modernization of Indian industry has become not only capital-intensive but also cost-intensive (see Ahluwalia, 1985).

Privatization has entailed legal changes in almost all countries. In India, for instance, the Companies Act, the Monopolies and Restrictive Trade Practices Act, and the Sick Industries Companies Act have been introduced, and it was necessary to amend the statutes of autonomous corporations to remove legal hurdles necessary to give effect to the policy changes. The long-awaited labour law changes, however, remain elusive, as they are considered politically suicidal.

4.2 Creating a climate for private sector investment

Business confidence — both domestic and foreign — in relation to further investments is generally low in view of political and economic uncertainties. Since the reforms started in June 1991, the US multinational Motorola has withdrawn from its project in the area of information technology because of bureaucratic delays. Another US multinational, Cargill, had its seeds plant in Karnataka ransacked in June 1993 by a farmers' lobby called the Karnataka Rajya Raitha Sangha. Cargill's salt project in Gujarat also suffered severe adverse publicity in the wake of protests by the Kutch Small Scale Salt Manufacturers' Association, which filed a writ petition in the High Court. Several political parties also joined issue over the salt project. Many foreign investors who were committed to invest in power projects are dragging their feet and asking for a package of incentives. Japanese investors are unwilling to make sizeable investments unless they are allowed to create "industrial communities" that are immune from the normal maladies of infrastructure breakdown and civic unrest.

Confidence in business — or the public image of business *per se* — is also rather low. The Government's acquiescence in the demands of the trade unions and perceived reluctance to face up to the challenges also affect the investment climate. A recent stock scam dampened the stock markets in India. The economies in the region are opening up at a time when, despite globalization and competitiveness, world markets have being showing signs of becoming recessionary (much publicized workforce reductions in the wake of corporate restructurings in most parts of the world) and regressive (regional trade groupings and protectionism). In these circumstances will private enterprise and investment be found wanting (owing to the "wait and see" syndrome) or will it rise to the occasion and seize the opportunities? The reforms seem to have stirred hopes. As CMIE (1993) reports, foreign investment, including foreign domestic investment and foreign portfolio investment, has emerged as a major factor behind the recent surge in capital flows in India. Its share in total capital formation increased sharply from a minuscule 3.3 per cent (US$158 million) in

1991-92, to 14 per cent (US$433 million) in 1992-93 and then to nearly 45 per cent (US$4,113 million) in 1993-94.

Policy reforms by themselves are inadequate if the infrastructure is not adequate and unfailing. In the past, under centralized planning, infrastructure development was limited by the availability of funds rather than being directed by demand. As part of the adjustment process, though plan outlays still envisage augmenting public investment in critical areas such as power, transport and telecommunications, the field is kept wide open for private and foreign investments to supplement the meagre budgetary resources so that market needs can be met more fully and more speedily than before.

5. Social consequences

Privatization — and the logical corollary steps to free the economy with a view to bringing about market orientation, reducing isolation from the rest of the world economy and enhancing competitiveness at macro and micro levels — involves complex social and labour issues. The heart of the dilemma is that it is difficult for affected employees to agree to a logic that dictates the necessity of undergoing change and even making sacrifices, if necessary, in the overall interests of the survival of an organization with which they have long been associated. Ideally the process of change should find acceptance at all levels and among all constituents of the organization. But often this is not easy to achieve. In what follows, employment and job security, trade unions, collective bargaining, industrial relations and tripartite consultation are briefly discussed.

5.1 Employment and job security

One of the major fears about privatization concerns the potential loss of present and future employment. Present organized sector jobs, which already account for less than 10 per cent of the total workforce, are likely to decline. If 20 per cent of the organized sector workforce is considered surplus, it could mean a loss of over 5 million jobs from a total of over 26 million. In the manufacturing sector alone, it could mean a loss of 2.4 million out of a total of 12 million jobs (see Mundle, 1991).

Job losses in the public sector are considered particularly worrying for two reasons: first, the annual rate of growth of organized sector employment during the period 1970-91 was much higher in the public sector (2.9 per cent) than in the private sector (0.7 per cent) (CMIE, 1991). Second, if public sector reform is to result in the loss of jobs in the central public sector, it means job losses in the high-wage segment. The non-departmental SOEs in the central sphere (the 237 SOEs usually covered in the BPE Survey of Public Enterprises) account for less than 1 per cent of the total labour force in the country or about 9 per cent of the organized sector labour force. The average wages of these employees as at 1 April 1992 was around Rs.50,000, one and a half times the average for all employees in private organized sector employment and about three times the national income for a family of three.

The relative decline of employment in the private sector and the growth of public service employment in the 1970s and 1980s may have further strengthened the notion that jobs in the public sector are more secure. Now that notion is on the verge of becoming a myth. According to official calculations, there are 58 chronically sick SOEs with accumulated losses of Rs.100 billion (Ratnam, 1992b; BIFR, 1991). Rs.150 billion would be needed to nurse these units and protect the jobs of about 400,000 people employed in them. It is argued in some quarters that the same amount, if properly channelled, can provide employment or livelihood opportunities for over 1.5 million people. It is also suggested that redeployment measures might militate against the interests of fresh entrants into the labour market.

Lack of modernization and lack of competition may eventually contribute to higher job losses. The long-term effects of privatization on employment depend on whether the enabling environment exists in which they can operate efficiently and, even if it does exist, how efficiently individual firms actually operate. It is easy to provide safeguards in profitable and expanding organizations but difficult in sick and unviable units. While it is extremely important to provide employment security, actual practice should be dictated by pragmatism.

At the macro level the ability to provide *social security* is conditioned by the structure of employment, the rate of unemployment and the health of the economy (Ratnam, 1991 and 1992a). If organized sector employment is significant, the labour market is facing shortages rather than surpluses, and the economy is buoyant, it is possible to provide and sustain better social security, in both form and content. But if the reverse is true, mere intentions alone will not suffice and social security becomes a casualty.

The Indian Finance Minister has of late begun to argue, along with various labour economists, that "the traditional approach to labour of providing the workers the maximum security in terms of employment and wages was not workable in the given situation . . . [there is] considerable evidence that our institutional structure of industrial relations discourages increased use of labour in production processes and therefore militates against the growth of employment itself . . . it is not possible to insulate workers altogether from the fortunes of the firms for which they work" (BPO, 1993).

5.2 *Safety net: The National Renewal Fund (NRF)*

In India, for centuries, the joint Hindu family system provided a measure of social security. Over the years the system is breaking down, partly as a result of industrialization and urbanization. The Government itself does not have any major social security programme such as unemployment insurance. Some states like Maharashtra and West Bengal have employment guarantee schemes while the Government of India has several employment generation programmes, but such schemes invariably have limitations and leakages. In organized industry, the trade unions, with tacit support from the Government, have for years been demanding that employers should provide for a measure of security. Employers, for their part, have been advocating an unemployment benefit scheme with tripartite contributions in the hope that this would make it easier for them to adjust their workforce in the face of economic compulsions. When the sickness in the textile industry became rampant and many mills were closed during and after the 1982 textile strike, the Textile

Workers' Rehabilitation Fund was set up along with the new textile policy in July 1985. Under the scheme, textile workers affected by the permanent closure of mills are given relief for three years on a tapering basis or until the date of superannuation, whichever is earlier. The scheme has not been implemented yet. Nor have efforts to establish a special scheme for coal workers on the British model borne fruit. In 1989, one of the state governments (Andhra Pradesh) passed a Bill providing for an insurance mechanism for workers affected by closures and retrenchment; this Bill was subsequently allowed to lapse.

While presenting the budget for 1991/92, the Finance Minister announced (see paragraph 53 of his budget speech) that "Government will establish a National Renewal Fund (NRF) ... to ensure that the cost of technical change and modernization of the productive apparatus will not devolve on the workers. The fund will provide a social safety net which will protect the workers from the adverse consequences of the technological transformation."

The Government set up the NRF in February 1992 to deal with sickness in both public and private sectors, particularly the former. The objectives of the NRF, as stated by the Union Finance Minister in the 1992/93 *Economic Survey*, are:

(a)   to provide assistance to firms to cover the costs of retraining and redeployment of employees arising as a result of modernization, technological upgrading of existing capacity and industrial restructuring;

(b)   to provide funds for compensation to employees affected by restructuring or closure of industrial units, in both public and private sectors;

(c)   to provide funds for employment generation schemes in the organized and unorganized sectors in order to create a social safety net for labour. The Department of Industrial Development, which administers the NRF, had now taken up the first set of cases relating to the National Textile Corporation units.

The NRF is thus designed to operate in three parts:

(1)   An Employment Generation Fund (EG), which will provide resources for approved employment generation schemes. These schemes will be designed to regenerate employment opportunities for employees affected by restructuring in the organized sector. It will also provide resources for employment generation for employees in the unorganized sector. Funds are to be disbursed in the form of grants even to non-governmental organizations (NGOs).

(2)   A National Renewal Grant Fund (NRGF), which will deal with the immediate requirements of labour in sick units arising from revival or closure of such units. Here, too, funds will be disbursed in the form of grants.

(3)   An Insurance Fund for Employees (IFE), which would allow industries to prepare themselves for future changes in their employment structures in the context of technological change and modernization.

The NRF also operates on the following assumptions:

(a)   An industrial undertaking should have the authority to restructure the staffing of its units to enable it to upgrade its technology and to modernize.

(b) There should be interaction and negotiation between the owner/management and labour unions on related matters.

(c) The Government will permit restructuring, including retrenchment, as long as it is reasonable.

(d) In cases where no agreement is arrived at between workers and employer, the employer can implement a reasonable restructuring scheme.

(e) The NRF will be utilized initially for the purpose of restructuring, that is, for the retrenchment, retraining and redeployment of labour in industrial units employing 100 or more workers.

Rs.2 billion was earmarked for the NRF in the 1991/92 budget; this was supplemented with another Rs.5 billion in the 1992/93 and 1993/94 budgets as special loans from the IDA at concessionary interest rates. Part of the proceeds of the SOE share disinvestment has also been transferred to the NRF. Six regions where industrial sickness is rampant were identified to undertake NRF activities on a pilot basis, with a view to replication elsewhere. In the wake of delays in formulating and disseminating details of the schemes, however, the NRF has come to be perceived, rightly or wrongly, as a programme whose scope is limited to offering sops to redundant employees, unable to make any substantial active labour market interventions to bring about meaningful retraining and job creation efforts. The Government has increased the compensation for voluntary separations from 15 to 45 days for each completed year of service and exempted such payments, subject to certain limits, from income tax. It is further proposing to dispense with prior permission for closure and to increase the retrenchment compensation from the present 15 days to 45 days or more for each completed year of service. The NRF initiatives have so far focused on retrenchment rather than renewal.

During the first 40 months since the NRF was announced, its major activity was to disburse funds to selected SOEs to meet the costs of their voluntary retirement scheme (VRS).[5] During 1992/93 the NRF contributed Rs.8,296.6 million towards VRSs for surplus workers and employees in the SOEs. The entire sum of Rs.7 billion earmarked under the 1993/94 budget has also been kept aside for implementing VRSs in the SOEs. Because of this the NRF has been dubbed the "National Retrenchment Fund". In fact, the funds earmarked are not sufficient even to meet the demand for voluntary retirement within the central public sector, not to mention the requirements of the unorganized and organized private sector. When the profit-making public sector steel company applied to the NRF for funds for voluntary retirement of surplus employees in two of its sick units, it was asked to provide the same amount from the surpluses generated by other profit-making units within the company.

Considering the estimates of large-scale redundancies, the expenditure on voluntary retirement seems high. In any case several SOEs cannot find enough money to administer the schemes. Some SOEs, for example the Mining and Allied Machinery Corporation, have had to withdraw the scheme for want of money; others, like the Steel Authority of India, have discontinued the scheme because they found that some of their "best people" were leaving the organization.

The budget allocations for the NRF are meagre, considering that the NRF concept paper prepared by the Government of India itself estimated the total requirement for assistance to 400,000 workers in 58 SOEs identified as sick according to the standards of the Sick Industrial Companies Act at Rs. 60 billion at the rate of Rs.150,000 per employee.

Concern about mobilizing additional funds to administer the NRF has led to the emergence of several possibilities of finding financial resources to create a social security net for surplus employees. Two ideas that have been put forward are (a) the sale of surplus land locked in sick and closed units and (b) a levy or contribution, to the tune of 1-2 per cent of wages and the wage bill, by employees and employers respectively, as insurance against future contingencies and compensation for flexibility. This could provide for additional benefits to surplus labour over and above normal terminal benefits and/or support for active labour market interventions through retraining for possible redeployment or resettlement in self-employment or special employment/livelihood programmes.

A tripartite committee was set up to oversee the functioning of the NRF. Unlike other tripartite committees, this one includes some management experts from industry and the academic world. But this committee did not meet until the middle of October 1993. The Government decided to establish six resource centres in areas where industrial sickness is particularly rife, with a view to advising workers who have lost their jobs, identifying their strengths and skills, and working out plans for retraining and redeployment. Institutions such as the Gandhi Labour Institute, Ahmedabad, and the Associated Chamber of Commerce and Industry were to undertake programmes under the NRF. The NRF scheme thus envisages direct responsibility for organizations representing the interests of either labour or management or both. It is over six months since the resource centre concept was proposed by the Government, but no progress has been made. While the programme design and objectives seem laudable, implementation is hampered by the lack of sustained political commitment and bureaucratic inertia.

6. Industrial relations

Trade unions in India, as elsewhere, and irrespective of their political affiliations, have generally opposed privatization for a variety of reasons: the rationale of the public sector and public services, and the need to preserve them in the long-term interests of the nation (Clements, 1988); and concern about security of employment, employment conditions, union security (membership strength and recognition), collective bargaining and industrial relations implications (for detailed statements from each of the tripartite actors in ASEAN countries, see ILO/UNDP, 1987).

Trade unions are weak in India, but they can influence — and, on occasion, even stall or reverse — privatization moves. This has more to do with government "tendermindedness" or calculations concerning the possible political fall-out for themselves than with the power of the unions (see Waterbury, 1988). Trade unions are not generally able actually to impede progress when government itself is less vacillating in its policy moves. For instance, the central Government set in motion a process of tripartite consultation over sick SOEs; it convened a special tripartite committee and set up seven tripartite industrial committees. But it soon realized the difficulties of achieving consensus and referred the cases of select sick SOEs over the heads of the tripartite committees to the Bureau of Industrial Finance and Reconstruction (BIFR), after an appropriate amendment to the relevant legislation. In 1992, the Japanese partner, Suzuki, acquired majority control in Maruti; a public sector unit thus had majority equity participation by a foreign company. This event took even the unions by surprise.

However, in view of political considerations and resistance from trade unions in existing SOEs and financial institutions, in India easing entry barriers and providing for increased private sector participation is considered the surest and safest way to achieve some of the major objectives of privatization without denationalization or wholesale disinvestment.

Privatization usually entails restructuring. This affects bargaining structures, the union membership base, and consequently the representative character of the unions. For example, when Suzuki acquired a majority shareholding in Maruti Udyog, the SOE was transformed into a foreign-owned private company. Company collective agreements would no longer have to be approved by the Department of Public Enterprises in the Union Ministry of Industry. Also, the earlier notion — following a Supreme Court ruling under Article 12-A of the Indian Constitution — that the public sector is State, would no longer apply in this case for its employees to claim any added protection. The reservation rules concerning employment of Scheduled Caste and Scheduled Tribe candidates applicable to the company when it was an SOE would no longer apply.

The Department of Public Enterprises used to issue guidelines for wage bargaining in the SOEs run by the Government of India and its ratification used to be mandatory. It announced a ban on wage revisions from 1 January 1992 onwards, but in April 1993 it lifted the ban and issued fresh directives that allow individual SOEs freedom to negotiate wage rises so long as (a) the SOEs do not depend upon the Government for budgetary support to meet the additional wage burden; (b) wage rises do not lead to consequential rises in the administered prices; and (c) the formula for dearness allowance is not altered.

The major change in industrial relations relates to the decentralization of bargaining at enterprise level, abandoning the principle of parity in basic wage and major items of employee benefits. The influence of the Government and of the national federations of trade unions may be reduced in future. But there is going to be a spate of litigation by trade unions in sick SOEs, as it will be hard for them to obtain wage rises when the SOEs no longer receive budgetary assistance from the Government. The parity principle and the Article 12-A rulings of the past should provide sufficient ammunition for the trade unions to drag the SOE managements to court if the latter fail to match their offers with the best in the public sector.

Along with privatization, several countries in the region are considering moves to reform labour law and company law to ease labour adjustment and increase labour flexibility. This may reduce the current level of protection afforded to workers in the organized sector. After considerable foot-dragging, the Union Minister for Labour assured industry representatives that the labour legislation would soon be amended to dispense with, among other things, prior approval for the closure of sick units. This announcement naturally met with stiff resistance from the trade unions. Managerial trade unionism is becoming more pronounced in the public sector than in the private sector (Sharma, 1993). Privatization may dampen the growth of the managerial trade union movement.

There may be a shift in emphasis in the skill composition of the workforce in privatized firms, with skilled workers gradually replacing unskilled ones, though not in the same proportion. This was evident in the privatized jute mills in Bangladesh (Lorsh, 1986). Major changes also await the human resources function if the changes are to be effected in such a way as to limit the negative effects on employment, employment conditions, and industrial relations and without violating the regulatory — moral, legal and contractual — framework defining the mutual rights and obligations of unions and employees.

Tripartite consultation may increasingly be found useful in achieving consensus on a controversial subject such as privatization. Present efforts to revive atrophied tripartite institutions — the Indian Labour Conference, the Standing Labour Committee, the special tripartite committees and industrial committees — seem to be more symbolic than substantive. The problem is that the Government may be finding the rigid timetables imposed by the debt burden and pressure from donors incompatible with time-consuming consensual approaches. The polarization among political parties and trade unions and the competing requirements of employers make it difficult to achieve social cohesion quickly. It is doubtful whether the central Government held full-scale consultations on the adjustment reforms with the state governments, let alone with the representative workers' and employers' organizations. On the other hand, the social partners might feel some hesitation about being involved in deciding merely the broad strategy rather than the details, for fear of being presented with a *fait accompli*. Genuine tripartite consultation should aim at going beyond privatization. It should be directed at collective endeavours to create a congenial environment and infrastructure in which the full potential of individual initiative and a free market economy can be realized.

In several countries efforts have been made to placate employees and their unions by offering a variety of concessions and preferences to promote employee ownership and facilitate employee buyouts. There are several cases of sick units being successfully turned around through trade union or worker initiative. Jaipur Metals and Electricals Ltd. is one such case. When the private sector unit became sick, the state Government took it over but could not make it viable. A fresh initiative by the company's managing director brought eight trade unions to respond to the crisis with a view to saving the threatened jobs. Workers agreed to job and pay cuts, and made several other concessions. In less than eight years, the workers' earnings had trebled and the unit provided more jobs than had been shed earlier. Workers began to own over two-thirds of the company's share capital through contributions from incentive earnings, and four worker representatives are on the company's board. Similar results are reported in the case of Kamani Tubes Ltd. in Bombay and Central Jute Mills at Calcutta, among others (Ratnam, 1990; Srinivas, 1994; Khandwalla, 1992). In India, the trade union response to worker ownership has generally been lukewarm, owing mainly to ideological reservations. In the case of sick nationalized textile mills, the Finance Minister offered to write off the bad debts and hand over the mills for worker takeover. For the first time, some trade unions and trade union leaders who had hitherto opposed employee ownership began to see it as a possible option to save threatened jobs.

7. Conclusions

The privatization programme in India has been a low-profile, selective and cautious affair, considerably decentralized to diffuse the attention of pressure groups. There is no official policy, as yet, on privatization. With a few exceptions, privatization is encouraged more by allowing the private sector to participate in hitherto forbidden fields than through outright sale of existing units. The limited disinvestment and public issue of SOE shares that have taken place have not been accompanied by consequential changes in the boards and management of enterprises. Disinvestment seems to have eased the burden of short-term fiscal deficit. The thrust of public sector reform, where there is a visible positive impact, has been towards reducing the budgetary dependence of the SOEs and allowing them to raise funds through internal generation of surpluses as well as from the market, without government guarantees. Much remains to be done, however, in restructuring relations between government and SOEs and in allowing enterprises greater autonomy. A spate of committees and commissions have addressed themselves to the ailments of the public sector, but there is still a lack of concerted action to bring about significant changes in culture and performance orientation.

There is considerable debate in India about whether liberalization should take place first, and whether domestic enterprises — both public and private sector — should be allowed some lead time to prepare themselves for competition before the economy is opened up. The sudden exposure to competition both from within and from outside, at a time when the global economy is reeling under recession, is thought to be increasing the mortality rate among already ailing Indian firms. There is a general shortage of funds, which are urgently required to expand units to reap the economies of scale and also to meet the needs of modernization. While industrialists are convinced of the need for a further forward thrust, they are lobbying for concessions by way of further changes in company law to facilitate the introduction of non-voting shares. This would allow the present captains of industry to retain their hold even as they expand the equity base; it would also facilitate inter-corporate mobility of investments for consolidation of their accounts with or without mergers, acquisitions, etc. After initial hesitation, the Government seems to be willing to accede to such overtures from indigenous industry.

Poor infrastructure continues to be a major impediment affecting the performance of enterprises. The bulk of liberalization, deregulation and privatization moves, and of fresh foreign and domestic investment, is directed at augmenting infrastructure, particularly power, transport and telecommunications. Unless infrastructure is developed, investments in manufacturing and services may become less attractive and less productive.

Since December 1992, the pace of reform seems to have decelerated. The initial first steps having been taken, this is inevitable. But the uncertainty about where to go from here is increased by fresh doubts about the political stability of the country — the communal strife over religious shrines and caste-based reservations; the stock and sugar scams; the dilemma of populism versus people orientation in economic policies; the lukewarm attitude of state governments to reform; the reliance of the Government on the leftist parties; the vulnerability of a government with a fragile majority based on support from factions of political parties and independents; the growing dissidence within the centre of the ruling party; and the results of elections (May 1996).

Discussions on the political economy of development often centre on comparisons with developments in the rest of the world. The tendency has been either to refer to success stories or to point at failures rather than to consider the issues holistically in the given context. The South-East Asian miracle is viewed with awe and apprehension. The spreading social tensions, indiscipline and unrest have led to a debate on the nexus between democracy and development. Some analysts point to restrictions on trade unions as one of the ingredients of the development strategy in South-East Asia. They question whether this is a price worth paying to ensure development. But such arguments do not seem to hold water in the 1990s, where one finds international trade and international aid being linked increasingly to national records on human rights and international labour standards. There is also a question about the continued relevance of the Nehruvian model of heavy industrialization, self-reliance, etc. Often the hypothetical question is raised: would India have done better if it had adopted policies and strategies similar to those adopted in South-East Asia? It appears that until the late 1960s the strategy of heavy industrialization that the country adopted, which involved a major role for the public sector, was appropriate: during the first two decades after independence not many entrepreneurs were available to undertake the kinds of tasks that the public sector undertook in building heavy industries requiring huge investments and long gestation periods. But once the base was built, the country could have shifted its strategy in the early 1970s and taken the lead in integrating its economy with the world economy. The consequences of not doing so are glaring: India was among the top two countries in the Asia-Pacific region in the early 1980s. By the late 1980s at least a dozen countries in the region had overtaken India in terms of both human development and economic progress.

If the climate for business is right, business confidence is restored and growth is accelerated, more jobs can be generated than are lost through competition and new technologies. It is not a question of private versus public. The developmental obligations, investment needs and opportunities are enormous: there is room for everyone. Both the public and private sectors, including the foreign sector, can — and need to — grow. During the last four decades the Indian economy grew at an average rate of 3.5 per cent per year while population growth was a little over 2 per cent. If the rate of growth is accelerated to a level that is at least four times the rate of population growth, the benefits of development will trickle down to reduce inequalities, poverty and deprivation, which would in turn contribute to social and human development.

References

Ahluwalia, I. J. 1985. *Industrial growth in India : Stagnation since the mid-sixties*. Delhi, Oxford University Press.

BIFR. 1991. *Industrial sickness — Case studies*. New Delhi, Bureau of Industrial Finance and Reconstruction, Ministry of Finance, Government of India.

BPO. 1993. "Unemployment insurance mooted", in *Business and Political Observer (BPO)*, 13 Jan. 1993.

Central Statistical Organization (CSO). 1993. *National Accounts Statistics*. New Delhi, CSO.

———. 1994a. *Economic Survey 1993-94*. New Delhi, CSO.

———. (Department of Public Enterprises). 1994b. *Public Enterprise Survey 1992-93 Highlights*. New Delhi, CSO.

———. 1992 and 1994. *Basic statistics relating to the Indian economy*. Bombay, CMIE, Aug.

Clements, L. 1988. *Privatization: Confronting the new Leviathan*. Iowa City, Labor Center, University of Iowa.

CMIE (Economic Intelligence Service). 1991. *Public sector in the Indian economy.* Bombay, CMIE, May.

———. 1993. *A Review of Central Budget: 1993-94.* Bombay, CMIE, Feb.

EIU. 1992. *India: Report 4 of 1992.* London, EIU.

Government of India. 1992. *Report on financial sector reforms* (Chairman, M. Narasimhan). New Delhi, Nabhi Publications.

Hakeem, M. A. 1993. "New industrial policy and public sector", in *Financial Express*, 15 Apr. 1993.

ILO/UNDP. 1987. *Privatization: Its impact on labour relations in ASEAN.* Geneva, ILO.

Khandwalla, P. 1992. *Innovative corporate turnarounds.* New Delhi, Sage Publications.

Kumar, S. 1991. "Public enterprise policy and reform measures: The Indian experience", in *Public Enterprise*, Vol. 11, No. 4, pp. 327-333.

Lorsh, K. 1986. *Privatization in Bangladesh.* Boston, Massachusetts, Kennedy School of Government, Harvard University.

Mishra, R. K., et al. 1993. "Disinvestment in public enterprises: Some lessons for the future", in *Decision*, 19 (3&4), July-Dec., pp. 175-183.

Mukul. 1991. "Workers against privatization", in *Economic and Political Weekly*, 27 July, pp. 1781-1785.

———. 1992. "Public sector employees: New agenda for action", in *Economic and Political Weekly*, 30 May, pp. 1125-1128.

Mundle, S. 1992. "The employment effects of stabilisation and related policy changes in India, 1991-92 to 1993-94", in ILO-ARTEP (ed.). *Social dimensions of structural adjustment in India.* Papers and proceedings of a Tripartite Workshop held in New Delhi, 10-11 Dec. 1991. New Delhi, ILO-ARTEP.

Ratnam, C. S. Venkata. 1990. "Role of employees and unions in turnaround management", in *Economic and Political Weekly*, Bombay, Nov. 1990.

———. 1991. *Privatization and the role of employers' organizations.* Geneva, ILO Bureau for Employers' Activities; mimeo.

———. 1992a. "Social and labour aspects of privatization", in *Indian Journal of Industrial Relations*, Oct. 1991.

———. 1992b. *Managing people.* New Delhi, Global Business Press.

SCOPE. 1989. *Reports/recommendations of various committees on public enterprises.* New Delhi, SCOPE.

Shankar, T. L. et al. 1992. "Role and relevance of state level public enterprises in 1990s", in *Decision*, pp. 183-214.

Sengupta, N. K. 1992. *New economic policy environment in India and early experience with privatization.* Mimeo.

Sharma, B. R. 1993. *Managerial unionism: Issues and perspectives.* New Delhi, Shri Ram Centre for Industrial Relations and Human Resources.

Srinivas, B. 1994. *Worker takeover in industry — The Kamani Tubes experiment.* New Delhi, Sage Publications.

Waterbury, John. 1988. *The political context of public sector reform and privatization in Egypt, India, Mexico and Turkey.* Princeton, Princeton University; mimeo.

Notes

[1] The public sector coal industry, which is virtually a monopoly, was always incurring losses during the era of budgetary support. But in the years 1991-93, when budgetary support was cut to around one-quarter of the 1990/91 figure, it was forced to stretch itself and reported profits for both years. During the late 1980s, it lost Rs.10 million each working day. During 1992/93 it reported a profit of nearly Rs.10 million each working day.

[2] Typically, a public enterprise is viewed as a company in which the Government holds almost all the equity. However, according to the Indian Companies Act, all companies where the Government has an equity holding of 51 per cent or more are considered government companies.

[3] Indian Petrochemicals Corporation Ltd. was among the first SOEs to make a public issue after the announcement of the structural adjustment reforms in June 1991. The immediate prospects of further disinvestment became grim in the wake of subdued stock market activity following a stock scam. Also, the secondary market for SOE shares is still to be developed.

[4] For instance, when copper prices in the former USSR crashed and simultaneously India reduced its import duties on copper, copper began to be dumped in India. The result was that the public sector copper corporation, until then healthy, became suddenly sick. Public sector power equipment suppliers have the potential to cater to the growing demand for power equipment, a sector in which demand is burgeoning. But, since the resource position of the Government and the tied trade-aid arrangements do not permit it to harness fully the potential of the local public sector corporations, it has to rely on outside suppliers. Even multinational corporations have paid a heavy price: a multinational pharmaceutical company which set up a plant exclusively to export its products to the former USSR has had to wind up its plant in Maharashtra.

[5] The Minister of State for Industry informed Parliament in September 1993 that 78,562 employees in 100 SOEs had opted for VRSs during the last three years, from 1990/91 to 1992/93 (*Indian Worker*, 20 Sep. 1993).

4. Privatization of telecommunications in Mexico

A. Botelho and C. Addis*

1. The Mexican privatization programme

Early this century Mexico pursued a policy of selective public control of enterprises in strategic economic activities, such as railroads, development banking, petroleum and electricity. Control was obtained either through the creation of new corporations, as in the case of development banking and electricity, or through purchases or expropriations, as with railroads and petroleum. After the Second World War, as Arena (1993) argues, public ownership of other economic activities gradually increased as a result of the following:

(a) strategic decisions that gave the State the sole right to carry out certain economic activities (uranium mining, telecommunications);

(b) lack of interest or insufficient capital in some industries considered at that time to be very important (steel, railroad cars);

(c) expansion in vertical or horizontal integration of former public enterprises (coal industry, petrochemicals, telephone directory publishing);

(d) the failure of some private enterprises, which frequently owed money to development banks and to the State through these banks, and subsequent decisions by the State to run them (sugar, mines, textiles, etc.).

The process reached its height around 1982 when the Government, with the peso grossly overvalued, seized most Mexican banks and affiliate companies in an effort to suppress demand for foreign currency.

Between 1982 and 1992, however, privatization programmes were an invariable part of structural adjustment policies undertaken (see table 4.1).

From 1982 to 1988 privatization progressed fairly rapidly in terms of numbers of companies privatized, but since 1989 privatization has involved a number of large enterprises, which has raised the amount of public ownership being privatized considerably. As a consequence subsidies to public sector enterprises dropped from 8.4 per cent of GDP in 1982 to 3.6 per cent of GDP in 1991.

* Kellogg Institute, Notre Dame University, South Bend, Indiana.

Table 4.1. Number of state-owned enterprises, Mexico, 1982-92

Type of enterprise	Dec. 1982	1983	1984	1985	1986	1987	1988	1989	1990	1991	May 1992
Decentralized organizations	102	97	95	96	94	94	89	88	82	77	77
Companies with a minority participation	744	700	703	629	528	437	252	229	147	119	106
Public trusts	231	199	173	147	108	83	71	62	51	43	40
Companies with a minority participation	78	78	78	69	7	3	0	0	0	0	0
Total	1 155	1 074	1 049	941	737	617	412	379	280	239	223

Source: OECD: *Economic Surveys: Mexico*, 1992.

Privatization brought the Mexican Government quite substantial revenues, amounting to an average of 6.3 per cent of GDP over the period 1989-92. According to one estimate, the revenues from privatization obtained in 1991 were used to reduce Mexico's internal public debt by almost 26 per cent (Salinas, 1992). Social expenditures in turn have increased dramatically, reaching the levels of the late 1970s.

Although general rules and procedures have guided the privatization process, it has, been largely a matter of trial and error, of tailoring the selling conditions to the peculiarities of the sector and its markets.[1] The Government has tried to keep the public enterprise labour force well informed about the privatization process. Preliminary screening of potential investors has eliminated unqualified buyers, so that bidding can focus on price. Labour has received some protection: the unions have the right of first refusal, and once the selling price is known they have the option of matching it and purchasing the enterprise (Tandon, 1992), though it is unlikely that the unions will be able to raise the funds for most of these purchases, particularly the larger firms. A second safeguard for labour is an understanding that buyers are not to lay off workers, but the extent to which this is respected remains unclear (Tandon, 1992). Finally, enterprises targeted for sale are transferred to the divestiture unit of the Ministry of Finance where it is hoped they will be turned around — via debt or company restructurings, renegotiated or new labour contracts, or other measures — so that the enterprise will command a higher price.

Regarding the decision about which firms to privatize, one analyst has written:

Although formally the sector ministry with administrative responsibility for an enterprise "proposes" it for disengagement [sale], the assumption now is that in principle all enterprises are to be disengaged, and the sector ministry actually has to justify retaining it. This subtle change in underlying attitude is partly responsible for the fact that very large numbers of enterprises have been disengaged (Tandon, 1992).

Although Tandon's observations are apparently borne out by the large number of privatizations, one conservative observer has noted that the decision to privatize firms boils down to political criteria:

Despite all this progress, the Salinas government still refuses to privatize the so-called "strategic sectors" of the economy — oil, petrochemicals and railroads.[2] The Mexican president continues to invoke Articles 25 and 26 of the Mexican Constitution, which endow the government with the right to administer economic affairs. . . . the argument that complete state ownership of these sectors is irreversible because they are strategic is unconvincing. Other strategic sectors of the economy, such as telecommunications, highways, airlines, and potable water distribution have been privatized. Why not railroads, electricity and oil? *The obstacles are not economic, but political* . . . (Salinas, 1992).

The turnaround process mentioned above, and the packaging of enterprises for privatization, again depend upon the particular condition of the firm and its market. In the case of the sugar refineries and banks, for example, to ensure that all the enterprises were purchased, one or two less desirable firms were bundled together with a desirable firm and sold as a package (Sanchez and Angel, 1992; Shapiro, 1993). In other cases, turning around the enterprise has meant micro-managing production and restructuring the labour force (Darling, 1991).

The rest of this chapter summarizes the background of Telmex and the sector's labour relations, examines the structural framework of changing labour relations, focuses on different components of the privatization agreement for labour and the financial health of the company, on the impact of technological change and the Consultation Agreement on the day-to-day lives of workers, concluding that the Telmex-STRM agreements are not, and should not be, a model for the restructuring of labour relations in privatized companies.

2. A case study of Telmex

2.1 Mexican telecommunications, employment growth and unionization

For the last three decades the central axis of Mexico's telecommunications system has been Telmex, the largest telephone service company in the country.[3] The Mexican State gained control of the firm in 1972, although 49 per cent remained in private hands. The Government appointed the majority of the company's executive board and subjected the firm to multiple regulatory agencies and regimes. In 1976, the Ministry of Communications and Transport (SCT) extended Telmex's monopoly of basic telephone services for 30 years (until 1996), with the possibility of renewal for an additional 20 years. The SCT was responsible for regulating the telecommunications sector, while the Budget and Programming Ministry supervised Telmex's annual budget. Rates for services were jointly decided by the Public Credit and Finance Ministry and the SCT in accordance with the Law on the General Channels of Communication of 1939.

Telecommunications was a neglected development priority in the early 1980s as the Mexican Government edged towards liberalization of the economy. The sector experienced a high average growth rate of 12 per cent until the early 1980s. After the 1982 economic crisis, growth slowed to an average of 6 per cent per annum until 1988. Only 16 per cent of Mexican households had a telephone in 1984. By the end of the decade the telecommunications system was plagued by poor basic service, high long-distance rates, uneven quality, continued disruptions and rampant corruption.

In 1988, telephone density was just five telephone sets per 100 inhabitants for an installed capacity of 8.8 million telephone sets. Only 17 per cent of households had telephones and there was a waiting list of 1.5 million. Density began to climb before the 1990 privatization, reaching 5.4 sets per 100 inhabitants in 1989 and 5.8 in 1988. Labour productivity measured in terms of workers per 1,000 lines has also improved since 1989. At the end of 1990, however, Telmex productivity was still only about half the average international standard (10.46 workers per 1,000 lines as against 6.02 for Telefónica Española).

Telmex employment increased from 29,600 in 1981 to 50,000 in 1988, and remained between 49,000 and 50,000 in the following three years. The employment growth of the 1980s was accompanied by an erosion in union membership, because many of the new employees were not unionized. At the time of privatization (1990), 64 per cent of the Telmex labour force was affiliated to the *Sindicato de Telefonistas de la República Mexicana* (STRM) and about 18 per cent to other unions. Although operators and exchange maintenance staff remain highly unionized, the greatest growth in Telmex has been in areas where workers are least unionized — administrative personnel, expansion, and engineering and construction.

The planning and installation of the telephone network, underground as well as outside, was carried out by outside firms and by Telmex subsidiaries. The installation of new digital exchange equipment was done by the suppliers, often foreign companies such as Ericsson, or by national contractors (Reintel, Telemontaje, Mactel). Telmex's construction department had 750 employees as against a total of 5,000 workers in subcontractor firms performing construction work. In the area of digital exchanges, Telmex created a subsidiary, Mitel, exclusively staffed by non-unionized personnel, undercutting the work of the Exchange Department (Felix, 1989). Given that much of Telmex's growth took place in its non-unionized subsidiaries, it has been estimated that by 1989, out of 100 hours' work on telephone services, only 20 were carried out by unionized personnel (Coparmex, 1989; Felix, 1989).

2.2 The Telmex balance sheet

Pre-privatization Mexican telecommunications has been characterized as conforming to the "cash-cow" model of state enterprise in which the cards are stacked against improvements in basic services (Cowhey and Aronson, 1989). The characteristics of this model are:

(a) key users, particularly urban users, and the federal treasury are subsidized;

(b) services are cross-subsidized: local rates are kept artificially low while long-distance and international rates are high;

(c) extending the service to all areas of the country is a political priority;

(d) The Government holds a monopoly in basic services;

(e) The firm has only moderate political clout so its investment needs are not given a high priority;

(f) Equipment suppliers are foreign but domestic production is encouraged.

Overall telephone rates have not kept pace with inflation over the past 15 years. International and domestic long-distance rates have eroded the least. Basic local rates in 1984 were less than half of their 1970 real value. Local calls represented 52 per cent of costs and 15 per cent of revenues. In 1986, international long-distance calls accounted for almost 60 per cent of total revenues, followed by national long-distance calls (27 per cent) and local use (13 per cent) (Escamilla, 1989).

Telmex's average annual growth rate in the 1980s was about half that of the previous decade. From 1982 to 1987, Telmex's revenues and net profits stagnated (Mendoza, 1989). Between 1983 and 1988, the distorted structure of charges, the closing of foreign financial markets to Mexican companies as a result of the debt crisis, the domestic recession and the Treasury's reluctance to reinvest the company's tax receipts led to a decline in investment capacity.[4] During this period Telmex's average annual growth rate was just 6 per cent, far short of growing demand.

In the second half of the 1980s, Telmex was allowed to reduce the gap between the rates it charged for telephone calls and marginal costs. Rates for local and domestic long distance calls increased while international long distance rates were reduced. Yet until 1989 the various taxes on local and (national) long distance telephone services that Telmex paid to the National Treasury kept the company from investing in the modernization of its basic infrastructure. In 1990, the various taxes on Telmex telephone services revenues represented 57 per cent of its operating expenses; little of this was reinvested in the firm.

3. Technological change, modernization and the new unionism

3.1 Telmex's structural and technological transformation

In 1980, Telmex embarked on a modernization programme centred on digital technology. Its objectives were to digitize 70 per cent of services by the year 2000 and to have an installed base of 30 million telephone sets. Although the first digital exchanges were installed in 1982, the programme was initially hampered by technical problems and investment shortages. By 1986, only 8 per cent of local lines, 35 per cent of local traffic exchanges and 25 per cent of long-distance exchanges had been digitized.

By the mid-1980s it became clear that the slow pace of digitization was not addressing Mexico's severe telecommunications problems. The growth in new lines was stagnating rather than accelerating, customer demand continued to outpace the supply of new lines, and the quality of service continued to decline. Other factors — in particular the country's growing communication needs, and also the significant destruction of the long distance public network caused by the 1985 earthquake — compounded the pressure on Telmex to support the modernization and opening up of the economy.

In 1987, Telmex responded to these challenges with the Programme for the Improvement of Services (PIES) based on a two-pronged strategy. On the one hand, it would concentrate on an overlay network which could rapidly provide much-needed and profitable services to large users. On the other, modernization of the basic network would continue.

This programme of structural change centred on three main axes: (1) growth; (2) modernization and diversification; and (3) quality. Objectives were delineated:

(a)   a new financing framework eliminating cross-subsidization of services; establishment of rules for state reinvestment; rationalization of services to government; and changes in charges and tax structures;

(b)   digitization of 80 per cent of the local network and 100 per cent of the long-distance network by the year 2000;

(c)   direct modernization permitting the construction of an ISDN network capable of generating new services which would be a source of future growth for the firm;

(d)   adaptation of the regulatory framework, particularly regarding concessions and the role of the State and the private sector in the development of new telecommunications services;

(e)   adoption of a decentralized administrative organization similar to that of equivalent international companies;

(f)   increased productivity and improvement in the quality of services through the constitution of Joint Enterprise-Union Committees for Productivity and Modernization.

The 1987 strategy formalized some *de facto* trends, most notably the increasing use of digital technology, which permitted Telmex to offer improved services customized to the needs of large users. After the destruction of long-distance equipment by the 1985 earthquake, Telmex accelerated the replacement of outdated equipment with decentralized digital exchanges. Modernization of the basic network, the second component of Telmex's strategy, was predicated upon a far-reaching administrative reorganization, replacing a pyramidal, centralized structure with a modular, decentralized one to gain greater operational flexibility. The new structure consisted of three corporate directorates (Finance and Administration, Planning and Corporate Development, and Human Resources and Labour Relations) and five autonomous directorates or profit centres (long-distance, telephone development, and three regional operations groups — North, South, and Metropolitan). A Centre for Advanced Telecommunications focusing on the development of new ISDN services was also created. In 1987, a programme focusing on automation as a means to improve services was launched. In 1989 Telmex introduced a long-distance system (LADA 800), thus automating about 80 per cent of this service. Telmex then had 21 subsidiaries organized in five activity groups, ranging from plant construction and engineering services to mobile communications and the production and marketing of telephone directories.

These structural developments quickened the pace of modernization, so that by 1990 29 per cent of lines were digital and 50 per cent by 1992. Digitization has presented workers with real challenges. Analogue equipment required eight people to operate one exchange controlling 10,000 lines, while digital equipment requires two workers per exchange of 100,000 lines. Although this would appear to presage massive lay-offs, they have not occurred. In fact, the installation, expansion and debugging of lines has led to a slight increase in the number of workers.

3.2 The STRM and the new unionism

Labour relations in Mexican telecommunications have undergone major changes since 1976. The next few years were marked by a series of labour confrontations, which in turn led to the gradual recognition of the STRM as an active and independent union, by both state officials and segments of labour. Telmex leadership, consistent with their platform of democratization, sponsored statutory changes such as delinking the union from the government party (PRI), limiting the terms of office of union executive members, greater financial transparency of union business, internal freedom of association, direct and secret balloting, and increased transfer of financial resources to regional offices. Work conditions and health demands moved to the top of the agenda along with wage claims. Initial efforts to democratize the decision-making process within the STRM were pursued through a decentralization of decision-making to smaller units with the aim of mobilizing a larger labour base. The STRM consists of a central section (in Mexico City), about 15 work centres, and 102 regional sections and subsections.

Although Hernández Juárez was elected on a platform of democratization and reform, he used his power to consolidate a "results-oriented approach" and reinforce his control over the union. He managed to change the statutes in order to extend his tenure in office and later to permit his re-election as well as that of other key officials. These actions belied the promises he had made in 1976. He successfully played opposing factions off against each other and managed to promote his own supporters within the union structure. Until the early 1980s, the STRM focused almost exclusively on economic issues, principally wages.

In the early 1980s, the union's focus began to shift from wage demands to issues of protecting workers from technological change and improving working conditions. The STRM accepted a management-drafted plan for the introduction of new technologies as well as its wage proposals. The company's expansion strategy focused on digitization of the system and the opening of the private PABX market to foreign companies. In 1981, maintenance workers led the first discussions on the impact of new technologies; individual departments also increasingly demanded a greater input in shaping the implementation of technological modernization.

In 1982 Telmex introduced its modernization plan and laid off over 500 workers, claiming that the redundancies were related to the new technology. An opposition movement emerged in the union *(Movimiento Democrático Telefonista)* and contended that the union leadership was not challenging the lay-offs. Ultimately, the fired workers were rehired, contingent upon their agreeing not to challenge the union's leadership.

A consequence of the internal struggles was that the union leadership, in order to defeat the opposition, was forced to give priority to the challenges of new technologies and began organizing around working conditions (health and safety policies). The tendency to look at areas other than wages was further reinforced by the implementation of various national austerity plans, which capped wage increases. The strategy was successful, and in 1986 an agreement was signed stating that technological change would not lead to lay-offs. Later that year, article 193 of the Collective Labour Contract (CCT) was revised. The article regulated the mixed commissions dealing with modernization, new technology, restructuring, health and safety, training and productivity. A mixed STRM-Telmex committee was created to negotiate the impact of the new technologies; this became the 1988 CCT Modernization Committee (Felix, 1989). (More will be said about this later. Many of these advances have come under fire as a result of the Consultation Agreement (CC), the pre-privatization labour accord reached in 1989.[5])

Until the 1985 earthquake, Telmex management had proceeded with modernization cautiously. New technologies were introduced gradually, and related support and administrative services were usually farmed out to subsidiaries and subcontractors to avoid confrontations with the union. During this period workers increasingly lost control of the labour process. The workers were kept in the dark about the overall direction and scope of the technological modernization plan (Felix, 1989). The 1985 earthquake laid bare management's strategy, leading to its challenge by labour. Telmex, forced to speed up the modernization programme *(Programa de Digitalización)*, extended the practice of subcontracting to non-unionized firms. In light of this sombre picture and the growing demands on telecommunications by the country's modernization drive, labour, government and management hammered out a tripartite agreement.

On the eve of the 1988 federal elections, some of the job losses were reversed and the quality of services became the target of an intergovernmental productivity committee which included union participation. In August 1987, Hernández Juárez joined the government party, the PRI, and exhorted STRM workers to disregard the opposition and vote for the PRI in the forthcoming elections. In April 1988, the PRI presidential candidate, Salinas de Gortari, visited the STRM. At the same time, the STRM expanded its external linkages to the national labour movement, through Juárez's participation in CTM's executive committee. After a strike in April 1988, the STRM negotiated an 18 per cent wage increase. Successive CCT negotiations led to significant wage increases for the rank and file, particularly for the network workers — traffic, external network, regional centres — which made up the union leadership's base of support.

In spite of 1987 tripartite agreement, by the end of 1988 Telmex had changed its tack and begun aggressively confronting the union. In the 1987 document spelling out its modernization plans (the aforementioned PIES), the company had publicly blamed workers for the increasingly poor quality of service.[6] The STRM, denying any blame for poor services, made a counter-proposal to PIES based on continuous improvements in quality linked to technological modernization and a simultaneous change in the pattern of labour relations. The ensuing negotiations had two main results: (a) the creation of a Joint Enterprise-Union Productivity Committee; and (b) a more solid plan for negotiating the introduction of new technologies, which was the basis for the revision of Clauses 136, 185 and 193 in the 1988 Collective Labour Contract (mentioned above).

To coordinate and support the union strategy and negotiations in these matters, STRM's National Executive Committee created a Modernization Committee in 1988. The existing agreement on new technologies was decentralized to the project level and minimum requirements for information on changes were instituted. At the end of the 1980s, the bulwark of STRM support was divided between operators (12,000) and maintenance workers (4,000), which together represented over one-third of Telmex's workforce. With their support, STRM's president Hernández Juárez effectively countered his opponents, many of whom were eventually coopted with administrative jobs in the union. Since 1989, negotiations have once again revolved around working conditions because the inflation-fighting National Economic Solidarity Pact strictly limits wage increases.

Internal union politics remain a major force driving the STRM's negotiating strategy. The National Executive Committee's priorities coincide with the demands of its traditional base of support, operators and maintenance workers. The only category-specific objectives of the Programme of Action presented at the September 1992 STRM General Assembly were for these groups. The union vociferously defeated the agreement hammered out with the company granting safeguards to operators threatened by technological change (for example, in relocation and retraining). It also sought to conclude negotiations on the impact of technological change on workers in the switching *(centrales)* and maintenance areas.

3.3 The privatization of Telmex

Among the reasons given for the privatization of Telmex was a five-year investment shortfall of US$10 billion that could not be met by the government budget, whose priorities were social programmes. There were also important political motives: an effort to weaken labour and experiment with a new model for the post-Fidel Velázquez/Confederación de Trabajadores Mexicanos period.

Privatization and labour reorganization were mutually reinforcing. In September 1989, during the STRM Annual General Assembly, President Salinas announced the impending privatization of Telmex. A new labour relations contract, codified in the 1989 Consultation Agreement *(Convenio de Concertación)*, was a prerequisite for the privatization and one reason the price paid for the firm was so high.

The privatization process was completed on 20 December 1990. The Mexican group CARSO led an international consortium which acquired a 26.7 per cent stake in the company, giving it effective control. At the time, Telmex was the largest company listed on the Mexican Stock Exchange, the third largest company in Mexico, and the second largest telecommunications company in Latin America (next to that of Brazil). The US$1.76 billion paid for 20.4 per cent of Telmex preferred stock by a consortium formed by Southwestern Bell (United States), France Telecom (France) and Grupo CARSO (Mexico) was the highest ever paid for a public enterprise since the inception of the privatization programme.[7] In addition, the Telmex privatization involved about 65,000 employees (including those in subsidiaries); this was the largest and most diverse group of employees in any privatized company. Preparing for privatization required protracted and far-reaching changes in the Collective Labour Contract, which will be discussed below. The Telmex privatization was also the largest that had taken place involving a service sector company.

Despite the privatization of Telmex the Government's stated intention was to retain regulatory control as a means of:

(a)   ensuring radically improved services;

(b)   promoting sustained expansion and modernization of the system;

(c)   promoting technological research and development;

(d)   guaranteeing the rights of workers and giving them some participation in the company; and

(e)   guaranteeing majority control by Mexican nationals.

In the privatized Telmex the Mexican CARSO group is responsible for human resources and labour relations. Its foreign partners in the consortium, Southwestern Bell and France Telecom/FCR, are responsible for commercial affairs, marketing, mobile phones, directories, and network modernization, including long-distance and international circuits.

4. The privatization of Telmex and labour relations

4.1 The Consultation Agreement

The new framework for labour relations was created prior to privatization by the *Convenio de Concertación* (Consultation Agreement — CC). The CC was signed in April 1989 between the STRM, Telmex and the Mexican Government. In return for a commitment to modernize and improve its services, Telmex demanded greater labour mobility, freedom to hire new workers, and leeway in the implementation of new technologies. This radical revision of the Collective Labour Contract (CTC) was hailed by political observers as a national model for labour relations.

While the price paid by labour in Telmex was less than that involved in restructuring in other companies such as the bankrupt AeroMexico,[8] the form in which the CC was negotiated compromised the future vitality of the union. One sceptic argued that the winner in the CC was the union leadership which, by reducing the number of departments and department-level agreements, effectively reinforced its control of negotiations with management and government. In the past, new leaders (and challengers to existing ones) had gained experience and visibility by negotiating department-level agreements. The reduction in the number of departments has thus reduced the opportunities for new leaders to emerge. Union dissidents saw the CC as a sell-out and claimed that the union had negotiated selective wage increases, for example to bring regional workers' wages up to those of the capital, to coopt workers into supporting the agreement.[9]

A general labour agreement covering all unionized workers replaced the 57 previous department-level agreements which, *de facto*, had constituted separate labour contracts.[10] The department-level agreements were very detailed, often setting the exact punch-in and punch-out times of workers. The new job descriptions *(perfiles de puesto)* were more general, delineating workers' responsibilities in broad terms such as "maintaining equipment, running tests, writing reports", and much shorter.

The number of work categories, at least on paper, was drastically reduced from 585 to 134, in turn classified into 31 specialties. The 585 salary levels were reduced to 41. General work areas were reduced from seven to five: (1) telephone operations; (2) commercialization; (3) maintenance; (4) administration; and (5) new services. In fact, actual rationalization is lagging behind.

As a result of the Consultation Agreement management obtained greater flexibility in hiring, replacing and transferring workers. Transfers could now be made at the discretion of the firm, and it gained new freedom to hire non-unionized staff — hereafter referred to as "discretionary hiring" — who usually had administrative and supervisory responsibilities. When transfers were to take place the union designated the workers to be transferred. If after two attempts the union could not identify a worker willing to be transferred, then the firm could designate the transferee. Furthermore, when transfers occurred, the old worker was not automatically replaced, which effectively limited job creation. A new job was created only in the event that the transferred worker was relocated on the basis of his/her particular skills. Finally, the required time that management had to replace workers was extended to two weeks from the previous limit of three days.

As regards modernization, the union lost its right to review new technologies and their implementation, and training was centralized and offered at the discretion of the firm. Management was required to provide information regarding the new technologies it introduced for training and information purposes only, rather than as a matter for negotiation. Management refused to accept a New Technology Committee and eliminated a clause in the earlier CCT calling for advance access to information by the union.

4.2 The worker-owned stock programme

To forge a new firm-based identity among workers and provide them with an incentive to increase productivity, workers were offered stock options. The Government guaranteed a low-interest loan of US$352 million to the STRM to acquire 4.4 per cent of Telmex public shares. Unionized workers bought 3 per cent as individuals, and the remaining 1.4 per cent was purchased by the union's retirement fund. Non-unionized employees were also authorized to purchase a certain number of shares through an additional fund established by the Government.

The union did not acquire a seat on the Telmex board but it was agreed that workers would be allowed to continue purchasing stock and that when they reached a 10 per cent share they would be entitled to a seat. The union leadership's goal of participating in Telmex's board is, however, a distant dream. Control of 10.1 per cent of company shares remains elusive, as many workers cash in their shares and others choose to exert direct control over their shares rather than consign them to the union's share fund management.

4.3 The emerging regulatory framework

As part of the privatization agreement, Telmex acquired sale rights to many tele-communications services. State regulation was to supplant the market in order to ensure that a privatized Telmex would continue to pursue social goals, such as extending service throughout the country and developing rural telecommunications. The monopoly regulations have important implications for the union; so far they have done little to strengthen it as the firm continues to farm out profitable services to non-unionized Telmex subsidiaries.

The Government set a number of investment and performance targets:

(a) annual growth of 12 per cent between 1989 and 1994 (equivalent to doubling the existing number of lines in service);

(b) extension of rural telephone services to give all villages with more than 500 inhabitants access to telephone services by 1994;

(c) installation of 80,000 public phones in popular urban areas (equivalent to a fourfold increase);

(d) expansion of the long-distance infrastructure by 60 per cent, including growth of the digital network to 8,500 kilometres, installation of 3,500 kilometres of fibre optics and replacement of 480,000 obsolete lines, with the aim of reaching a level of 65 per cent digitization.

The existing monopoly which granted the company exclusive right to provide international long-distance services until 1996 remained in place. However, Telmex lost its monopoly on the sale of integrated telephone services and equipment. Sales of equipment to final users were opened to foreign firms, as was the provision of value added services: equipment for interconnection, data transmission equipment, private networks, fibre optics, satellite support services, cellular telephony, digital exchange, television and broadcasting equipment. Only satellite transmissions and telegraphic services remained closed to foreign capital.

Changes in the telephone services concession title extended Telmex's monopoly on basic telephone services an additional 20 years (until 2026 rather than 1996) and created limited regulated competition in certain areas of activity: cellular telephony, private networks, equipment manufacture, and earth stations for satellite communication. Telmex has experienced the greatest competition in the area of cellular telephony, where the private company Iusacel (a rival of Telmex's cellular subsidiaries) has experienced a dramatic expansion.[11] Telmex and its competitors were freed to broadcast any type of signal in their networks, except radio and television. The Government retained the regulatory control over tariffs, through a system of ceiling prices.[12] The State became the regulator of negotiations between Telmex and value added service suppliers for interconnection.

At the fiscal level, some previous taxes (IEPS) were incorporated in the new rate structure and a new tax on telephone services revenues (29 per cent) was created. The company was allowed an investment deduction of up to 65 per cent of this new tax. The general impact on Telmex's revenue structure was to increase the share of revenues from the local basic and national long-distance services and diminish the share of international long-distance services.

Notwithstanding the new regulatory framework and telecommunications code, the basic law on telecommunications, the LVGC, was not changed. The discretionary power of the Minister of Communications and Transport (STC) over Telmex and the telecommunications sector in general was thus preserved. For example, the STC retained discretionary powers to regulate rates in the "open" value added services areas (ISDN), private circuits, directory assistance, and new subscriber services such as call waiting, if it seemed that price liberalization was not working and/or that Telmex was unfairly exercising its monopoly power.

The regulatory framework of the newly privatized company compromises the future size and strength of the union, which in many ways is tied to the fate of the basic network. The basic network continues to deteriorate and to lag behind the country's telecommunications needs. Although 55 per cent of lines are digitized — a figure which surpasses the international average — Telmex continues to outstrip other companies in terms of the number of complaints reported to the Consumer Protection Agency.[13] The basic network is not being sustained, while efforts to modernize and opportunities for profitable services are focused on subsidiaries outside the union's purview. This strategy, concentrating on the modernization of services to large firms and industrial zone areas, serves two goals: it creates more streamlined service firms and simultaneously sidesteps organized labour.

5. The impact of privatization

5.1 Improved services and economic performance

Telmex and the STRM worked together to identify the bottlenecks to productivity growth. The problematic areas in decreasing order of importance are: material resources, external plant, exchanges and support, and infrastructure. The efforts did pay off, as productivity improved markedly from 1985 to 1991 (table 4.2). In the two years following privatization, Telmex installed 1.5 million new digital lines, reaching a level of digitization of 55 per cent. In 1992, it also replaced obsolete analogue lines with 400,000 digital ones; this meant a net gain of 34,000 lines, which is still far below demand. In 1991, Telmex met one of its targets and considerably increased the number of rural communities connected to the telephone network.[14]

5.2 The transformation of the workplace

More than privatization *per se*, the introduction of new (digital) technologies since the early 1980s, and particularly after 1987, has had a considerable impact on the definition of work categories and tasks. The introduction of new technologies has been of variable pace and has had a variety of implications for different groups of workers. All workers find, however, that the intensity of work has increased and that they are often poorly trained to meet the challenges; the new technologies thus pose threats as well as opportunities for workers and their union.

   As the modernization of the company has progressed, labour has lost much of its ability to control the content and pace of changes in working conditions, whether these are a result of changes in technology or of recent administrative restructuring. The operators, in particular, have suffered from intensification of work, while maintenance workers are insufficiently trained to work with digital switches. The future of wage increases is uncertain as they have been linked to productivity increases, but the rules for defining these increases

Table 4.2. Telmex business profile, 1985-91

	1985	1987	1989	1991
Revenues (US$m)	1 032	1 047	2 070	5 400
Net profits (US$m)	175	289	687	2 300
Telephone lines (000s)	3 575	3 985	4 700	6 782

Source: Escamilla, 1989; Mendoza, 1989; PTTI, 1992.

have yet to be fixed. New work-related hazards have emerged, yet they remain unrecognized by the firm. Furthermore, retraining and its attendant promise of improve- ment in workers' futures have not materialized.

5.2.1 Operators

The operators, constituting over 20 per cent of the workforce, are the group of union workers most threatened by new technologies but, despite the changes, the expected lay-offs have not materialized. Although one operator can now handle many more calls, the number of calls has increased as more lines have been installed. Additionally, many generations of equipment exist side by side and the need for old skills has not been eliminated. The majority of the over 13,000 operators, for example, use a switchboard, which limits them to processing about seven calls simultaneously.

As many of the skills that operators previously needed are being displaced by the computers, the typical concept of the workplace is disappearing. A new one, however, has not emerged to take its place:

The seniority privileges that you had earned are in jeopardy ... Anyone can acquire the knowledge that you needed to use the "little machine" [computer], it does not require a lot of time. With the analogue equipment, it took you a month and a half to learn, in addition to the practice you needed. With the new equipment, in a week and a half, any *compañera* that speaks English, any one from the street can do it. You no longer need experience as an operator, you learn the equipment and operate it quickly.[15]

These trends towards automation will accelerate because the rate structure makes direct international dialling cheaper than operator-assisted calls.

Other issues are work-related injuries and retraining. Operators are experiencing increasing stress as the number of calls increases. In addition, they are suffering from injuries such as carpal tunnel syndrome, eye strain, and other problems related to poorly installed lighting, poorly adjusted chairs and other equipment. Few studies are made, and the way the firm and the union address these problems is symptomatic of the increasing loss of contact with the rank and file. The union leadership and management make a deal regarding the installation of new lighting or the purchase of new chairs, but the workers who use the equipment are barely consulted.

Regarding training, although an agreement has been signed between the Technological Institute of Telmex (Inttelmex) and France Telecom to train workers, workers complain that the courses are theoretical rather than practical and that training begins only after new equipment has been installed, rather than before.[16] As a result, workers are penalized for mistakes stemming from inadequate training.

5.2.2 External plant

Digital systems are capable of automatic self-diagnosis and correction, and main-tenance takes place in a modular and centralized manner. Whereas old crossbar telephone exchanges required seven to ten technicians per exchange with 10,000 lines, the new digital exchanges require just one technician per 60,000 lines. Finally, since 1979 a variety of administrative and financial services have been computerized, a trend that intensified after 1987 (Coparmex, 1989). Yet the debugging of the system and the persistent problems of old lines have led to a 10 to 15 per cent increase in the number of maintenance workers. As with the operators, predictions that the number of maintenance workers would fall by 25 per cent between 1980 and 1995 never materialized. In fact, the number of maintenance workers has probably increased by about 10 per cent since 1982.[17]

As far as "external plant" (installation and repair) is concerned, according to one departmental delegate, the principal changes are on intensification of work and the fact that a previously specialized worker now has to do many tasks. In the past, for example, one person installed lines, another repaired them, and another injected gas. Although the installation of fibre optic cables is similar to the installation of copper ones,[18] installation is very different from maintenance and gas injection. Now, workers are given two weeks' training and are supposed to be able to do all the tasks. Another change is that several maintenance centres can now control one exchange, so there is no longer a dedicated relationship between a centre and an exchange.

Work has been intensifying since the early 1980s with the firm's modernization plan. Since privatization, however, repair work has increased by 30-40 per cent, and as the rules tying wages to productivity are being hammered out, the rhythm of work has intensified again. Worst of all, repair people are not being given the training or even the tools they need to do their jobs.

Finally, though workers are organized into teams, the levelling of wages that has taken place is undermining the teams' functioning. The lowest increases have gone to highly skilled workers who become team leaders. Thus, as their responsibilities have increased, their relative wages have decreased. The new post-Consultation Agreement worker identity that was to have emerged has not materialized, leaving workers frustrated and feeling unfairly treated.

5.2.3 Non-union hiring by Telmex

The Consultation Agreement gave Telmex more liberty to hire non-unionized workers, generally administrative and supervisory personnel *(personal de confianza)*, who in turn acquired more authority over workers. One critic argues that the union made a strategic error by not negotiating stricter limits on discretionary (non-union) hiring (Felix, 1989). In interviews, workers have complained that the discretionary personnel in Telmex are often too new or ill-prepared to meet the challenges of setting up a framework for tying wages to productivity, a key aspect of the new era of labour relations. They also claim that the discretionary personnel best trained to implement and use the new technology are in the subsidiaries; their expertise is therefore unavailable to Telmex workers.[19]

5.3 The retraining mirage

There is a widespread perception among workers that the retraining agreements established in the Consultation Agreement and Collective Labour Contract have not been implemented.[20] For example, retraining of workers to install and maintain the fibre optics network has been too limited. Retraining courses have been too short and often too late. There is a general feeling of disorientation and frustration. Furthermore, training has not succeeded in motivating workers to embrace a new technological culture.

In spite of Telmex's repeated pledges to continue the Intensive Programme of Permanent Quality,[21] experience seems to show otherwise. Workers are poorly prepared for participating in quality circles. When the circles are started, they are strictly controlled and issues tend to be limited to ones that workers consider insignificant; workers believe the circles skirt the fundamental problems. Workers, both unionized and low-level supervisory, are unaware of the firm's commitment to quality, and perpetuate traditional forms of labour organization. A damaging consequence of this general ignorance, combined with mistrust about quality, is that middle-level line managers have increased their power and tightened supervisory practices rather than decentralizing control.

5.4 Productivity agreements

In so far as the opportunities for significant wage gains have been limited — given government directives encouraging wage restraint and the political agreements between the union leadership and key government political actors — productivity agreements have gained a crucial importance. General wage negotiations are part of the Collective Labour Contract negotiations which take place every two years, and annual increases are fixed by government authorities. Sustained productivity increases are vital if the union leadership is to retain the support of the rank and file; they are also fundamental for an effective and durable pattern of labour relations.

Although productivity increases have in theory increased the possibilities for workers to attain higher pay, there have been considerable disparities across different areas. Up to January 1993 only the traffic area had received productivity incentives, whereas negotiations on measuring parameters and economic incentives had stalled in most other areas. In some, such as maintenance centres, after a year of negotiations, management had come up with unacceptable demands that had practically halted the process. In some regions after long and extensive discussions, negotiations over productivity incentives were called off by management, who argued that workers were already performing at or above the negotiated level. A dangerous consequence of the productivity drive noted by workers and union is the intensification of work. Workers express a legitimate concern about being caught in a vicious circle of intensifying work just to maintain reasonable wage levels.

At the root of the problems with productivity incentives is the fact that the union jumped on to the bandwagon without really knowing what was involved. As a member of the STRM executive committee puts it: "The negotiation of productivity incentives was done a bit in the dark, as its characteristics weren't very well known. So the idea was to jump in to learn and to get the incentives, and to try to solve the problems as they appeared."

Workers and union delegates involved in actual negotiations confirm this impression, adding that their management counterparts are often even less well prepared than they are. A top-level union-company committee, the Analysis Committee, is responsible for discussing these productivity problems as well as issues related to quality. However, Telmex management fears that such a body might acquire a too central and all-embracing role by linking issues that it would have preferred to negotiate separately.

The problems were compounded by the fact that the top-level negotiations between the union and Telmex did not set general criteria but rather attempted to base particular ones on individual specialties. When these specialty-grounded criteria were transposed to diverse labour processes with differing characteristics and labour relations traditions (e.g. mechanics in different areas of the company), intractable problems surfaced. Finally, these negotiations were carried out very quickly and were overshadowed by the then politically more salient problem of share acquisition by workers. Telmex initially wished to link productivity incentives only to improvements in services that involved direct contact with subscribers, such as external plant and commercial areas. Secondary priority areas were subscriber registry and telephone exchanges. The area where productivity incentives began to be implemented (November 1992) was external plant, because it already had a record of improvements, which helped to set up measurement parameters.

5.5 Technological change, worker participation and labour relations

Clauses in the Consultation Agreement regarding worker participation have become a dead letter: committees are frequently reorganized but remain centralized within the upper echelons. Moreover, the 1987 administrative reorganization, which was supposed to produce greater decentralization and increased responsibility at the lower levels, never materialized. Workers claim that channels to administration/management that were previously open, allowing workers to participate in the introduction of technological change, are now blocked (see section 4.1).

According to members of the executive committee, there have not been any major structural changes in STRM-Telmex labour relations. With regard to the negotiating framework, they argue that the 1987 decentralization transformed the structure of power relations within the firm, strengthening the negotiating power of individual department managers vis-à-vis the management executive committee negotiating team. However, several workers and departmental delegates observe that the decentralization has not had a similar effect in the union negotiating structure, where workers at the departmental level have in fact been weakened owing to the new job classifications, vis-à-vis both their immediate management superiors and the union executive committee. This discrepancy in the power and negotiating structures of labour and management could have negative consequences for the long-term negotiating strength of labour as the rank and file lose their negotiating power, without a corresponding increase in the effective power of the union leadership.

6. The non-replicability and shortcomings of labour relations at Telmex

The far-reaching changes in labour relations at Telmex are part of a larger process of technological change, increasing international competition, and national and internal union politics. Privatization and the Consultation Agreement are two turning points in the tortuous and often unpredictable trajectory. We would argue that the Telmex-STRM agreements are particular to the political conjuncture in which they unfolded and are not therefore generalizable to other sectors of the Mexican economy.

Telmex's record in maintaining employment has been impressive compared to that of other Mexican companies that have undergone restructuring. This can be attributed to several factors, including the recent growth and investment in the company; the safeguards negotiated for labour prior to privatization; STRM president Hernández Juárez's centralizing leadership; and the personal ties between Hernández Juárez and President Salinas as both strove to forge a new model of labour relations to support the country's modernization drive and advance their political goals. As a result the STRM is in the enviable position of having not only survived but strengthened itself. The record as regards creating a committed and dedicated workforce capable of confronting the daunting challenges is, however, less laudable. The increasing centralization of the STRM and the corresponding rift with the rank and file may impair the union's credibility in its role as spokesman and channel of communication between firm and labour force.

In 1991, TELMEX reported a huge profit of US$2.3 billion on revenues of US$5.4 billion, with annual growth at 20 per cent. The turnaround from the sluggishness of the 1980s was spectacular by any measure.[22] Increased charges, in line with the regulatory mechanisms of the privatization agreement, allowed new investment which fuelled investment and growth.[23] Telmex's US$8 billion modernization programme was completed in 1993. The replacement of analogue with digital lines has gone ahead rapidly, although its efficiency has been hampered by the poor condition of the basic network.[24] The modernization of the basic network continues to require massive resources, well beyond the millions of dollars already spent. In 1991 only about half of all calls were completed.[25] The poor quality of the domestic telecommunications system pushes Telmex and other firms to concentrate on high-value services which are provided by non-unionized firms. Telmex has also given a high priority to the overlay network, which serves the largest domestic and foreign companies.[26]

Although the STRM succeeded in including in the 1992 Collective Labour Agreement an article requiring Telmex to contract unionized personnel through the STRM when it creates new subsidiaries (negotiated as part of the privatization settlement), by and large the path to modernization is not a unionized one.

By reducing the number of labour categories and work areas, the Consultation Agreement was intended to bring about a more efficient allocation of labour resources. Without disputing that the number of categories and work areas was excessive and that greater flexibility was needed, it appears that Telmex management have been unable to benefit from this new-found flexibility. As a result, the reorganization of work tasks has been a stumbling and ad hoc process. Workers complain that there is no coherent strategy. More importantly, they claim that their efforts to organize quality circles have been stunted by management, who pursue short-term but limited efficiency gains rather than address structural problems. The limited efficiency gains achieved by the company can be attributed to a long overdue policy of sustained investment in equipment, rather than to the establishment of a modern framework of labour relations and the flexibility this would bring.

Although workers' ownership of a share of Telmex was to be another element in the structure of cooperative and profitable growth, the underlying reality is quite different. It has been argued that the lack of union opposition to the sale and the subsequent changes in the Collective Labour Contract can be attributed to the profit-sharing agreement, but this view seems to be mistaken.[27] Although the STRM embraced the Consultation Agreement, it was only after bitter internal struggles in which dissidents were defeated. Furthermore, as interviews with workers and union delegates revealed, the profit-sharing plan had not produced the expected identification of workers with the firm that is so important in defining a new role for labour in the restructured firm.

The STRM leadership's strategy was to accept management's plans for introducing new technology without lay-offs. In return, it would mobilize the rank and file to work towards productivity incentives and leave behind old-style wage demands. It would also bargain to regain jobs lost to outside subcontractors and non-unionized personnel appointed by Telmex *(personal de confianza)*. If successful, the strategy would have been a self-reinforcing one, promoting productivity and increasing unionization. But union leaders, despite their rhetoric about co-responsibility and cooperation to increase productivity and profits, have been unable to establish rules for productivity incentives. They have also increasingly closed off input from the rank and file. Negotiations over productivity incentives stalled as management dragged its feet in an effort to sabotage them. The January 1993 strikes by external plant area personnel in Mexico City was a recent example of growing discontent with the union's handling of the emerging work rules and productivity incentives. This was the first strike in protest at the way in which the March 1992 productivity programme is being implemented. Workers complained that there was little discussion about it and criticized the methodology for measuring productivity.

The ties between government, union leadership and workers are strained to the point where workers are demanding a return to old-style collective action centring on wages rather than the alliance of productivity to which their leaders aspire. The National Executive Committee's response to these trends has been threefold. First, it is strengthening its traditional base of support at the same time as it calls for a new union identity that aggregates a larger number of workers. Second, it is modernizing its structure from the top down, training new union cadres in modern industrial relations techniques and establishing a centralized system of documentation and information. Third, it has increased its external activities: it has sponsored the creation of a new union movement, FESEBS; and pursued alliances with domestic and foreign unions and other external entities. However, these overtures are usually perceived by workers as superficial — a palliative that will not correct the erosion of real wages.

The STRM signed the Consultation Agreement in part because it was forced to: it was losing strength as more profitable services were farmed out to non-unionized Telmex subsidiaries, as technology was eliminating many skilled professions, and as industrial restructuring in other firms was taking its toll on labour.[28] The union leadership's enthusiasm for policies that compromised the union's future growth and produced no guaranteed wage agreements further aggravated the growing split between the leadership and the rank and file, who perceived the union's enthusiastic support as politically motivated, narrow and short-term. The signing of the Consultation Agreement saved the union but many of its provisions mortgage the STRM's long-term growth and bargaining power. Profitable services go to non-unionized companies; workers' identification with the job is eroding which complicates negotiations; centralization within the union is leading to growing disaffection among its supporters. A union that is more responsive to rank and file needs may be able to reverse some of these trends. It must struggle for advance information on the introduction of new technologies so that it can keep its members informed about what will be happening and devise strategies to minimize the negative impact. It must strive for continual training and rotation of workers, not only to protect workers from lay-offs and alleviate the boredom and hazards of repetitive tasks but also to create a wider company-level identity. It must maintain control over assignments and transfers but permit decisions to be made at the lower echelons. And it must create institutional structures that permit a flow of information between workers and union officials. Centralization of negotiation and decentralization in response to workers needs must reinforce each other.

References

Arena, E. 1993. "Privatization and training. The Mexican case", Interdepartmental Project on Structural Adjustment Occasional Paper 19. Geneva, ILO.

Comisión de Modernización. 1988. *Comisión de Modernización — Proyecto (propuesta)*. Informe presentado por la Comisión de Modernización a la XIII. Convención Nacional Ordinaria Democrática de Telefonistas, Sep.

Coparmex. 1989. *El sindicato de telefonistas de la República Mexicana (STRM): Una muestra de reestructuración tecnológica y flexibilización del contrato colectivo*. Mexico City; mimeo.

Cowhey, P. F.; Aronson, J. D. 1989. "Trade in services and changes in the world telecommunications system", in Cowhey et al., 1989.

————; Aronson, J. D.; Székely (eds.). 1989. *Changing networks: Mexico's telecommunications options*. Monograph Series, 32. San Diego, Center for U.S.-Mexico Studies/University of California.

Darling, J. 1991. "On the ground floor of Mexico's privatization: Alfredo Lelo de Larrea is the government's turnaround expert, and he's doing just that, turning troubled firms into companies that will sell quickly in the private sector", in *Los Angeles Times*, 10 Sep.

Denton, D. 1992. "Selling cellular: Competition is fierce, but there are plenty of customers to go around (Mexico)", in *Business Mexico*, 2 July, pp. 26-27.

Escamilla, J. R. P. 1989. "Telephone policy in Mexico: Rates and investment", in Cowhey et al., 1989, pp. 101-123.

Félix, R. E. 1989. "La pérdida de la materia de trabajo en el sindicato de telefonistas", in E. G. Garza (ed.). 1989. *Reconversión industrial y lucha sindical*. Mexico City, Fundación Friedrich Ebert-México/Editorial Nueva Sociedad, pp. 135-142.

Grant, J. 1991. "Mobile mania (cellular phones increasingly popular in Mexico)", in *Business Mexico*, 1 June, p. 23.

————. 1990. "Going mobile (Mexico)", in *Business Mexico*, No. 7, Sep., p. 44.

Mendoza, A. P. 1989. "Teléfonos de México: Development and perspectives", in Cowhey et al., 1989, pp. 91-99.

Ortiz, R. M.; Iriarte, R. 1988. "Reconversión industrial y lucha obrera", in *Revista Brecha*, Mar.

Postal Telegraph and Telephone International (PTTI). 1992. "Multinationals in telecommunications: Update". Spring 1992; mimeo.

Ramirez, A. 1992. "Woes at Telmex not of its making", in *New York Times (Business Section)*, 18 Sep.

Rogozinski, J. 1992. "Learning the ABCs of Mexico's privatization", in *Wall Street Journal*, 15 May.

Romo, R. C. 1992. "Teléfonos de México", in M. S. Gonzales, (ed.). *El proceso de privatización en México: Un estudio de casos*. Washington, DC, Inter-American Development Bank.

Salinas, R. 1992. "Privatization in Mexico: Much better, but still not enough", in *Heritage Foundation Reports*, 20 Jan.

Sanchez, L.; Angel, M. 1992. *Productividad y trabajo. El caso de Telmex.* Serie Analisis del Trabajo, Centro de Investigaciones del Trabajo y Estudios Económicosociales, AC, July 1992.

Shapiro, H. D. 1993. "A year of new boundaries. Privatization in Mexico gets out of the banking business", in *Institutional Investor*, Jan.

Solís, V. 1992. "La modernización de teléfonos de México", in *El Cotidiano*, No. 46, Mar.-Apr., pp. 60-68.

Székely, Gabriel, (ed.). 1989. *Changing networks: Mexico's telecommunications options.* Monograph Series, 32. San Diego, Centre for US-Mexican Studies/University of California, pp. 5-49.

Tandon, P. (ed.). *World Bank Conference on the Welfare Consequences of Selling Public Enterprises — Case studies from Chile, Malaysia, Mexico and the U.K.* (CDP Summary Volume). Washington, DC, 11-12 June 1992, Chapter 16, pp. 1-42.

Notes

[1] On the mechanics of privatization see Tandon, 1992; Rogozinski, 1992; Darling, 1991.

[2] Other sectors where the State plans to remain include the corn and beans distribution networks and the development banks (Darling, 1991).

[3] Teléfonos de México, a private firm, was created in December 1947 through the incorporation of the assets and concessions of Teléfonos Ericsson, SA. A few years later, Telmex acquired its sole competitor and became the single most important telephone services firm in the country, controlling 95 per cent of all lines. During the 1950s an investment programme based on the acquisition of shares by subscribers began. Until August 1958, however, the company's majority capital was in foreign hands. In that year a Mexican investment group acquired the majority of shares in Telmex.

State participation in Telmex began in 1963 through credits derived from taxes on telephone services. Finally, in 1972, the State became the majority shareholder with 51 per cent of the company's social capital. In 1984 Teléfonos de México SA became a corporate entity, Teléfonos de México, SA de CV, and in 1987 it became the only national telephone services enterprise when it absorbed two smaller regional companies.

[4] Public phone rates were frozen from 1952 until the early 1980s, representing a decline in real terms of almost 100 per cent. In 1975 local and national long-distance rates in Mexico were the lowest among 21 countries with more than 2 million lines, and the real cost of the basic service infrastructure was twice the revenues it brought in.

[5] Interview with delegate from central maintenance department.

[6] Between January and July 1987 the number of complaints not dealt with increased from 16,000 to 44,000 and productivity of repairs declined by 55 per cent.

[7] Not even the privatization of one of the most important banks, Banamex, brought so much money into the coffers of the Mexican treasury.

[8] AeroMexico was in a poor financial position. It was declared bankrupt by the Government, and its assets were transferred to another company, which was sold to a group of private investors. The bankruptcy proceedings gave the Government leeway to fire workers and the workforce was halved.

[9] Interview with international operator, January 1993. See also Dubb, 1992, on this point.

[10] Analysis based on Solis, 1992; Coparmex, 1989; interviews.

[11] Firms competing with Telmex had 200,000 subscribers at the end of 1991 (Denton, 1992; Grant, 1990 and 1991).

[12] The regulatory system for prices and charges is based on the real prices of a basket of all services offered by Telmex, weighted by consumption levels per service in the preceding period. After 1996, prices will be reduced by 3 per cent per year in order to transfer to users the benefits of improvements in productivity and efficiency. After 1999 the Government will adjust ceiling prices, so that the company at least receives a constant return based on its capital costs. This system, in principle, gives Telmex the flexibility to set competitive rates for specific services.

[13] "Instalación de un millón y medio de nuevas lineas: Telmex se moderniza con nueva tecnología digital", in *La Jornada*, 2 Jan. 1993.

[14] This expansion had started in 1990, when the number of communities served reached 10,221 in comparison with just 7,322 in 1989. By June 1991 the number was 11,107.

[15] Interview with a long-distance operator who had previously been a union delegate, January 1993.

[16] Inttelmex was created in 1991. In that year 5,701 operators, 500 supervisory personnel and 110 technicians participated in intensive courses.

[17] Interview with a union delegate from the external plant, December 1992.

[18] In addition to installing cables, workers install a diagnostic system which lets subscribers check their own lines. If there are problems, subscribers who have paid a service agreement with Telmex call the company. The repair can also be done by outside companies.

[19] Interview with a union delegate from the maintenance department.

[20] The training programme is an elaborate one, incorporating the Joint National Committee on Training. It reviews and defines training needs for new technologies. In theory, it also decides which job specialities should be involved, the course description and its contents, the number of participants, and when and where the course will be given (Modelo de capacitación Telmex, n.d.).

[21] In the April 1992-94 Collective Labour Agreements, a "General Programme of Incentive for Quality and Productivity" was signed by the STRM and Telmex. It was an outgrowth of the March 1992 Permanent Quality Programme, modelled on programmes pioneered by Japanese firms. They include statistical process control, methods for analysing and solving problems, quality circles and cost analysis systems. The programme explicitly states that increases in productivity are intimately tied to quality considerations.

[22] Between 1987 and 1991 revenues grew fivefold and profits leapt tenfold.

[23] Real increases in charges in the first quarter of 1991 fully reflected inflation between June and November 1990. Further adjustments, according to revisions in the concession title, were below the rate of inflation.

[24] In 1992 almost 180,000 analogue lines were replaced with digital lines, permitting a wider range of services.

[25] In 1991 only 55 per cent of calls were completed, a small improvement from 47 per cent in 1987 (PTTI, 1992; Ramirez, 1992).

[26] Telmex invested US$400 million to further develop the overlaid network (RDSI) to serve the telecommunications and data transmission needs of the country's 700 companies.

[27] Romo contends that the profit-sharing plan was one of the most important elements in labour relations negotiations leading to the successful privatization (Romo, 1992).

[28] For a discussion of the threats to unions from industrial restructuring and the climate of uncertainty and fear prevailing in the 1980s, see Ortiz and Iriarte, 1988.

5. Privatization and employment in Bulgaria's reform

Charles Rock*

1. Introduction

This chapter addresses the problem of privatization and the labour market in post-communist Bulgaria. Privatization is a complicated political process which has made slow progress in Bulgaria. The uncertainties of the outcome of this process appear to have been a major contributor to the worsening economic situation during the period of reforms.

A brief review of political constraints and macroeconomic reforms is followed by an examination of employment effects and other microeconomic responses of the state enterprise sector to the reforms. The laborious steps made so far towards privatizing the economy are then detailed. Finally, some conclusions about the process of transformation of Bulgaria's economy are elaborated.

1.1 Democracy and political polarization

Bulgaria began a difficult process of political, economic and social transformation following the downfall of the longtime communist leader, Todor Zhivkov, in November 1989. During the previous decades, political, economic and social life were highly centralized, with party coordination of nearly all functions of society making Bulgaria a mirror image of the former USSR. Despite initial optimism, the years of transformation have been much more exhausting and perplexing than anticipated. The economic collapse has been one of the most severe of all the former socialist countries of Central and Eastern Europe. Political life has been characterized by an electoral polarization around two blocs — the anti-communist UDF coalition (Union of Democratic Forces) and the BSP (the Bulgarian Socialist Party) formed out of the Communist Party at the start of the transition. Neither group was able to fully dominate the 1990 Constitutional Assembly elections nor the parliamentary elections of 1991. Only with the BSP majority control in parliament following the December 1994 vote did one party govern alone.

This political instability has meant that until 1995 no government has had the security of office which might have facilitated more successful economic reforms. Politics has

* Department of Economics, Rollins College, Winter Park, Florida.

dominated economics. Relatively frequent changes in office holders and other government appointments have meant that economic actors have faced tremendous uncertainty. The application of many laws has varied, laws in place have been regularly questioned and amended, and many other regulations and decisions about economic life have evolved along with the shifts in government power.

In addition to the domestic barriers to a successful economic transition, the external situation has also been unfavourable in the early 1990s. The sudden collapse of the coordinated Comecon international trading system, the wars and conflicts affecting former Bulgarian markets in the Balkans, the Middle East and the former USSR, and the worldwide recession of the early 1990s have all added further obstacles for the Bulgarians. The cumulative effects of all these foreign and domestic factors have exacerbated the economic collapse in Bulgaria, and hence the material pain of the process of transformation.

1.2 Liberalization, stabilization and macroeconomics

By the time of the first elections of 1990, all the major parties in Bulgaria openly agreed on the need for a market economy. The major questions in 1990 were who would lead the Government, how fast the economic transformation would be, and which existing model of a market economy to emulate. Although the reformed communist bloc (reconstituted as the Bulgarian Socialist Party — BSP) won the June 1990 elections, it proved unwilling and unable to govern alone; by the end of the year it had placed representatives of the opposition in key ministries dealing with economic reform.[1] As the economy was in free-fall, and since foreign debt payments had been suspended in 1990, by the beginning of 1991 there was little political will to oppose those ministers who successfully moved the Government to adopt policies advocated by the International Monetary Fund and supported by the World Bank. There seemed little alternative to "shock therapy", and in February 1991 the liberalization and stabilization programmes went into effect.

The main goals of the agreement of 1991 with the IMF were: (a) to stop the decline in output; (b) to reduce inflation; and (c) to reduce the external deficit. The stabilization programme included five parts:

(i)   price reform to reduce the excess supply of money savings (or "monetary overhang");

(ii)   exchange rate reform to create a unified rate permitting freer and more market price-based trading;

(iii) limitations on increases in money income and reductions in real wages;

(iv)   reduction of the Government deficit and measures to keep it within strict limits in the future; and

(v)   limitations on credit expansion, mainly through increasing the interest rate ("Letter of Intent (to IMF) of February 1991").

The IMF would provide standby financing mainly to support the Government's efforts to avoid a balance of payments crisis and to keep the currency (lev) exchange rate stable while fighting domestic inflation.

The policy package outlined above has proved only partially successful. Output steadily and significantly declined after 1990, with only the briefest of indications that the bottom might have been reached in mid-1994. Inflation in 1991 was several hundred per cent; it has fluctuated since 1992, but it is still considered too high. The more than US$10 billion external debt has continued to be problematic.[2] The price shock effectively cancelled out most people's monetary savings by the end of 1991. The managed float and the unified exchange rate were relatively successful during 1991-93, with the Bulgarian lev appreciating during 1992 and part of 1993. However, the lev has periodically come under attack (at the beginning of 1994 it was effectively devalued by about 50 per cent; a similar exchange rate crisis developed in spring 1996).

Despite the desire for much freer trade in currency, the Central Bank has had to monitor the exchange markets closely and a truly free market in currency is still to be attained. Real wages fell by more than half during 1991. There was some growth when collective bargaining procedures began in late 1991, but in general real wages have stagnated since 1992. Coupled with the large drop in total employment, this means that family incomes have been severely affected.

The government deficit has continued to be a major problem. Most of the taxes in the old system were turnover taxes. The tax authorities have had great difficulties in collecting these and the reformed income taxes, especially from private enterprises; the budget deficit has not been controlled as hoped. Attempts to limit the expansion of credit have not been successful, in part owing to inter-enterprise extension of credit. There has been a virtual disappearance of bank-financed net investment by state enterprises. The IMF policies have been continued by all governments since 1991; no government could imagine any other option which did not rely on continuing financial support by the IMF and the World Bank.[3]

2. Employment, management strategies, unions and industrial relations in the transition period

2.1 Reducing the labour supply

At the end of the communist era, most people in Bulgaria knew that almost all enterprises were overstaffed and that many workers might be shed with no effect on output. Towards the end of the first year of post-communist reforms, mandatory and early retirement were selected as the initial means of stimulating state enterprises to shed labour. Those near pensionable age were offered 90 per cent of their normal retirement pension if they voluntarily agreed to end their contract. Some enterprises offered to pay the 10 per cent difference in order to stimulate more people to accept this offer. If firms insisted on keeping employees who were past retirement age, they had to pay a large recurring tax to the Government for each post-retirement age employee retained on regular contract. Also, there were penalties for increases in enterprise wage bills; the use of a tax-based incomes policy has continued throughout the five years of the reform period. All together, these (push and pull) policies led to a large exodus of people of retirement age or near it from most state enterprises.[4] Table 5.1 shows changes in employment in Bulgaria between 1989 and 1995.

The government strategy to reduce the state sector labour force after this initial move was not so precisely geared as its policies to remove older workers. The 1991 liberal government wished state enterprise managers to behave like profit-oriented capitalist

Table 5.1. Annual average employment level by sector and percentage change in employed, 1989-94

Sector	Annual average number of persons (000s)					
	1989	1990	1991	1992	1993	1994
Industry	1 646	1 498	1 230	1 064	979	943
Construction	361	337	253	204	209	192
Agriculture	789	735	679	674	698	738
Forestry	25	22	17	17	14	13
Transport	247	242	223	193	197	188
Communications	44	45	44	44	44	44
Commerce, trade	394	372	344	336	333	371
Other kinds of material production	25	29	28	27	31	33
Housing, public utilities and services	97	92	80	68	66	75
Science research	97	91	67	53	36	30
Education	277	273	268	263	263	255
Culture and art	46	47	38	34	41	41
Health services, social security, sports and tourism	214	221	207	204	200	195
Financial services	26	25	27	35	37	44
Administration (government)	61	54	50	52	67	75
Other services	16	14	9	6	7	5

Sector	Percentage change in annual average employment					
	1989-90	1990-91	1991-92	1992-93	1993-94	1989-94
Industry	−9.0	−17.9	−13.3	−8.3	−3.7	−42.7
Construction	−6.7	−24.9	−19.4	2.5	−8.1	−46.8
Agriculture	−6.8	−7.6	−0.3	3.1	5.7	−6.5
Forestry	−12.0	−22.7	0	−17.7	−7.1	−48.0
Transport	−2.0	−7.9	−13.5	2.1	−4.6	−23.9
Communications	2.3	−2.2	0	0	0	0
Commerce, trade	−5.8	−8.1	−3.8	0.9	11.1	−6.6
Other kinds of material production	16.0	−3.5	−3.6	14.8	6.5	32.0
Housing, public utilities and services	−5.2	−13.0	−15.0	−2.9	13.6	−22.7
Science research	−6.2	−26.4	−20.9	−32.1	−16.7	−69.1
Education	−1.4	−1.8	−1.9	0	−3.0	−7.9
Culture and art	2.3	−19.2	−10.5	20.6	0	−10.9
Health services, social security, sports and tourism	3.3	−6.3	−1.5	−2.0	−2.5	−8.9
Financial services	−3.9	8.0	29.6	5.7	18.9	69.2
Administration (government)	−11.5	−7.4	4.0	28.9	11.9	23.0
Other services	−12.5	−35.7	−33.3	16.7	−28.6	−68.8
Total employed	*−6.1*	*−13.0*	*−8.1*	*−1.6*	*0.6*	*−25.7*

Source: National Statistical Institute, *Statisticheski Godishnik*, 1995, p. 86 (1990-94); 1993, p. 57 (1989-90).

Table 5.2. Unemployment (numbers, rates) and labour force activity rate in Bulgaria, 1990-95 (numbers in 000s)

Date end of period	Registered unemployed at labour bureaux	Estimated unemployed from survey	Unemployment rate calculated from surveys or from registered*	"Activity rate" (= lab. force/pop. with more than 15 years)
1990 Dec.	65	n.a.	1.7*	61.3*
1991 Dec.	419	n.a.	12.3*	58.7*
1992 Dec. 4	—	646	21.8*	58.3
1992 Dec.	577	—	—	57.1*
1993 Sept.	599	814	21.4	55.4
1993 Dec.	626	n.a.	16.3*	55.9*
1994 June	—	734	20.1	54.4
1994 Oct.	—	740	20.5	52.4
1994 Dec.	488	n.a.	13.1*	55.0*
1995 Mar.	—	684	19.2	51.7
1995 June	—	565	15.7	52.2
1995 Oct.	—	521	14.7	51.5

Note: Unemployed must register at Labour Offices to receive unemployment payments for limited time. Hence registered unemployed may underestimate the rate, since not all workers are eligible for payments. The surveys are better methodologically to measure unemployment accurately; however, they may overestimate the rate, since some subjects may hide their work for fear of income tax implications of accurately reporting private work or self-employment. The survey methodology is equivalent to American unemployment survey techniques, so is a better comparison in this case, assuming respondents are equally forthright in Bulgaria. A national census was carried out on 4 Dec. 1992. Note the large difference in unemployment totals from two methods; a subject of some dispute in Bulgaria. "Activity" rate is for trend in participation in labour market; trend remains when age cut-off is 65 years.

n.a. = not available.

* Calculation done with data from registrations at labour bureaux and data from the Ministry of Labour and Social Affairs.

Sources: NSI, "Employment & Unemployment", 2/94, pp. 28-29; 3/95, pp. 26-27, for survey data. NSI, *Statisticheski Godishnik*, 1995, pp. 71, 92; 1993, p. 62. Registered unemployed = those registered regularly at Labour Offices. Ministry of Labour and Social Affairs, unpublished data, 1991-93.

managers. The Government wanted to change the economic environment surrounding the state enterprises. Enterprises would no longer be sure of subsidies nor of credit availability; in theory, their financial resources would be limited to the revenues they received from sales. "Corporatization" — greater autonomy for management — would separate enterprises from direct government administrative control so that managers could be expected (required) to act independently to ensure the survival of the enterprise. "Marketization" of the economy also meant that enterprises were free to change the prices of the products they sold as they looked for buyers in the decentralized networks of market exchange.[5]

During the 1991-92 period, the State progressively cut budget subsidies to state enterprises, and lay-offs became more frequent. People who voluntarily left jobs found it increasingly difficult to find new employment in the state sector. Many voluntary and involuntary leavers re-entered the labour market, but in the private sector. Others left the country. The number of officially recorded unemployed rose from zero at the beginning of 1990 to half a million by mid-1992. The numbers of registered unemployed rose to a peak of more than 20 per cent of the labour force by the end of 1993 (table 5.2). The unemployment rate fell slowly thereafter, mainly due to people leaving the labour force. The number of employed has barely increased since the end of 1993; the number of registered unemployed has fallen since the end of 1993. Table 5.3 summarizes the labour market aggregate figures during the period under review.

Table 5.3. Bulgarian labour market in transition, 1989-94

	1989	1990	1991	1992	1993	1994
Population (millions)	8 767	8 669	8 596	8 485	8 460	8 427
Working age population (millions)	4 852	4 806	4 781	4 733	4 739	4 741
Labour force (millions)	4 365	4 162	3 983	3 851	3 848	3 730
Labour force participation rate (%)	89.9	86.6	83.3	81.1	81.2	78.7
Total employment (millions)	4 365	4 097	3 564	3 274	3 222	3 242
Employment in private sector (% of total)	n.a.	5.9	10.1	17.7	28.3	36.0
Unemployment, registered (000s)	—	65	419	577	626	488
Unemployment rate (%)	—	1.6	11.8	17.6	19.4	15.1
GDP at constant prices (%)	0.5	−9.1	−11.7	−7.3	−2.4	1.4
Industrial production (%)	−1.1	−16.1	−27.8	−15.1	−7.1	4.1
Industry employment (%)	−2.9	−9.0	−17.9	−13.3	−8.3	−3.7

Note: working age population is 16-54 for females, 16-59 for males. Registered unemployed at labour offices. Employed are annual averages, all workers. Participation rate is ratio of labour force to the working age population.

Sources: NSI, *Statisticheski Godishnik*, 1995, pp. 39, 43, 86, 92, 223; 1993, p. 25; 1992, pp. 45, 49. NSI, *Statistical Reference Book*, 1994, p. 28. "Economics of Transition", 1995, Vol. 3, No. 4, p. 526 (for output indices).

2.2 The varied responses of managers to the new economic environment

At the outset of the post-communist transition, there was a political consensus (at least in public discourse) that enterprises should rapidly be made to respond to decentralized market signals rather than to the fiat of political decision-makers. However, politics has continued to be a dominant force, at least equal to the market. Government policies have not been sufficiently ruthless, focused or comprehensive to impose a clear and consistent economic "hard budget" constraint on state enterprise managements. Constraints on enterprises have changed from the old system, but they have involved a continuously and unpredictably shifting array of incentives and sanctions, owing in large part to the highly politicized policy-making climate of the nearly six years of transition. Managers, predictably, have reacted to these uncertainties and constraints in diverse ways. They have not always "rationalized" their enterprises according to any easily observable market-based criteria.

Even when managers have attempted retrenchment policies in response to market demands, they have not always been allowed to succeed. If the workers have complained loudly enough and either threatened or engaged in industrial action, the Government has frequently backed down from its promised policies and sometimes helped bring about a change in the enterprise's management. Management groups have repeatedly complained that the Government and its ministries are sending them mixed messages and enacting contradictory policies.

Following the October 1991 elections which put the UDF in power, many managers of state enterprises were replaced. Ministers, politicians and others called for the replacement of particular groups of the management *nomenklatura* because these Communist Party careerists were incompetent, corrupt, or both. But even the liberal, anti-communist Government of 1991-92 was not uniformly hostile to managers. In certain branches, repeated meetings were held between the ministries, other representatives of the Government and management to enable the Government better to communicate its goals to the state enterprise managers. Many managers had risen to their positions at least in part because of their competence in running a highly complex production organization. Others had been chosen by workers (following the "self-management" provisions of the 1986 Labour Code under which workers had the legal right to elect/impeach managers at least until the revised Labour Code of 1993) from among eligible candidates put forward by the state authorities.

Understandably, especially considering the unanticipated severity and duration of the economic crisis, state enterprise managers have displayed a diversity of styles of reacting to the new environment. Initially, many perceived their best allies to be the workers. These managers sought to maintain employment by whatever means they could. Many felt that they had first and foremost to pay attention to the desires and fears of the workforce. At the other extreme, there were a few management groups which decided that large-scale and immediate lay-offs were the best response to a massive drop in demand for their products.

The great majority of general directors or management teams fell in between these extremes and had differing mixtures of objectives, priorities and information.[6] Some managers focused on lining up potential foreign investors for an immediate joint venture or future privatization. Others spent most of their time in search of new markets and new customers. Others focused on developing new product lines which they thought would have a better chance at gaining access to new markets, or in some cases which could be sold domestically and would thus ensure some employment was retained at the enterprise. Still others focused on acquiring assets for themselves or their friends. They worked to provide themselves with (privatized) economic alternatives for the uncertain future.

The different goals espoused by managers are evident also in the reaction of workers and trade unions to specific cases. Workers frequently went on strike to call for the dismissal of their enterprise management (under the old 1986 Labour Code, workers had this right). In other cases, managers did not ally themselves with workers or the Government in any explicit way. The managers then pursued their own agendas, constrained by workers' demands on the one hand and the Government's attempts to impose its requirements on the other. Needless to say, all but the most self-confident managers in the state sector were anxious about their personal future and confused about government intentions; this tended to make them focus on immediate problems rather than on medium- or long-term strategies (apart from personal survival in the new system). Managers, trained in the old system to hoard labour in the enterprise, failed to reduce their workforces at a rate that anywhere near matched the rate of decrease in demand for their products or services. This has had an ironic result. Labour productivity (output per worker) has actually declined during the transition in the vast majority of state-owned enterprises.[7]

3. Privatization

3.1 Privatization and marketization: Definition problems

Forcing state firms to face the hard reality of possible bankruptcy was one aspect of the 1991-92 liberal Government's stated intention of privatizing the economic decision-making of the country — taking microeconomic decisions out of the hands of government officials and putting them into those of non-state economic agents. That government often complained of obstructive management teams who were slowing down or even actively subverting moves towards a responsible, equitable and fiscally sound full privatization of state enterprises. The Government was dissatisfied with its progress — something which has been true of all the different governments of the transition period. Each one has claimed to want more rapid privatization.

"Privatization", as the term is used in Bulgaria, specifically refers to the *actual transfer of ownership* of state property to private individuals or firms. This is the narrow sense of the term. In spite of governments' publicly stated desires for speed, actual transfers of ownership of major state enterprises have been very few in number.

There are broader concepts of "privatization", and in this paper a broad variant is used. In addition to outright sale of state assets, *other aspects of restructuring* are included — those which aim to create a large number of autonomous or entirely private economic actors which are not controlled directly by the Government. This broader version of "privatization" might just as well be called the re-creation of the independent and private sectors. In summary, it includes the following:

(a) selling uncontested state property (for example, property which has traditionally been state-owned, or has been developed entirely in the state sector or as a result of a fully compensated and largely voluntary nationalization process);

(b) leasing or contracting out such state property;

(c) cutting loose informal lines of state control over certain units of the economy (notably the renewal of the independence of the cooperative sector);

(d) restitution (restoration) of illegitimately seized property (e.g. land and factories nationalized through legislation returned to the pre-communist owners; control of property which was more informally placed under state controls restored to former owners);

(e) promoting the development of wholly new private enterprises (creating new businesses or even sometimes trying to stimulate the entry into open, lawful activity of formerly underground, black market entrepreneurs);

(f)   attracting private foreign firms to open up operations in the country;

(g)   giving private businesses the right to provide goods and services which have formerly been monopolized by the state sector (this may not involve any transfer of assets, but more often elimination of a legal state monopoly to engage in specific lines of production).

This broader meaning of the term leads to discussion of policies and economic mechanisms besides outright transfer of ownership — one of which is the "marketization" of state-owned enterprises.[8] Marketization refers to attempts to restructure management, administrative controls and the regulatory environment to enable existing state enterprises to act more (or entirely) like autonomous, private, market-oriented firms. Eventually, like private firms, they will buy inputs and sell outputs at market prices without any preferences in the bidding processes. Ultimately, they should have little ad hoc flexibility or recourse to additional public budget subsidies in hard times. The main additional public aid (beyond planned funding) they would receive would be identical to special programmes available for private firms. There would be few if any special privileges, although management might be aware that public goals may be somewhat broader than those of the classic profit-maximizing investor. Management teams would be able to take decisions independently, without consulting public authorities on a day-to-day basis. The management would be answerable to the enterprise's board of directors (or supervisory board) just like the management in purely private corporations.[9] The board's main mechanism for controlling top managers would be the power to replace them, just as in the private sector joint stock company.

In Bulgaria, the enterprises earmarked for such potential autonomy do *not* necessarily include those involved in services traditionally provided by the public sector which, in the more developed market economies of Western Europe, are provided publicly by agencies under direct state management (e.g. health, education). They are rather those which are currently publicly owned (not necessarily permanently) and for which, in the short term, no superior alternative private arrangement seems to be economically feasible.

In contrast, for the sectors seen as *fully* privatizable, the general movement toward marketization of state enterprises is seen as only a temporary and partial step towards full private ownership. For these sectors, the goal is to prepare current state enterprises for outright sale (privatization) in the future. One result of marketization may be to provide better information to private buyers as to which state firms are viable concerns and attractive investments. The Government may also become better informed as to which state companies are potentially viable operations and which are not. If the marketization process is success- ful, it could reduce the negative budgetary impact of the state enterprise sector (reducing subsidies, increasing tax revenues). If the goods or services provided involve a natural monopoly but sales still do not cover production costs, operating in the market may help make clear the level of public subsidy required to maintain (politically decided) production levels at current prices. Where no significant natural monopoly exists, competition can be enhanced by private producers of similar goods or services entering the market.

3.2 The politics and economics of privatization in Bulgaria

The multi-faceted "privatization" programme described above has not developed in a coherently planned or organized fashion in Bulgaria. It has been the outcome of continuing political struggles. It has taken place in the context of a revolutionary change in political power in which antagonisms are deep-rooted and many politicians appear to be focused largely on self-vindication, on the just punishment of past collaborators in totalitarianism, or on outright revenge. The elections of October 1991 eliminated most independent representation of the middle-ground parties, which might have contributed to creating a democracy that was more tolerant of differences, more understanding of the seemingly unavoidable personal compromises of the past, and more accepting of a significantly pluralistic democratic system. The 1991 elections, however, produced a Union of Democratic Forces (UDF) Government that perceived little need for a broader consensus on economic reforms, at least within parliament making the laws. This divided, bipolar political development has had significant implications for the economic reform process.

The Union of Democratic Forces legislation to introduce economic reforms was carefully designed to meet a dual aim. They wanted a dynamic, modern market economic system. They also wanted this new system to hold out little or no chance for the previous regime's ruling élite, and their numerous "collaborators" in the old centralized system, to rise again, this time through economic power. Economic reforms were thus structured with the goal of preventing former communist "profiteers" (e.g. with difficult-to-trace hard currency accounts secreted abroad), and former *nomenklatura* and active careerist party members, from translating their many advantages into dominance in the new market system. These advantages (better educational opportunities, more experience in commerce and foreign travel, more contacts with foreigners, more knowledge of how to manage money and hard currency, etc.) were seen as their means of emerging as the main new "red" capitalist entrepreneurial class in a free market economy. The main privatization law passed in mid-1992, for example, has a clause requiring buyers to disclose the "origins" of the money used to purchase any enterprise assets.

In this sense, the process of economic reform has been strongly politicized. Without a political understanding of the reform process, some changes would appear economically illogical, even irrational. There seem to be many simpler, probably more effective mechanisms to achieve certain economic goals — but not, however, if one seeks to achieve both economic change and political retribution.

Paradoxically, economists representing both the communist ruling groups and the anti-communist opposition forces could agree within four months of Zhivkov's overthrow that a private property-based market system was a *sine qua non* of a modern Bulgarian economy. Groups at both political poles saw privatization as a crucial step in the right direction. What continues to be a matter of dispute is the precise manner of creating the autonomous private sector which is expected to dominate economic life in the future.

When the socialists (reformed communists) formed a majority in parliament (June 1990 to October 1991) the UDF opposition criticized them for holding back the speed of privatization. The anti-communist UDF was the leader in the coalition government in power from October 1991 to late 1992 and had control of the Ministries of Finance and Industry even before. The same criticism of inadequate progress towards privatization was levelled at them by the parliamentary BSP faction. The 1993-94 Berov government and the BSP government since then were both seen to be too slow on privatization. Others — including IMF officials — have complained about every transition government's slow progress towards privatization.

Specific matters relating to privatization which have been the subject of serious political debate in Bulgaria include:

(a) "sequencing", or the order of reforms, and whether privatization should occur first, continuously, or only after a set of prior steps has been taken;

(b) the issue of fairness and equity in the process, especially who would get preferential treatment;

(c) what kind of new ownership structure should be aimed at, "strong"/concentrated, "weak"/dispersed, a mixture of these, or some middle way;

(d) whether there should be a "free" distribution of shares or only the budget-enhancing sale of assets;

(e) political control and public accountability of the agencies (e.g. the State Privatization Agency) responsible for the actual process of privatization;

(f) participation of the trade unions in the formulation of privatization mechanisms and later in the actual process of privatization in individual enterprises;

(g) retention of a state share — or a share of some quasi-autonomous government organization/fund — in the ownership of assets of the privatized enterprises;

(h) the purposes to which the sales revenues should be put;

(i) the relationship (contradictions) between restitution (either the same actual physical assets or by means of financial compensation) of nationalized property and the privatization process;

(j) the amount of flexibility regarding methods and procedures for privatization permitted to the agencies in charge;

(k) restrictions on participation of foreign buyers or foreign companies in the process (protection of the national patrimony); and

(l) restrictions on former high communist officials participating in privatization.[10]

Many technical issues (some with political implications) have been debated as well: establishing minimum prices; valuation procedures and training/licensing of specialists; methods for selling enterprises or parts of them; rules/methods/criteria for selecting enterprises to be privatized; methods of payment for the assets; rights of creditors of privatized enterprises, and so on. Nearly all these issues have been debated in other Eastern and Central European countries (von Brabant, 1992). Many have been debated in the dozens of countries around the world which have been involved in setting up privatization procedures in the last few years.[11] The major Bulgarian privatization law of April/May 1992 decided some of these issues but left many still unresolved. Moreover, even some of the decisions that have been made can be interpreted or implemented in a variety of ways.[12]

3.3 Legal reforms, privatization and state enterprises: The history of privatizations and privatization laws, 1989-93

The maze of laws, decrees and regulations which has affected the transfer of state-owned property[13] makes it difficult to determine how much privatization has already occurred in Bulgaria.[14] Nevertheless, some tentative conclusions can be drawn. Most of the state property which has been transferred (fully privatized) so far consists of land, buildings, other real estate, office supplies, small-scale equipment or vehicles. This section will focus on transition period attempts to set in motion the full privatization of the main state-owned enterprises.[15]

For exposition purposes, we will distinguish five phases in the privatization of state-owned assets in Bulgaria.[16] The first is the period of "spontaneous" (or "wild" or "self" or "quiet") privatizations early in the transition period. The second phase is the so-called "small privatization" process begun early in 1991, halted towards the end of that year and, after some delay, continued intermittently since. The third phase began with the passage of the main privatization law in mid-1992, while a fourth might be identified with the replacement, in mid-1993, of much of the Supervisory Board and somewhat later, of the Executive Director of the State Privatization Agency. A fifth phase, beginning in 1994 with the "mass privatization" law involves the sale of subsidized vouchers for all Bulgarian adults to purchase shares of a selected group of larger SOEs.

Phase one: "Wild" privatization

The majority of "wild" privatizations appear to have occurred before August 1990. At that moment, the newly elected president (a compromise candidate, Zhelyu Zhelev) declared a moratorium on any further transfer of state assets. This action was taken because of charges that managers and other personnel connected with state firms were enriching themselves by transferring assets to their own or other related persons' businesses at very low prices.

There are many cases where state enterprise assets were in fact sold at extremely favourable (low) prices compared to what they could have fetched at an open public auction. Setting very low prices was technically legal. Bulgarian enterprises only put values on physical and financial assets. Physical assets were valued in the company books at purchase prices minus a fixed depreciation. Inflation in previous years was hardly accounted for. Trademarks, technical processes, inventions and general corporate "good will" had no explicit valuation under socialist accounting methodology. The old enterprise book values thus bore little relationship to any reasonable market or auction price.

The process of "wild" privatization was supported by Decree 56 of January 1989, enacted under the communist Zhivkov regime. This important decree recognized private business of various corporate forms and also described asset transfer procedures. It allowed Bulgarians to establish private companies (to which, implicitly, assets from state enterprises could be sold). Other regulations made by the Council of Ministers in 1989 and 1990 also specifically permitted the leasing or full transfer of assets. Transactions which were specified in each of these various measures included:

(a)   the leasing of retail and distribution outlets to their staffs;

(b)   the leasing or transfer of assets or enterprises in tourism, distribution and trade, or services;

(c)   the sale of used vehicles and farm machinery.

Another measure which aided "wild" privatization was an amendment to Decree 56 in spring 1990 transforming directly administered state-owned enterprises (those directly administered by state authorities) into state-owned corporations. This seemingly innocuous change had the effect of requiring the transformed enterprise to establish a board of directors to govern the enterprise (which meant only an indirect connection to state authorities). The amendment also allowed the enterprise to auction off fixed assets. Significant pieces of property could thus be sold at an "auction", which was apparently whatever form of sale the company board decided on, since no precise rules for conducting an auction were specified.

Another provision in the supplemental regulations for Decree 56 seems to have helped make it possible for newly issued stocks in an enterprise to be sold to its employees. In some enterprises, it appears that this was the technical loophole that enabled part of the company assets to be transferred to some of its employees. The board and management could determine both the price per share and the specific rights attached to these shares.

Strong criticisms have been made of this process of "wild" privatization; many include charges that these transfers were done illegally. Until mid-1991, with the passage of the Commercial Code (voiding much of Decree 56 of 1989) and another Act on the formation of state sole proprietorship companies (which explicitly put a stop to stock or ownership share transfers), there was no clear legal regime regulating all possible means of transferring — or leasing at rock-bottom prices — state property. The regulations were often contradictory. Thus, if the parties involved in the spontaneous privatizations were clever enough, what they did may be considered immoral but in most cases it can probably be claimed that their actions were technically legal.

Phase two: "Small" privatization

The second phase of enterprise privatization was the attempt at so-called "small" privatization that began in 1991. A legal opening was provided, in December 1990, when the moratorium suspending all transfers of property made the preceding August was partially voided. This allowed small enterprises or small parts of large firms to be sold through open, publicly announced auctions or through a tendering process. A special resolution required specific government authorization for such sales. The Ministry of Industry and Trade made plans to sell gas stations, shops, small workshops, machines and vehicles. Several dozen sales were made, both through announced, solicited bids and through open auction procedures; the total initial value was about 100 million leva (approximately US$5 million). Sales were suspended in the second half of 1991 following enactment of the Commercial Code and pending the passage of a full-scale privatization law.

Phase three: Passing of the 1992 privatization law

Passage of the formally recognized privatization law in mid-1992 was preceded by a great volume of public discussion, media attention and energetic parliamentary debate. This can be considered the beginning of the third phase of enterprise privatization in Bulgaria. The passage of the law was politically very difficult and occurred only as soon as it did because of intense pressure from international financial organizations. The process of debating more or less specific proposed versions of the law lasted over a year outside parliament and for six months in the UDF-dominated parliament. The law is quite complex and very flexible; it appears to have taken a great deal from the flexible Hungarian privatization arrangements as well as some components from Polish law (on workers' preferences). The law gives the cabinet and parliament — and their agents, the State Privatization Agency, and several ministries responsible for enterprises in their domain — a great deal of latitude in deciding the fate of each individual enterprise. Municipal governments are similarly responsible for privatizing firms under their jurisdiction. No single method of sale is required. The timing and sequence of privatization are unspecified. Several matters were left for further resolution by decree, regulations, or even more ad hoc decisions in the future. With these additional regulations, the law does provide a general legal framework in which specific privatizations can proceed. The State Privatization Agency, together with the relevant ministries, proposed the first major enterprises for privatization within a few months of the passage of the privatization law.

Other developments prior to that are relevant to the process of privatization. As discussed earlier, the Government wished state-owned enterprises to face market constraints and to be in a position to take advantage of market opportunities. It also wanted more competition than existed. A variety of laws and decrees were therefore enacted during 1991 and 1992 which provided some of the context for making enterprises face more competition and harder budget constraints. "Demonopolization" of state enterprises (the breaking up of the big multi-establishment "firms" or "*kombinats*" into separate units) began even before the mandates of the Protection of Competition Law in mid-1991; it accelerated afterwards. Some enterprise managements complained, however, that demonopolization had gone too far, since some of the separated enterprises were still entirely dependent on other parts of the big state firms (for inputs, for marketing output, for exports and imports).

Most large state enterprises have been "corporatized".[17] This means that they have been transformed into state-owned joint stock or limited liability partnerships (indirectly state controlled). This facilitates their sale, especially if only part of an enterprise is sold (and subjects them to shared ownership with other partners/shareholders). Thus, transformation has also provided a legal form for the enterprise to act autonomously on its own behalf and be distinguishable from directly controlled government agencies. The board of directors (or supervisory board in a two-tiered corporate governance arrangement system) has become the accountable and liable party for the corporate "juridical person" in law. Government ownership (like that of any other owner) gives the right to vote/appoint directors to the board.

The Commercial Code requires the initial capital investment creating a corporation to be specified. Valuation procedures were established in the autumn of 1991 which required all state-owned enterprises to hire licensed accountant appraisers. Firms had to provide these experts with full information on all assets controlled by the enterprise. This process anticipated the similar problem of how much the State should demand when selling (privatizing) the enterprise later. This was preceded by an Accountancy Act in early 1991 establishing a West European accounting framework in Bulgaria to replace the old Marxist-based system. This solution of the valuation problem was slightly revised within the 1992 Privatization Act.

Other laws and institutions supporting privatization and marketization have also been passed, but gaps persisted in the institutional environment necessary for market constraints to operate effectively. Perhaps most notable was the lack of a bankruptcy law until mid-1994, and of laws governing public securities and capital markets. Other factors also hinder rapid privatization. State enterprise bad debts — to each other, to the banking system and to the Government — make valuation of the assets for sale difficult. In some cases, state enterprise managements have acted in ways calculated to slow down or prevent privatization. At the end of 1993 a new law was proposed imposing a large personal monetary fine on managers who try to obstruct the process.

Phase four: Selling major enterprises

The political crises of the second half of 1992 eventually led to the creation of a new government at the beginning of 1993. This brought about (after several months) replacement of the Government's appointed representatives on the State Privatization Agency's Supervisory Board; the new appointees in turn elected a new chair and also helped bring about the replacement of the UDF-connected Executive Director. This may be seen as the beginning of the fourth, and much more active, phase of privatization. In the last half of 1993 the SPA concluded its first sales agreements with a handful of foreign buyers — for three major enterprises.[18]

Since January 1993, under the new government, there appears to have been an acceleration of privatization actions by certain ministries with state enterprises under their jurisdiction. This is particularly true of the second half of 1993 and 1994. Most of Bulgaria's municipalities have also moved more quickly than in the past to sell or auction off some of the local enterprises they are responsible for. By the end of 1995, over 500 enterprise full privatizations had been concluded, 75 per cent of them by municipal governments (NSI, 1995, p. 405).

Phase five: "Mass" privatization

In the late summer of 1993, to try to accelerate the slow-moving privatization process, Prime Minister Berov and his cabinet proposed a "mass" privatization programme involving subsidized vouchers for all Bulgarian adults. During the next year, many different versions were debated and introduced in parliament. When the 1992 privatization law was redone in mid-1994, a "mass" privatization scheme was added to this new version. It lacked detail and little more progress was made on it during the run-up to the December 1994 parliamentary elections.

The new government moved slowly on the specifications for the scheme. A new Centre for Mass Privatization had to be created and staffed. The sale of the vouchers did not begin until January of 1996. The vouchers, with a nominal value of 25,000 Bulgarian leva (less than half a year's average salary), cost 500 leva (less than US$10). The vouchers received a rather cool reception, with less than 20 per cent of those eligible actually purchasing them as the early spring 1996 deadline approached. The Government extended the deadline to allow more people to buy them. The final results of the sale are not yet available.

In essence, this would be a programme similar to those carried out in other post-socialist transforming economies. The vouchers may be used as one form of payment for auctioned shares of the 1,000-odd enterprises which are to be privatized and are part of the "mass" privatization scheme. The vouchers may not be sold, although they may be placed with investment funds as a means of indirect investment in enterprise shares. If this process succeeds, it will involve enterprises with large numbers of employees. One characteristic of all previous privatizations discussed so far is that, cumulatively, they have affected directly a relatively small number of workers — probably less than 10 per cent of all Bulgarian employees.

3.4 Other "privatizations": Sales, restitutions, confiscations and new private firms

The previous section focused on privatizing state-owned enterprises outside of agriculture. This section reviews the following:

(a) the restitution of nationalized and non-nationalized personal property and cooperative property to former owners;[19]

(b) the sale of housing;

(c) new confiscations of the property controlled by Communist Party/regime organizations;

(d) the promotion of new private firms.

Since 1989 one of the most contentious issues in Bulgaria has been how to dispose of *agricultural land*. Bulgarian agriculture was almost entirely collectivized under the Communists; in the recent past there was relatively little substantive difference between state collective farms and cooperative farms. Neither were considered adequate to create an efficient system of agricultural production. Even the Communists, recognizing the usefulness of individual incentives in agricultural work, granted individual households the right to use a small plot of land to cultivate and market crops. This small plot of land was important for producing a large proportion of key (mostly perishable) items.

In the late 1980s the Government promoted the involvement of what were essentially privately controlled small cooperatives in agricultural work, especially where the very large-scale collectives had trouble finding workers who would take the necessary care in harvesting to ensure quality production and distribution. After the overthrow of Zhivkov, debate (especially in the cities) began on the need to return to private farming. The first government following the change of November 1989 soon acted to permit private individuals to lease up to 30 hectares of land. Several weeks after the change of ministers in December 1990, parliament passed the first land ownership act, which permitted individuals to get back land which had been theirs before nationalization. The law was difficult to implement owing to the lack of records and administrative procedures. Few collective farm administrators appear to have taken much initiative in this first phase of land restitution. In addition, many farm workers had stated repeatedly in polls that they preferred, in some way or other, to remain part of a cooperatively organized business. There was no strong, unified rural consensus backing a precise form of restitution.

The July 1991 law on cooperatives set up a procedure for creating democratically controlled cooperatives out of the existing cooperatives — if the owners wished to do so. Farm owners in the still formally cooperatively organized farms had never had their land legally nationalized, so no legislation was required to restitute their property.

The UDF, who controlled parliament after October 1991, wished to create a private property-based agricultural system and at the same time to eliminate the power base of the rural ("red" or communist/socialist-leaning) farm managers.[20] Major amendments to the land act were passed in 1992 to achieve these joint goals. All collective farms in the country were required first to privatize the land; this would then be returned to the former owners, with some being allocated to landless farmworkers who had worked in the collectives for a certain number of years. Only after this restitution and privatization had taken place could the new owners form a cooperative business if they wished. It still seems likely that some form of cooperative agriculture will continue to exist in most parts of the country. The average size of landholdings is too small to be efficient otherwise; the average age of farm workers is in their fifties, and most of the existing machinery is designed for large-scale farming.

Decisions on the allocation of land are made by special government-appointed land (or "liquidation") commissions. Not all commissions have been sufficiently sensitive to local issues, and many disputes over their decisions have been vividly reported in the mass media. The restitution process also required new land surveys of borders and valuations of land quality to ensure some rationality in the process. This was a long, laborious process, even when helped by foreign financial aid for training surveyors and for computer equipment to enter the complex data collected. Not all of the land owned by the state farms was to be given to current farmworkers; some land was to be made available to urban people. The Government hoped to attract urban dwellers, especially the unemployed, to live and farm in the rural areas, although opinion polls seem to contradict the likelihood of any large urban-rural migration.[21]

The complicated land distribution procedures have compounded the economic failures of Bulgarian agriculture during the transition. The reforms have further aggravated the disruption of the complex economic linkages among farms, agricultural machinery centres, transport, credit, etc. The story of agricultural reform is quite a sorry one even now, six years after 1989.

Most *production cooperatives outside of agriculture* never had their property formally nationalized. Many of them have simply had control of the factory or workshop returned to the staff. Most production cooperatives are in light industry. Over 300 cooperative manufacturing firms were operating autonomously by mid-1996. One problem was how to deal with former members (now dead or retired) who were in the cooperative when it was taken under the wing of the party-dominated central cooperative union or later transferred to local government authorities. Another problem was how to treat current workers who had only joined after the imposition of state/party/municipality control. In many cases, cooperative members held general assembly meetings in which present and former workers participated and decided on the allocation of property rights within the cooperative. Several other issues remained unresolved (Meurs and Rock, 1992).

The *restitution* of real estate and of enterprises expropriated in the past had to await specific and comprehensive legislation, which was finally completed in February 1992. The Restitution of Immovable Property Act had one feature which might have stood in the way of the privatization of other state enterprises without nationalized personal property. Initially, it set no deadline for making a claim on state property, and in principle the actual physical assets were to be returned to the previous owner or his/her heirs (a similar problem existed in the restitution process in the former German Democratic Republic, whereas Hungary compensated only former owners, either in kind or financially). Thus the status of much property in Bulgaria would have remained uncertain for the indefinite future. This was partially resolved by a clause in the 1992 privatization law which stipulated a one-year limit for making a claim and gave previous owners the right to have a share in the privatized state enterprise equivalent to the value of the previously owned property.

Housing in Bulgaria is very largely privately owned. This was the case even before 1989. The main problem has been a shortage of apartments in certain urban centres. During the three-year period from 1989 to 1992, over 6 per cent of the housing stock was purchased from the State and the central cooperative authorities in charge of the property (*Bulgarian Business News*, 7-14 June 1992). Prior to 1989, potential purchasers had to go through a long queuing process, which involved making a deposit and later paying a subsidized interest and principal payment over several years. The Government speeded up the purchasing process after 1989 and introduced a special provision to further subsidize people who already had the deposit but needed to save more money before buying an apartment. This rapid purchase was very beneficial to purchasers, since housing costs have increased much more rapidly than the average rate of inflation for other goods. Those most disadvantaged by the inflation in housing costs are renters and young households who might wish to purchase housing in the future. Asking prices for apartments continued to be relatively high, but the fact that purchasing power has collapsed suggests that the market has not operated as hoped in this case. Despite the large number of private construction firms, the construction of multi-unit housing has almost come to a halt. This, combined with the conversion of many urban apartments into business offices and the restitution of apartments to former owners or their heirs, has led some people to make dire predictions about an approaching housing crisis.

In the 1991-92 period, the liberal Government passed laws to *confiscate* or "renationalize" certain properties. Best known was the December 1991 bill which confiscated the property of the Communist Party and other organizations contaminated by their association with the old regime. This included the property of the former monopoly Bulgarian Trade Union organization. The heir of this organization was the Confederation of Independent Trade Unions of Bulgaria (CITUB), which had already voluntarily returned to the Government two-thirds of the property it had controlled before 1990. It had also offered repeatedly to share its remaining properties with the other major labour movement organization, Podkrepa. The Government did not budge from implementing the confiscation law and ultimately the case went to litigation. West European labour confederation officials publicly declared their concern over the Bulgarian government's action of nationalizing all CITUB's property and threatening the leadership with criminal penalties for non- compliance.

The 1991-92 UDF Government actively sought to discover if former communist officials had illegally (even if under previous laws of the old regime) taken financial assets from parts of the public treasury, ministries or enterprises. The Government even engaged international researchers to help locate the allegedly stolen funds. The Government also hoped to reacquire most of the property which it felt had been obtained wrongfully through insider dealing and other chicanery. It had little success in locating any such funds or proving the illegality of property transfers.

The 1991-92 government hoped for a rapid growth of *new private enterprises*, as did later governments. Private entrepreneurs have become quite numerous in retailing and wholesaling, import-export, and business and consumer services. Relatively few foreign firms have made large-scale investments so far, and many of them have only made token investments in order to have some representation in Bulgaria. The total foreign direct investment for 1990-95 was only half a billion dollars. Policies to promote the development of both domestic and foreign private businesses have been adopted. The Foreign Investment Act of 1991 was substantially revised in 1992 to make it easier for foreign investors to buy property and invest in Bulgaria. Profits can be fully repatriated and foreign investors get a tax holiday for a period after investing. Joint manufacturing ventures with foreigners get several years of tax relief. Private enterprises face fewer regulations and red tape than state enterprises. In 1992, private businesses had to fill in only a simple form with a few basic items on it for the tax and statistical authorities, while state enterprises were filling in literally hundreds of detailed forms. There are no wage bill limits for private businesses. Nevertheless, the slow development of the non-merchant private sector has continually disappointed liberals during the transition years.

In manufacturing, private firms are still very rare. Completely new private manufacturers are even more rare. One might expect this, given the collapse of domestic demand. Most foreign investments have been joint ventures and in sectors allowing easy export to sure markets. The cooperatives which have got their property back are relatively few in number, though some private owners of establishments have already formed lobbying organizations to protect and promote their interests. The development of private manufacturing faces many hurdles which may hinder its development for some time.

For example:

(a) the costs of borrowing are perceived as formidable (even if the *real* interest rate is not large or even negative);

(b) domestic demand for any intermediate inputs and producers' goods will remain dominated by state-owned enterprises for some time;

(c) state-owned enterprises are used to paying their bills at their convenience, so promised payments are uncertain;

(d) business support organizations are relatively new and inexperienced; and

(e) production and management skills are in short supply among potential small business people.

4. Conclusions: Complexities of economic transformation, privatization and the Bulgarian case

4.1 Separating the effects of privatization from other economic changes affecting labour markets

At present, it is scarcely possible to separate out the effects of the privatization process on employment, labour markets and economic welfare in Bulgaria — there are so many complications. First, many changes are occurring simultaneously in the Bulgarian economy, all of which have some impact — direct or indirect — on the labour market. Second, "privatization" must be precisely defined.[22] Third, relatively few of the larger state assets have so far been fully transferred to private ownership; identifying the quantitative (and perhaps qualitative) effects of an incomplete, ongoing process requires more subtlety and detail than the available data provide. Excepting agiculture, privatization leading to full control has occurred in enterprises with barely 10 per cent of the labour force.

Here we review only the first problem, by simply reiterating some of the main changes which interfere with identifying the effects of privatization *per se*. External changes affecting employment and privatization include:

(a) general slow growth in the world economy during the whole period of transition up to the present;

(b) collapse and disintegration of the CMEA "rouble market" and evaporation of traditional demand channels for Bulgarian exports;

(c) continuing reluctance on the part of Western economies (especially the crucially important European Union) to open their markets fully to countries in Central and Eastern Europe (they are especially reluctant to open their markets in agriculture, processed food and heavy industry — all of them important for Bulgaria);

(d) wars and attendant economic dislocation (e.g. blockades) in the Middle East, former Yugoslavia, Moldova, Georgia;

(e) sudden exposure to world market prices for energy imports and other crucial raw material inputs;

(f) reduction in trade credits, and limitations on banking services for Bulgarian exporters owing to a moratorium on foreign debt servicing (beginning in spring 1990; ending with an agreement with foreign creditors late in 1993) and recurring exchange crises;

(g) intense competition for foreign investors from large-scale privatization projects in dozens of other countries in all regions of the world;

(h) huge demands from many other transforming or restructuring economies on the limited resources of international financial and aid agencies (as well as on countries traditionally involved in bilateral aid).

Domestic economic policy changes important for the economic activity of Bulgarian enterprises include:

(a)   rapid price liberalization (price "shock") and profound shifts in domestic relative prices since February 1991;

(b)   high rates of inflation since February 1991 and difficult-to-forecast future inflationary developments;

(c)   restrictions on credit expansion, high nominal interest rates, and an initial reduction in real money supply;

(d)   reductions in budgetary subsidies to certain sectors, and a shifting of continued, limited subsidies from some sectors to others;

(e)   quasi-market determination of foreign exchange prices and frequent interventions which effectively ration inadequate foreign exchange among importers (especially important for enterprises dependent on foreign inputs);

(f)   price freedom (within certain restrictions which limit increases in the rate of profit) for state-owned enterprises.

Changes more closely connected to privatization, which differentially affect enterprises' economic opportunities and managers' perceptions, include:

(a)   Demonopolization and corporatization of state enterprises, involving the breaking up of integrated multi-establishment firms. Sometimes smaller monopolies or oligopolies are created in place of bigger monopolies directly controlled by the State. Occasionally, these supposedly independent units are recombined into holding companies.

(b)   Theoretical autonomy for firm managements — but government/ministries make ad hoc and frequently unpredictable interventions in management. Possible politicization of enterprise affairs and management appointments (by government, political parties, unions/workforces). There is also potential for workers to intervene to seek management dismissal, government subsidies, re-regulation, etc.

(c)   Separation of exporting/marketing functions from subsidiary production establishments as big conglomerate firms are broken up into several smaller units, and recombination of some of the units into new foreign marketing operations. Inexperienced management teams in demonopolized units have faced marketing problems.

(d)   Widespread insolvency in the state-owned productive sector, though there have been very few outright liquidations or bankruptcies. All/most enterprises owe money to each other, to the Government, to the tax authorities, or to the (primarily) government-owned banking sector. Revenue flows from contracted work or deliveries are unreliable; enterprises/agencies simply defer payments.

(e)   Very uncertain incentives, as privatization lies ahead but will be carried out in a time frame and manner that is not completely predictable (at least for each individual enterprise). This is one effect of the instability (or inconsistency) and polarization of Bulgarian political life and institutions.

To add to these complicating factors, there is at present no control group which might be used as a benchmark for assessing the independent effects of policies, external changes, and the internal dynamics of the privatization process. The typical private establishment differs in several ways from a state sector enterprise. The current private sector enterprise tends to be much smaller and more independent of other economic units; it faces a different tax regime, has new subsidized consulting agencies (with aid from foreign experts) set up specifically to aid private business development, and had no wage rate restrictions until 1993. Most private firms are not in manufacturing. Only as full privatization occurs in more cases and in more sectors can a more complete story be told, and the specific effects of full privatization perhaps be identified more adequately.

4.2 Tentative conclusions on the lessons of transformation policies in Bulgaria

In the first year after the downfall of Zhivkov in November 1989, the inertia of the old system kept the economy operating much as in the past. In 1991, the emphasis was placed on macroeconomic balancing, accompanied by the sudden freeing of prices, exchange rates and trade rules. During the period 1991-92, the State tried to withdraw from active direction of state enterprises (SOEs), while at the same time hoping for propertyless managers (facing unknown rules and regulations) to imitate the property-owning capitalists in economies where rules are enforced relatively consistently. The SOE managers *did* imitate the drive for personal gain and security of Western business people, but in the Bulgarian context this translated into many severely negative social consequences. Janos Kornai was surely right in *The road to a free economy* when he emphasized the absolute need for "real" property ownership for those who might try to transform the old SOEs of the Communist systems. Otherwise, any potential value of the existing SOEs might be dissipated by purely opportunistic behaviour. This was predicted by other analysts as well; to a large extent it has occurred in Bulgaria.

For economists, it is not the opportunism itself which was "wrong" or "bad". Rather, it was the absence of appropriate constraints to guide this opportunism and turn it to socially beneficial purposes.

The following are some of the lessons that can be drawn from the Bulgarian experience:

(a) Do not apply shock treatment to economies entirely dominated by oligopolistic state-owned enterprises — at least not until one can be very sure that constrained and truly autonomous economic agents exist. They must be constrained to respond effectively to the results of price movements. The constraints (e.g. competition, enforceable and enforced rules, visible and predictable benefits and sanctions) must operate effectively; otherwise, clever people will find out how to avoid the sanctions and grab the most easily obtainable and least risky benefits.

(b) If shock treatment is chosen, then state property should be given away. Shock treatment requires rapid privatization. This should occur even *before* the shock.

(c) Usually, the people who have the most to gain and the most to lose from the changing fate of an existing enterprise are the people whose lives are most closely connected with it: the workers and managers who work in it.

(d)   Unless there are buyers waiting at the door, give the enterprise away to the workers and managers.[23] They will probably need help in creating a workable system of governance so that they can get on with the business of producing.

(e)   Do not give *anyone* permanent control over an unregulated monopoly or quasi-monopoly which makes products or services that someone or some enterprise or some public agency *has to* buy. The monopoly enterprise will eventually exploit its position, no matter who is in control of it.

(f)   Make these enterprises truly autonomous. Make the new owners clear about what they will lose if the enterprise folds (jobs, part of their pension, unemployment benefits, etc.).

(g)   Perhaps keep a minority government stake in the enterprises. Make the owners' dividends a function of employees' total and individual compensation levels *and* profitability. This can be used to help compensate those workers and citizens who are offered nothing in the privatization game. It also improves the compatibility of incentives among owners and employees.

(h)   Do not withdraw the State from the micro-economy and meso-economy in the transition. Historically, successful market economies have not developed in a vacuum. More attention ought to be given to the Japanese and East Asian processes of economic development, as well as to the last decade of Chinese economic reforms. Financial issues and institutions are social organizations which take years to create and adopt appropriate regulations for.[24]

(i)   Develop a coherent set of industrial policies to stimulate production, investment and employment. These policies should also identify and take account of the constraints from trade barriers which may persist over the medium term, even if one can imagine them decreasing in the longer term. As the Japanese (and others) have shown, comparative advantage can evolve over time and be guided by government policies to do so in different ways.

References

Bulgarian Business News (168 Hours BBN). Miscellaneous issues. Sofia.

Central Statistical Office (CSO — now the National Statistical Institute). 1990. *Ikonomikata na Bulgaria: Statisticheski Sbornik (The economy of Bulgaria in figures)*. Sofia, CSO.

——. 1990-95. *Statisticheshki Godishnik na Republika Bulgariak (Statistical Yearbook of Bulgaria)*. Sofia, CSO.

——. 1991. *Statistical Handbook: Economics of Bulgaria*. Prepared for the IMF. Sofia, CSO.

——. 1991-95. *Statistical Reference Book (Statisticheski Spravochnik)*. Sofia, CSO.

Donahue, John D. 1989. *The privatization decision: Public ends, private means*. New York, Basic Books.

Economic Commission for Europe. 1993. *Economic Survey of Europe 1992/93*. Geneva, United Nations.

Frydman, R. et al. (eds.). 1993. *The privatization process in Central Europe*, London, Central European University Press.

Gormley, W. T. Jr. (ed.). 1990. *Privatization and its alternatives*. Madison, Wisconsin, University of Wisconsin Press.

Kornai, J. 1991. *The road to a free economy: Shifting from a socialist system. The example of Hungary*. New York and London, W. W. Norton.

"Letter of Intent to the IMF, Feb. 14, 1991", in *Bulgarian National Bank News Bulletin*, 16-29 Feb. 1990, pp. 2-34.

McKinnon, R. 1993. "Gradual versus rapid liberalization in socialist economies" in *Proceedings of World Bank Annual Conference on Development Economics 1993*, pp. 63-112.

Meurs, M.; Rock, C. 1993. "Recent evolution of Bulgarian cooperatives", in *Yearbook of Cooperation 1993*. London, Plunkett Foundation, pp. 39-52.

National Statistical Institute (NSI) *see* Central Statistical Office.

Organization for Economic Co-operation and Development (OECD). 1992, 1993. *Short-Term Economic Indicators Central and Eastern Europe*.

Pamouktchiev, H. 1992. "Sindikalen pogled vurkhu zakona za privatizatsiata" (Union view on the privatization law), in *Sindikalna praktika*, 6/1992, pp. 12-22.

——. 1993. "Shareholding and the dynamics of enterprise reform in Central and Eastern Europe: The implications for Bulgaria." Unpublished manuscript. Sofia, May, 135pp.

Petkov, K.; Gradev, G. 1995. "Bulgaria". Chapter 3 in J. Thirkell et al. (eds.) *Labour relations and political change in eastern Europe*. Ithaca, New York, ILR Press.

Rock, C. 1992, "Employment, labour and privatization in Bulgaria's reforms: 1989 to mid-1992." Unpublished manuscript. Geneva, ILO, July, 88 pp.

Rock, C. 1993. "Workers' ownership: Prospects in Bulgaria". Paper presented at the ILO Conference on Employment Restructuring in Bulgarian Industry, Sofia, May 1993.

Suleiman, E. N.; Waterbury, J. (eds.). 1990. *The political economy of public sector reform and privatization*. San Francisco, Oxford and Boulder, Colorado, Westview Press.

Tzanov, Vassil. 1995. "For a negotiated alternative to tax-based income policy" in *Reforming wage policy in Central and Eastern Europe*, Geneva, ILO. pp. 87-122.

von Brabant, J. M. 1992. "On property rights and privatization in the transition economies", in *Economic Survey of Europe in 1991-92*. Geneva, United Nations.

World Bank. 1991. *Bulgaria: Crisis and transition to a market economy*, 2 vols. Washington, DC, World Bank Country Study.

Notes

[1] Although the elections of June 1990 led to a nominal majority in the Constitutional Assembly for the BSP, it was not unified and faced ongoing popular protests and demonstrations led by the opposition coalition, the Union of Democratic Forces (UDF). The BSP-led assembly elected as president a well-known dissident and one of the leaders of the UDF, Zhelyu Zhelev, in August 1990. In December 1990, the BSP cabinet collapsed, leading to the appointment of opposition member as Minister of Finance and Minister of Industry. These ministers led the agreement with the IMF and initiated the shock therapy beginning in February 1991. The parliamentary elections of October 1991 put the UDF slightly ahead of the BSP, but did not give it an outright majority of the members. From 1991 to 1994, all governements depended on the implicit support of the Movement for Rights and Freedom (MRF), the ethnic Turkish party, since it has held the balance of power between the UDF and the

BSP. At the end of 1992, the UDF-led government of Philip Dimitrov fell and was replaced by one led by the non-partisan Lyuben Berov, former adviser to President Zhelev. Berov lasted until the autumn of 1994, when a caretaker cabinet was established under the former head of the Privatization Agency. Renata Indjova ruled for a few months before the second democratic parliamentary elections of the transition period. These December 1994 elections gave a single party, the Socialists, an outright parliamentary majority for the first time (even though the popular vote results remained substantially polarized). Prime Minister Zhan Videnov and the BSP has governed since then.

[2] The spring 1994 renegotiation agreement involved state assumption of liabilities, some debt forgiveness, extended repayment terms and possible equity swaps. The currency exchange crisis of 1996 threatens ongoing repayments.

[3] Although they have been quite critical of the slow speed of privatization and the faulty implementation of the prescribed policies in Bulgaria, IMF and World Bank economists have mysteriously come to a relatively positive assessment of the consequences of macroeconomic reforms in the early transition years.

[4] Perhaps some 100,000 pensioners and early retirees left the labour force in 1989-91. The number of pensions only increased by a quarter of this amount; also, people can receive more than one pension based on their work history.

[5] Although there was a cap on price mark-ups, many enterprises used creative accounting to reduce the effect of the cap.

[6] One thoughtful Bulgarian economist thinks that there is one consistent goal of state enterprise managers in the reform period: managerial survival through the reforms and into the actual process of privatization. This seems very plausible, but does not necessarily help predict the behaviour of any particular manager. Their information and assessment of the situation may differ, and actions may differ considerably across firms. Even so, managers seem generally to have acted to secure their personal fortunes for the future, and this is only accidentally the same as profit maximization (Pamouktchiev, 1993). For an intimate trade union perspective on managerial actions and motivations see the four very interesting enterprise case-studies in the paper by Petkov and Gradev (1995). They also state that during 1991-92 some 2,000 state enterprise directors were replaced (p. 43), which should be a majority of them (depending on how multi-enterprise firms are counted). In any case, this lack of job security motivated managers to look for allies, wherever they might find them, to help them survive the political and economic chaos of the early transition period.

[7] It is arguable that this result is to be expected. A fall in labour productivity during an economic contraction is not unusual in the sense that it is characteristic of developed market economies in the recessionary phase of the business cycle. What is unusual, perhaps, is the severity of the collapse of production in Bulgaria. There was some reversal of this productivity fall during 1994-1995. However, the banking, exchange and debt crises of 1996 may disrupt this growth trend.

[8] These could be similar to, say, the French manufacturing SOEs, which operate autonomously and are primarily responsive to market signals rather than to government preferences. Thus, as discussed above, the attempt to impose "hard budget" constraints on them is part of this process.

[9] Thus, public goals as such would only be represented among the directors on the supervisory boards. Management would have to respond to them but only in the same way as managers in purely private companies do to the variety of interests which exists among their own board members.

[10] Many of these have been discussed *ad nauseum*, especially the mainly political issues. See e.g. *Monitor na Privatizatsiyata*, 1992.

[11] Bulgaria is not very unusual. See the discussions in Gormley, 1990; Suleiman and Waterbury, 1990; Donahue, 1989; and for a survey of privatization in many countries in Central and Eastern Europe, including the former Soviet republics, see Frydman et al., 1993.

[12] Certain additional decrees and laws have been passed clarifying some, but by no means all, of the uncovered issues since the law was passed.

[13] The major laws affecting privatization in Bulgaria until mid-1992 are included in Rock, 1992, appendix. A second major privatization law for enterprises was enacted in mid-1994, which clarified some of the provisions

of the 1992 act and included further measures to promote employee and managerial buy-outs. It also contained a rather vague mass privatization scheme using vouchers, strongly supported by the non-partisan Prime Minister Berov.

[14] Tables of restituted and privatized property do exist, but they are not very useful for assessing effective control (i.e. "full" privatization) of the properties listed. For example, agricultural lands have been restituted, but Western and Bulgarian academics working on a major research project on the transformation of Bulgarian agriculture have found that the nominally private lands are often not controlled/farmed by the supposed owners. The current data are probably most adequate for assessing full privatization of urban retail/commercial real estate restitutions.

[15] By SOEs we mean both national and local enterprises owned by governments at both levels. For convenience we also include the cooperative enterprises under this heading.

[16] These are not perfectly sequential "phases". The second phase overlaps with both the third and fourth. "Quiet" or "wild" (illegal or quasi-legal) acquisition of state property has apparently continued to be a problem throughout the transition period. This is due in part to the sometimes mutually contradictory laws in place and in part to the cleverness of Bulgarians in the new environment in testing the limits of new restrictions on self-dealing. For example, a "White Paper" in late 1993 by the Governor of the Bulgarian National Bank (BNB) outlined apparently unpunished irregularities in nine major banks, where new shares were issued without permission of the BNB. One of the Bulgarian legal advisers aiding the State Privatization Agency sardonically commented to me, "In Bulgaria, we have the most clever quiet privatizers in all of Eastern Europe".

[17] Although the corporatized enterprises do not form a majority of all state enterprises, it appears that they represent a large majority of all state enterprise assets. This conclusion is based on interviews as well as an extrapolation of research on a subset of these SOE corporations by Pamouktchiev (1993).

[18] The three deals were for companies involved in chocolate production (Swiss buyer), grains processing (Belgian buyer) and beer manufacture (German buyer). Another previous deal with an American buyer went sour since the buyer did not pay the amount stipulated in the deal. To be fair, it should be mentioned that at least some of the credit for these deals belongs to the administrators in place even before January 1993. Concluding such deals can take many months, sometimes over a year.

[19] Near the end of 1994, a total of nearly 40,000 non-agricultural properties had been formally restituted. These included over 12,000 parcels of urban land, over 8,000 shops, nearly 10,000 housing units, nearly 1,000 warehouses, 400 office buildings, 700 milling operations and a variety of other properties. These restituted properties represent over 55 per cent of the total properties — both the number and appraised value — on which claims for restitution had been made. (National Statistical Institute, "Restitutsiata v Republika Bulgaria — 3" 1994, p. 20.)

[20] In all elections since 1989, the Bulgarian Socialist Party (BSP, created by former Communist Party activists) enjoyed its strongest voting support in the rural agricultural areas of the country.

[21] There were some people interested in this possibility, but with very little credit availability in rural areas, the number actually moving appears to be insignificant.

[22] Our broad definition, described in section 3.1, includes not only the actual transfer of current state assets but also the creation of the necessary environmental conditions for a reasonably functioning market economy and the creation of privately owned, independent enterprises — both domestic and foreign.

[23] This is argued more expansively in Rock, 1993.

[24] If a freer capitalism is desired, it would seem appropriate to take lessons on it from its more moderate advocates such as Ronald McKinnon rather than from monetarists and many in the IMF. See his 1993 article and the discussions following it.

6. Privatization and its labour market effects in eastern Germany

Jürgen Kühl*

·1. Introduction

Contrary to the approach adopted by Central and Eastern European countries, Germany established a new public institution, the Treuhandanstalt (THA), to manage the privatization, reconstruction and reorganization of all state-owned enterprises. It was set up under German Democratic Republic law and began operations on 1 July 1990. The centralized THA was supported by 15 regional sub-agencies dealing with firms employing a workforce of fewer than 1,500 workers. The THA's basic principles of operation were not changed by the unification treaty, but its credit limit was increased to DM25 billion per year; the figure was DM37 billion in July 1993. The THA operated under the supervision of the Federal Ministry of Finance. As owner of more than 8,000 former state-owned companies, the THA initially had control of over 45,000 plants, with a total workforce of 4.1 million, about half the total workforce in the German Democratic Republic in the second part of 1989 when the Berlin Wall fell. By the end of 1994 the THA's operations had ended: 98 per cent of all companies in the THA portfolio (12,354) had been privatized or closed; 192 firms employing 66,000 employees were transferred to the follow-up institution, and one-third of these firms and jobs are expected to be privatized soon.

Table 6.1 summarizes enterprise transformations by the THA during 1991-94. Out of a total of 12,162 enterprises transformed over the whole period, 6,546 (54 per cent) were sold to the private sector; management buy-outs (MBOs) made up 22 per cent; and 13 per cent of all privatizations were sold to foreigners. Although there are some surviving parts of enterprises, 3,718 firms have been closed, i.e. 31 per cent. The new owners of firms have promised to invest DM211 billion (over the entire decade) and to keep 1.5 million jobs. Up until the end of THA operations on 31 December 1994, the new owners had paid DM49.4 billion to the THA and total resources amounted to DM73 billion. The portfolio of all THA enterprises increased over time due to splitting up, mergers etc.

The THA activities and their employment consequences (unemployment, earlier retirement, migration or commuting to western Germany) were based on a "rich uncle" solution. The THA and the Federal Labour Office (*Bundesanstalt für Arbeit* — BA)

*Institute for Employment Research, Nuremberg.

Table 6.1. Survey on enterprise transformation by the Treuhandanstalt (THA), 1991-94

	End of 1991	End of 1992	End of 1993	End of 1994
Portfolio — all THA enterprises	10 663	11 787	12 246	12 354
Enterprises in THA ownership	7 502	3 143	1 059	192
Rate of privatization[1] (per cent)	39	75	91	98
Employment in THA-owned enterprises (000s)	1 837	780	187	66
Transformation total	4 852	9 212	11 295	12 162
Privatized enterprises[2]	3 315	5 456	6 180	6 546
Re-privatized enterprises[3]	527	1 188	1 573	1 588
Community ownership	145	319	261	265
Other privatizations	0	0	85	45
Closed down, liquidation[4]	865	2 249	3 196	3 718
Investments promised (DM billion)	114.2	169.5	183.2	211.1
Jobs promised (000s)	880.1	1 350.5	1 448.1	1 487.3
Enterprises sold to foreigners	248	548	806	855
Revenue from firm sales (DM billion)	19.5	40.1	45.0	49.4
Management buy-outs	854	1 946	2 425	2 697

[1] Total number of enterprises transformed as per cent of portfolio by end of 1994; [2] Including 7,600 parts of firms and 25,030 "small" privatizations, e.g. retail trades, restaurants; [3] Including 2,670 parts of firms which were given back to their previous owners; [4] There are some surviving parts of enterprises that were to be closed down.

Source: THA.

expenditures accounted for 28 per cent of the eastern GDP (constant 1991 prices) in 1991 and 40 per cent in 1992 and 1993; in 1994 this share was 35.4 per cent (table 6.2). Except in 1994, the BA had to spend even more than the THA in order to cope with the labour market and social consequences of rapid privatization.

Thus, the THA and the BA had an important impact on the process of restructuring and employment in eastern Germany. However, neither institution had any structural or industrial policy aims. The THA had no explicit targets relating to preserving or creating jobs or to industrial or regional structures of employment.

By the end of 1994 the THA had stopped dealing with privatization but its successor institution, *Bundesanstalt für Vereinigungsbedingte Sonderaufgaben* (BVS), continued to control contracts, sell land and real estate, and help the remaining firms which could not be sold or closed down for which a solution had not been found. The number of THA employees had reached a peak of 4,200 by mid-1993 but was to be reduced to 2,800 in 1994 after the privatization process ended. One difficult issue in reforming the industrial structure of a centralized economy is the policy on liquidation. By the end of May 1993 only 49 firms had been completely liquidated, but 2,653 were still in the process of liquidation. In total 2,702 firms employing 303,700 people had been closed down; there was some hope that 82,300 of these jobs (27 per cent) might survive.

The THA strategy may be summarized by its slogan: rapid privatization, decisive reconstruction, smooth liquidation of firms. It involved considerable costs, and it

**Table 6.2. Expenditures of the THA and the Federal Labour Office (BA),
eastern Germany, 1991-95**

	Expenditure (DM billion)		GDP	Expenditure as % of GDP	
	THA	BA	1991 prices	THA	BA
1991[1]	27.6	29.9	206.0	13.4	14.5
1992	41.2	46.0	222.1	18.6	20.7
1993	46.6	50.6	238.1	19.5	21.3
1994	49.8	41.6	258.3	19.3	16.1
1995	—[2]	35.8	272.7	—	13.1

[1] In the second half of 1990 the THA expenditure was DM5.9 billion; [2] The budget of the THA follow-up institute, i.e. *Bundesanstalt für Vereinigungsbedingte Sonderaufgaben* (BVS), is DM24 billion for 1995-97 and DM21 billion for 1998 and later.

Source: GDP: THA, BA, own calculations.

completely reshaped the industrial landscape in eastern Germany, with a severe impact on employment. In order to gain a better insight into this process, section 2 of this chapter concentrates on the operations of the THA, followed by a review of privatization criteria in section 3. Section 4 presents employment trends in THA companies and in privatized firms, based on the results of eight representative surveys carried out between April 1991 and October 1995. Sections 5 and 6 analyse the labour market status of workers after leaving THA firms, the effect of labour market programmes and the role of employment companies. Section 7 compares the performance of investment, while the last section shows how the method of privatization has resulted in large-scale deindustrialization in eastern Germany.

2. THA operations: Main activities, progress in privatization, and the costs involved

As a government agency, the THA was charged with the following duties (Trusteeship Act, Treuhandgesetz, 17 June 1990):

(a)   Administration of state-owned firms according to the principles of a social market economy; disengagement of company structures and promotion of marketable firms and efficient economic structures; assistance in preparing opening balance sheets on a Deutschmark basis and organizing firms according to western laws.

(b)   Transfer of companies into the private sector as quickly as possible, the priority being to privatize rather than to reconstruct firms or parts of firms. Transfer means selling to the private sector — even at "negative prices" — returning firms to former owners who lost them in 1972, or restoring public ownership by communities.

(c)   Reorganization of firms which can be reconstructed into competitive companies and then privatized. Reconstruction was intended to be achieved by splitting up firms into marketable units, downsizing the remaining companies, and rearranging local economic networks.

(d)   Provision of real estate for economic purposes; reorganization and privatization of THA assets in agriculture and forestry, considering the special nature of these sectors.

The economic activity of state-owned firms was to be reduced as soon and as much as possible, while privatized firms were to be made competitive in markets in western Germany and the European Union, thereby securing existing jobs and creating new ones. The THA had no decisive obligation to revitalize eastern Germany's economic base, or to create enough good jobs and preserve a high enough level of employment to secure wages and standards of living in the east comparable to those in the west.

Accordingly, THA activities can be divided into six periods:

(a)   Until the unification of Germany, the THA had to guarantee the liquidity of its firms by offering cash. It had to take an inventory of firms and their capital stock, real estate and obligations. Firms were asked for a certain opening balance and their business plan; they had to be reorganized according to the economic and legal system of the Federal Republic of Germany. By October 1990 only 34 firms had been privatized.

(b)   From October 1990 until the end of the year the THA remained passive while west Germans began to buy the best firms.

(c)   From the beginning of 1991 the THA offered "company information services" and an "Official Register of Treuhandanstalt Companies". Official and mass media advertising of firms to be sold supported a policy of rapid privatization. About 70 per cent of all firms were judged to be reconstructable, mainly after being sold to the private sector or transferred to public authorities.

(d)   Active marketing by the THA started in 1992. This included looking for foreign investors[1] and promoting management buy-outs and buy-ins (MBOs, MBIs); workers could also take a 20 per cent share in their company. Small and medium-sized firms (SMEs) were offered to SME owners in western Germany. Registers of all firms to be privatized were published. THA initiatives aimed to boost public and private sector orders to THA firms. A "Match Making" operation promoted cooperation with THA firms.

(e)   In late 1992 the THA started active reorganization of firms because many companies could not be sold immediately. Reconstructable firms were combined into management partnerships (ten to 15 firms would enter a management company). The *Länder* (states) of eastern Germany began to take responsibility for the industrial firms within their borders. Large firms essential to the industrial base and labour market of the whole region came to be seen as "core companies". Although no private investors had yet been found, the THA and state government officials agreed to reconstruct certain firms and to share the costs. But the THA always made the final decision unless the State alone was paying for the reconstruction of a firm. In July 1993 the THA introduced a kind of portfolio privatization by selling 13 firms *en bloc* to the Deutsche Industrie Holding (DIH).

(f)   During 1993-94 the THA changed its policy towards necessary investments in its firms, which had to be "neutral" to potential investors, and later on the THA even actively reconstructed firms before they could be sold to private owners.

Carlin and Mayer (1992, p. 336) have documented highly active restructuring by the THA: creation of opening balance sheets; evaluation of the viability of firms; the writing off of debts for firms believed to be viable; creation of supervisory boards; identification and evaluation of potential buyers; negotiation of employment and investment guarantees and sale prices; break-up of enterprises, liquidation of assets, and closure of firms.

The THA approach to privatization was thus a single-company one: it sold downsized firms to investors without regard to the industrial or regional structures of employment. The main criteria were the number of firms to be transferred, the number of jobs to be preserved and amounts to be invested. The THA showed little interest in productive potential, preservation of a qualified labour force, research and development facilities, training resources, creation of new products, marketing, or reconstruction of competitive firms before selling them to the private sector at decent prices.

Table 6.3 shows the progress of privatization from late 1990 to the end of 1994: altogether about 15,000 firms were wholly or partially sold by the THA during that period. The pace of privatization reached a peak in 1992. It slowed down thereafter because mainly hard-to-sell companies were left.

Table 6.3. Privatization of firms and the THA debt, 1990-94 (DM million)

Year	Number of firms privatized[1]	Total THA debt	Credit market	Takeover of firms' debt	Debt due to equalization claims of firms
1990	4 082[2]	14 058	4 330	9 728	0
1991	5 210	39 402	24 192	15 210	0
1992	11 043	106 792	54 669	38 010	14 113
1993	13 429	168 322	134 488	19 684	14 150
1994	14 576	204 619	203 504	752	363

[1] All forms of privatization: complete companies or majority shares, parts of firms, MBOs, minority shares up to 49 per cent.   [2] Includes 34 privatizations before October 1990.

Sources: THA, Bundesbankbericht, own calculations.

The estimated "value" of all THA firms has shrunk rapidly, from an estimated DM600 billion to as little as DM81 billion. The opening balance of the THA was estimated at DM114 billion, including no equity capital at all. In fact, the THA started with a deficit. The "supply shock" of firms to be sold quickly led to lower prices; prices fell even further owing to shrinking markets, and the recession in western Germany and the European Union. Some of the new owners of firms received more financial support or comparable advantages from the THA than they had to pay for the firm and to promise to invest in it. "Negative prices" of firms were the result of the THA's writing off of firms' old debts, the equity capital offered, the takeover of ecological burdens, and some risk-sharing by minority shareholdings of the THA. The consequences of low and even "negative prices" and subsidies to THA firms were large deficits.

At the end of 1992 the THA's total debt was DM107 billion, and by May 1993 it had increased to over DM168 billion; 80 per cent was borrowed on the credit market, 12 per cent stemmed from the THA's taking over of firms' debts, and 8 per cent was due to "equalization claims" by THA firms. The THA allowed firms to make equalization claims in order to compensate for their severe losses owing to the general lack of competitiveness, the loss of eastern markets and a widespread lack of capital. The THA's increasing indebtedness is closely linked to the progress of privatization, not only because of the THA's writing off of firms' debts and paying equalization claims, but also because of the supply of equity capital to firms — the amount depending on the industrial sector involved. In spring 1993 the THA debt per privatization could be estimated at DM10 million. At the end of THA operations in 1994, the THA had a total debt of DM205 billion. During the years after 1994 additional expenditure of DM60 billion is planned, bringing the total deficit up to DM265 billion. Taking this expenditure into account, DM101 billion was spent on taking over firms' debts (including DM26 billion in interest payments), DM44 billion was devoted to ecological reconstruction, and DM154 billion was spent on privatization or closing down of firms, including social plans. The huge burden of all THA/BVS activities will further increase the public debt, leaving future generations to pay for this.

3. THA privatization criteria: Jobs, investments, revenues

Table 6.4 elaborates on the THA's own privatization criteria. Out of the initial 8,000 firms (with 45,000 plants), the plan was to privatize about 6,100. The gross number of firms under THA control (its "portfolio") increased rapidly as firms were split up into smaller, more marketable units. By mid-1993 almost 13,000 firms had been under THA control. The privatization of complete firms or parts of firms proceeded rapidly, with 12,360 units privatized by the end of May 1993. The privatization rate — the proportion of privatized firms in the THA portfolio — rose to 24.7 per cent by mid-1991, 69.5 per cent by mid-1992 and 95.4 per cent by mid-1993. In addition to these privatizations, 1,588 firms had been reprivatized; 265 community privatizations had taken place by the end of 1994 (see table 6.1).

According to the principle of rapid privatization, the THA proceeded very fast in wholesale and retail trade, restaurants, hotels and services. The privatization rate in manufacturing industries was much lower. However, looking simply at numbers of firms privatized neglects factors such as firm size (number of jobs) and the regional and industrial distribution of firms. In the beginning, no targets for jobs or investments were included in sales contracts. Later on, buyers promised certain numbers of jobs and levels of investment, and later still contracts contained penalty payments if the promised figures were not met after privatization. Out of the 1.46 million jobs promised at the end of May 1993 (table 6.4), only 58 per cent were backed up with fines if the new owners broke the agreement. By that time 1,015 contracts securing 106,000 jobs had been broken.

On average, firms reduced their workforce by 20-30 per cent after the THA's responsibility ended. Some firms had made no promises on jobs; some had no agreements on penalties; some kept on parts of the workforce for some time before dismissals; some found their initial expectations of a rapid upswing disappointed, having made this a condition for retaining jobs. Only a very few privatized firms have been asked to pay the fine of DM5,000-DM20,000 per job promised — a sum which would bring firms close to bankruptcy if they had to pay it.

For similar reasons, less than half (DM88 billion) of DM179 billion worth of investment promises was backed up by fines. The majority of investments promised were

Table 6.4. Privatizations out of the THA portfolio of firms, promised jobs and investments, and gross revenues from sales of firms, 1991-93

Quarter and year	Portfolio of THA firms[1]	Privatization	Firms to be privatized	Promised jobs[2]		Promised investments[2]			Gross revenues from THA sales[2]		
				Total (000s)	Per firm privatized	Total (DM bn)	Per firm (DM m)	Per job (DM 000)	Total (DM bn)	Per firm (DM m)	Per job (DM 000)
II 1991	10 334	2 583	7 200	449	174	35.3	13.7	78.6	11.6	3.9	24.4
III 1991	10 357	3 788	6 500	643	170	55.2	14.6	85.8	13.9	3.7	21.6
IV 1991	10 970	5 210	6 000	853	164	84.0	16.1	98.5	19.5	3.7	22.9
I 1992	11 555	6 579	5 117	1 001	152	98.8	15.0	98.7	26.8	4.1	26.8
II 1992	11 759	8 175	4 340	1 147	140	114.0	13.9	99.4	30.7	3.8	26.8
III 1992	12 142	9 338	3 810	n.a.	n.a.	n.a.	n.a.	n.a.	n.a.	n.a.	n.a.
IV 1992	12 599	11 043	2 843	1 260	114	150.2[3]	13.6	119.2	39.2	3.5	31.1
I 1993	12 892	11 530	2 173	1 440	125	176.7[3]	15.3	122.7	41.6	3.6	28.9
II 1993	12 952	12 360	1 871	1 457	118	178.9[3]	14.5	122.8	43.0	3.5	29.5

n.a. = not available.
[1] Gross number of firms under THA control. Mergers, splitting up of firms, property rights in mining industries, firms without employment and firms in foreign countries mean a permanently fluctuating number of firms in the THA portfolio.
[2] According to contract.
[3] Includes DM30 billion investments in energy industries offering 77,000 jobs. These are excluded from the upper part of the table because they were blocked until an agreement had been reached between the big energy suppliers in western Germany and local firms in eastern Germany.

to be undertaken in 1994 and 1995; one-quarter of all investments have no specified timescale. Many investment plans have been revised downwards because of slack economic conditions in western Germany and a slow-down of real economic GDP growth from +7.8 per cent in 1992 to +5.6 per cent in 1995.

The number of jobs promised per firm privatized was quite high, an average of 174 in mid-1991, declining to 118 by mid-1993. But that is still eight times as large as the average firm size in western Germany. Downsizing is thus expected to continue. The levels of promised investments per firm were quite stable over time, DM15 million on average. The level of investment per job promised, on the other hand — an indicator of the capital-labour ratio of privatized firms — increased by 56 per cent within two years, up to DM123,000 per job. As more than four out of five privatizations had been completed in 1993, table 6.4 ends in that year. However, the above trends might have changed slightly in the following year because in 1994 many hard-to-privatize firms had to be dealt with by the THA. Table 6.5 shows the structure of investments and jobs promised by industry at the end of 1993. The most important investments were promised outside the manufacturing core of production, that is in energy, water and mining; in real estate activities (THA-Liegenschaften); in local business areas and agriculture; and in trade, transport and services. These four sectors had two-thirds of all investments promised and half of all jobs.

Gross revenues from THA sales of firms had reached DM43 billion by the end of May 1993. Net revenues were probably lower because some firms would have had difficulties paying the sum agreed. A few firms were given back to the THA, and there were many renegotiations concerning prices, conditions, and job or investment promises. If we

Table 6.5. Investments and jobs promised by the new owner of firms, by the end of 1993

Industry	Investments promised (DM billion)			Jobs promised (000s)		
	All	Fixed in contracts	With fines	All	Fixed in contracts	With fines
Energy, water, mining	51.6	38.4	31.0	52.1	40.8	36.5
Chemicals, synthetics	9.8	8.9	6.2	52.6	41.0	32.4
Stone, glass, ceramics	7.8	6.5	4.1	53.3	37.9	28.9
Iron, steel, machinery, auto	18.0	13.7	8.4	212.8	159.8	135.9
Electrical, electronic, precision machinery	4.7	3.9	2.5	107.1	73.3	61.3
Food, drink	8.1	6.4	3.1	51.4	41.4	33.5
Textiles, leather, wood, paper	5.4	3.9	3.0	74.5	64.5	52.5
Construction	4.1	4.1	3.6	129.6	120.9	102.3
Trade, transport, services	17.5	12.9	10.2	234.1	144.0	118.4
Local business areas, agriculture	26.8	6.2	4.2	180.9	31.5	11.6
Real estate *(Liegenschaften)*	41.3	30.4	24.8	247.3	173.3	112.2
Other	9.1	6.3	3.7	73.3	52.9	34.4
Total	204.2	141.6	104.9	1 469.1	981.3	759.9

Source: Treuhandanstalt.

accept the official THA figures, gross revenue per firm privatized remained fairly stable at around DM4 million, showing a slight decline from mid-1992. Gross revenue per job promised increased slightly to just under DM30,000 at the end of May 1993. For comparison, average gross wages/salary per full-time worker in privatized firms was DM2,811 per month in March 1993, which is around DM34,000 a year.

Total THA revenues during 1990-94 from selling firms, real estate and land was estimated by the THA at DM73 billion. These revenues should be compared to the overall deficit of DM260-270 billion over the 1990s, although this deficit is lower than expected by the Government.

On the face of it, the THA's achievements were impressive: the overall rate of privatization, the promised number of jobs, the promised level of investment, and the gross revenues were remarkable. Sometimes actual employment figures and investment levels lagged far behind the promises.

Many promises were limited in duration, only two-thirds had been fixed in contracts, just 80 per cent of the contracts included penalties. By the end of November 1994 official statistics of the THA follow-up agency reported that 447,000 jobs in firms with job promises were 16 per cent above those promised. But the decisive question is: Why were only 1.5 million promises of jobs given out of 3.5 million jobs in THA firms, and why were only two-thirds (i.e. 1.02 million) contracted and only 790,000 jobs penalized? After promises expire, 55 per cent of firms want to keep their staff unchanged, 20 per cent want to hire, and 25 per cent want to dismiss employees — employment will decline. The following data for THA firms may help explain why the privatization process was so problematic. Earnings from operations and cash flow per unit of sales were negative in almost all industries in 1991 and 1992 for the majority of THA firms. In 1991, 84 per cent of 3,425 THA firms showed a loss of DM12.2 billion for the financial year, which represents 25 per cent of the value of sales. Just 16 per cent of firms made some profit or broke even.[2] Some progress may be seen in the figures for the end of March 1992: three-quarters of all firms suffered from severe losses (13 per cent of the value of sales on average), while only 764 out of 3,135 firms made some profit and 28 firms broke even.

Finally, if we compare total subsidies to privatize or close down firms of DM154 billion to the sum of investments promised of DM211 billion, much public money has been devoted to transform the former state-owned economy. If we take into account that less investment had been made than was promised, there was almost DM1 subsidy per DM of private investment.

4. Employment trends and employment prospects in THA firms and in privatized firms

Between April 1991 and 1995, eight representative surveys were conducted in order to monitor the development of employment and employment prospects in THA firms and in privatized (ex-THA) firms.[3] By 1 April 1991, THA firms had reduced their workforce by 35 per cent down to 2.65 million (table 6.6). Many workers commuted to western Germany in pursuit of higher wages. Some early retirement schemes had been introduced by the German Democratic Republic government. Only a minority of the total job losses of

1.4 million from January 1990 until April 1991 stemmed from privatization (some privatization had taken place before the THA started operations). At that time, THA firms expected their workforce to decline further to 1.2 million by the beginning of 1994. That figure is close to that reached in each of the subsequent surveys. By April 1994, for example, THA companies had 161,000 employees, while completely privatized firms had 989,000. If we add jobs in partly privatized firms, expectations about jobs three years later were quite realistic.

The employment record of privatization has not changed much over time. In general, privatized firms have hastened the decline in employment. In addition, employment prospects have become even worse over time. This finding is reinforced if we look at the job projections of individual firms over all survey dates, indicating that initial hopes of a rapid recovery were disappointed.

The development of employment in privatized firms is the result of two opposite effects: because of privatization by the THA, employment has risen in privatized firms; and because of employment losses, downsizing and plan closures, employment is declining in

Table 6.6. Employment in privatized companies and THA firms, 1990-95;[1] employment projections up to 1998

Month	Year	Privatized firms		THA firms		
		Employment (000s)	Change	Employment (000s)	Change	Index July 1990 = 100
January	1990	—	—	4 080	—	117
July	1990	—	—	3 500	−580	100
January	1991	—	—	2 937	−563	84
April	1991	—	—	2 653	−284	76
October	1991	410	—	2 000	−653	57
April	1992	560	+150	1 235	−765	35
October	1992	885	+325	626 (560^2)	−609	18
April	1993	1 047	+162	392 (337^2)	−244	11
October	1993	999	−48	252 (213^2)	−130	7
April	1994	989	−10	161 (137^2)	−91	5
October	1994	980	−9	116 (94^2)	−45	3
October	1995	950	−30	—[3]		
January	1996	883	−67	n.a.		
January	1997	830	−53	n.a.		
January	1998	816	−14	n.a.		

[1] In July 1990 the THA started its activities with 3.5 million jobs in THA firms. Reliable figures exist from the beginning of 1991.   [2] Employment in economically active companies (excluding companies in liquidation).   [3] In October 1995 former THA companies now under the supervision of the BVS, i.e. *Bundesanstalt für Vereinigungsbedingte Sonderaufgaben*, had 7,600 employees. In addition, companies in liquidation had 17,000 jobs. Furthermore, there were 11,000 jobs in specific management companies.

Source: Surveys on THA activities and privatized firms by SOESTRA on behalf of the *Bundesanstalt für Arbeit* (BN, IAB).

privatized firms. At the beginning of 1993 employment in privatized firms reached its peak. Later on, privatized firms lost more jobs than jobs were added due to privatization, as the pace of THA activities slowed down during 1994. Maximum employment in privatized firms continued to decline until 1995, and is expected to continue until the beginning of 1998 (overall loss of more than 200,000 jobs). Expected job losses by industry were as follows: mining 55 per cent; manufacturing 11 per cent; construction 20 per cent; employment companies 51 per cent. By the end of 1995 eastern Germany had less than 950,000 jobs in completely privatized firms plus about 350,000 jobs in partly privatized firms. In manufacturing industries half of all jobs were offered by fully or partly privatized firms.

5. *Workers leaving THA firms and labour market policy*

Table 6.7 shows the labour market status of different workers leaving THA firms. In 1991 ordinary retirement and special early retirement schemes — *Vorruhestandsgeld* up to 2 October 1990, *Altersübergangsgeld* after unification — accounted for one in eight workers leaving THA firms. In 1992 the figure was a little more than 4 per cent, and by 1993 the retirement possibility seems to have been exhausted. About one-quarter of all THA leavers in 1991 found new jobs in privatized firms, management buy-outs (MBOs) or management buy-ins (MBIs), mostly as a result of voluntary moves to other firms or attempts to start a new business. During the phase of active privatization in 1992 a greater proportion of leavers

Table 6.7. Labour market status of workers after leaving THA firms, 1991-93
(per cent)

Labour force status	1.4.1991	1.10.1991	1.4.1992	1.10.1992	1.4.1993
Retirement	4.4	1.2	1.0	4.4	0.6
Early retirement	7.1	12.9	3.2	0.4	0.0
Total	11.5	14.1	4.2	4.8	0.6
Privatization, MBO, MBI	12.6	5.8	15.2	15.8	6.7
Move into another firm, founding new firm	15.4	15.7	13.3	10.8	7.2
Total	28.0	21.5	28.5	26.6	13.9
Employment companies	0	8.4	10.7	8.4	16.4
Job creation programmes	10.3	8.1	3.1	1.5	1.2
Training and retraining	6.3	5.2	3.7	1.9	1.9
Total participation in labour market policy measures	16.6	21.7	17.5	11.8	19.5
Unemployment	44.0	24.0	34.5	42.7	43.0
Other, unknown	—	18.5	15.5	14.1	23.0
Total	100.0	100.0	100.0	100.0	100.0

Source: Surveys of THA firms and privatized firms.

Table 6.8. Short-time workers, 1991-93

	1.4.91		1.10.91		1.4.92		1.10.92		1.4.93	
	000s	%	000s	%	000s	%	000s	%	000s	%
THA firms	1 271	47.9	709	35.5	237	19.2	104	18.6	58	17.2
Privatized firms	n.a.	n.a.	n.a.	n.a.	47	8.5	50	6.0	97	10.1
Eastern Germany	1 990	22.6	1 333	15.1	494	6.5	251	4.4	246	4.3
Western Germany	139	0.6	133	0.6	266	1.1	204	0.9	1 061	4.6

Note: n.a. = Figures not available.

were absorbed by privatized firms. Moving to other firms and setting up new businesses declined in importance as economic conditions worsened in eastern Germany.

In accordance with the THA strategy of reducing the workforce of firms to be sold until an investor was willing to buy, and relying on labour market policy measures and unemployment benefits to cater for redundant workers, almost one in five workers benefited from labour market policy measures.[4] At first job creation via wage subsidies and vocational training/retraining schemes accounted for impressive numbers, but the figure dropped to 3 per cent of THA leavers in 1993 as the financial resources of the Federal Employment Office (BA) became gradually exhausted.

Increasingly large shares of THA leavers were taken into employment companies with different obligations relating to training, job creation, and regional or industrial restructuring to cope with labour market slack. Employment companies became a precondition of privatization as they took on increasing numbers of workers who had to be made redundant before privatization could take place. As employment companies offered training and job creation measures financed out of the BA budget, their expansion may explain why the relative importance of these measures fell over time. If we leave aside leavers of unknown and other status (less than 20 per cent), an ever-increasing share of former workers in THA firms became unemployed, up to 43 per cent in the spring of 1993.

Table 6.9. Expenditures on active labour market policy and on unemployment benefits/assistance, 1991-95 (DM billion)

Selected expenditures	1991	1992	1993	1994	1995
Individual and institutional promotion of vocational training and retraining	4 267	10 721	10 307	6 989	7 194
Job creation	3 076	7 803	8 586	6 812	7 294
Short-time working allowance	10 006	2 653	919	499	448
Early retirement	2 680	9 330	13 460	9 033	2 453
Unemployment benefits	7 810	11 809	12 868	12 663	12 507
Total expenditures of BA	29 875	46 032	50 615	41 647	38 284
Unemployment assistance paid out of the federal budget	271	1 489	3 658	5 057	7 576

Source: BA, 1995 budget figures.

Labour market policy attempted to cushion the effects of dismissals in THA firms and to stabilize employment in privatized firms by means of short-time working allowances. Table 6.8 looks at the extent of that scheme, showing that almost two-thirds of all short-time workers in eastern Germany were in THA firms and privatized (ex-THA) firms. On 1 April 1993 about 17 per cent of workers in THA firms were working reduced hours and about 10 per cent of those in privatized firms did so. Both groups received wage subsidies for short-time workers from the BA budget.

Table 6.9 sums up total expenditure by the BA on labour market policy measures in eastern Germany, although it is not possible to calculate the shares of spending related to THA firms and privatized firms. In 1993 more than 17 per cent of GDP in eastern Germany was spent by the BA on labour market policy measures. If we combine expenditures on early retirement, unemployment benefit and unemployment assistance, more than DM26 billion was paid to economically inactive people in 1993, which represents more than 10 per cent of GDP in eastern Germany. It has already been argued that the BA incurred larger annual expenditures than the THA because the employment consequences of privatization were largely transferred to the BA. In 1995, unemployment benefits and assistance accounted for DM20 billion while outlays on early retirement had declined to DM2.5 billion, which still means that 9 per cent of GDP was spent on passive purposes.

The enormous expenditures of the BA on labour market policies aimed at both active and inactive workers may explain why the tremendous decline in employment in THA firms — which resulted in just over 1 million workers transferred to new jobs in privatized firms and left almost 3 million at the mercy of slack labour markets — was implemented without large-scale unrest and social resistance.

6. Employment companies and counselling services

Labour market policies accompanying privatization in eastern Germany did not create new instruments but they did introduce some new measures and counselling services/ institutions. These were introduced as a kind of "bridge over troubled waters" of slack labour markets, until such time as self-sustained growth offered enough good jobs and real incomes that were up to the standard of living in western Germany.

Employment companies were established to employ and retrain redundant workers, namely those leaving THA firms to be sold after downsizing. They have implemented training and job creation measures, largely financed by the BA. Additional means have come from the THA firms (money, rooms, training staff and facilities, organizational help, management), from severance payments (on average DM5,000 per redundant worker), from public programmes financed out of federal, state and local budgets, and — sometimes — from the employment companies' own earnings. Aiming at the promotion of employment and structural development (*Gesellschaften zur Arbeitsförderung, Beschäftigung und Strukturentwicklung* — ABS companies), they have tried to cooperate at the regional level in order to formulate and implement industrial policies.

The THA and the BA agreed to establish employment companies only after very controversial discussions with the trade unions. The THA even joined some of them. Furthermore, some employment companies adjusted their activities in the light of regional planning and projects, training workers according to the needs of local firms and attempting to combine subsidized and market operations. There was a general consensus that employment companies were a necessary precondition for the reconstruction of the economy and the reorganization of industrial structures through training and job creation.

In 1991-92 there were 333 ABS companies operating, with more than 130,000 workers under contract, about one-tenth of all participants in labour market policy measures (Kaiser and Otto, 1993). Of these 130,000 workers about 40 per cent of participants worked in job creation schemes; 35 per cent stayed in short-time working schemes, some of these in fact do not work at all (zero hours — *Null Kurzarbeit*); almost 17 per cent were trained or retrained; 2 per cent received vocational education.

After leaving the employment companies, about one-third found a new job outside, one-quarter became unemployed, and one-tenth went to work in western Germany. One in 20 joined another job creation scheme, one in 25 retired early, and just under 1 per cent tried to survive as entrepreneurs. Starting your own business while under contract to an employment company was initially believed to be a good idea, but experience has shown that such businesses seldom operate successfully.

Parallel to the employment companies, a large variety of counselling services/ institutions were founded in order to provide information and promote investment and job creation (Fritzsche et al., 1993). Coordinating bodies were created at the state, regional and industry levels to support and advise employment and training companies. Teams, consultants, "round tables" and promotion agencies were established to shape and coordinate policies. Both public bodies and private institutes, such as chambers of commerce, have promoted technology centres and the setting up of new firms. Regional labour offices, operating on a tripartite basis, implement labour market policies. Unemployed people and other groups particularly affected by the employment crisis have organized their own associations. Trade unions and employers' organizations have started counselling and training efforts.

Consultants and coordinating bodies always tend to proliferate if much money is involved. In addition to the expenditures of the THA and the BA, about 5 per cent of western Germany's GDP (roughly DM150 billion) is transferred annually to the east. Nevertheless it is necessary to have good counselling agencies to implement the transformation of a system.

Some of the eastern states — Saxony, Mecklenburg-Vorpommern, Brandenburg and Berlin — tried to cooperate with the THA in order to reconstruct some of the "core firms" which remained under the THA. They either established special agencies (ATLAS in Saxony, ANKER in Mecklenburg-Vorpommern) or involved the state ministries responsible for economic and structural policies. There was some co-financing for three years of reconstruction for individual firms, but the THA made the final decisions. The states have not participated in supporting individual firms, but offer money out of European and federal funds for regional and social policies. The lack of policy formation and coordination, the absence of industrial policies, and the general need for counselling services are seen as the most important reasons for the industrial decline of eastern Germany. More state action has emerged in the past few years, the banking sector has been involved in privatization, and state funds have been created in order to deal with privatization failures. Finally, the THA had started to reconstruct firms completely before privatization.

7. Comparison between THA firms and privatized firms: Size, wages, productivity and investment

To obtain a deeper insight into the employment consequences of privatization, it is worthwhile to compare different aspects of THA firms and privatized firms: size of firms, wages, productivity and investment.

Table 6.10 reveals a very similar average size for THA and privatized firms: 166 and 162 workers per firm respectively in spring 1993. While the THA pointed out that 47 per cent of the total of 1,871 firms still to be transferred out of its responsibility had a workforce of 20 employees or fewer, it is interesting to note that only 1.5 per cent of the firms accounted for 47 per cent of all jobs to be privatized. If we define small and medium-sized firms as those with a workforce of up to 500 employees, about 95 per cent of all THA firms and privatized firms belong to that group. They employed 35 per cent of workers in THA firms in 1993 and just over 50 per cent of employees in privatized firms in 1993 and 1995. Privatization thus brought about a decisive downsizing of firms. The THA's difficulties in privatizing firms were mainly due to the very large size of their workforce. The THA published a list of the "big 30", giving the name, industry and workforce of the firms; these are seen as the core industrial sectors.

The size distribution of privatized firms seems to have remained quite stable over 1993-95. In 1995 the average size of fully privatized firms was still 160 workers. Wages in the German Democratic Republic were fairly low and the industrial wage structure was flat. Soon after unification on 3 October 1990, the western system of wage-setting through collective bargaining was introduced in eastern Germany, and employers' organizations and unions in the different industries started negotiations on a decentralized basis. They agreed to try to close the huge wage gap between east and west by the end of 1994, thus stressing the fact that eastern Germany was not to be a low-wage country in the future. Investors were told to use the most recent technologies; workers were offered incentives to

Table 6.10. Size of THA firms and privatized firms, spring 1993 and autumn 1995

Employment size	THA firms (31 May 1993)			Privatized firms (1 April 1993)			Privatized firms (1 October 1995)	
	Firms (%)	Workers (%)	Workers per firm	Firms (%)	Workers (%)	Workers per firm	Firms (%)	Workers (%)
1-20	46.6	1.3	5.9	17.9	1.3	11.3	20.1	1.4
21-50	16.8	3.5	34.1	26.7	5.4	32.5	26.3	5.4
51-100	12.1	5.4	73.7	21.1	9.3	71.7	20.7	9.2
101-250	13.5	12.9	158.5	20.8	19.8	154.7	20.8	19.2
251-500	5.7	11.8	343.4	7.2	14.8	332.3	7.1	15.1
501-1 000	2.7	10.8	657.0	3.6	15.5	695.1	3.2	14.2
1 001-1 500	1.0	7.4	1 204.2	1.3	9.6	1 199.7	1.1	8.2
+1 500	1.5	46.9	5 026.6	1.3	24.3	2 939.4	1.6	27.5
Total	100.0	100.0	166.0	100.0	100.0	162.1	100.0	100.0
Number	1 871	310 536		2 385	386 517		2 249	361 700

Source: THA survey of 2,385 privatized firms in 1993, and of 2,249 firms in 1995.

Table 6.11. Eastern wages as a percentage of western wages, 1991-95, in privatized firms

Year September	Gross monthly wages in manufacturing industries		All industries	
	Wages DM	Index western Germany = 100[1]	Wages DM	Increase per cent
1991	1 818	43	1 991	–
1992	2 435	54	2 679	35
1993	2 826	60	3 073	15
1994	3 296	68	3 407	11
1995	3 636	72	3 655	7

[1] Companies employing 20 and more workers. Social security contributions and other non-wage labour costs are excluded.

Source: Survey of privatized firms.

stay in their region to reconstruct firms. Both the State and the social security system had reasons to expect good revenues from productive workplaces.

During the four years between 1991 and 1995, the average wage in privatized firms almost doubled to DM3,626 per month in 1995, which is about 72 per cent of western wages. Wages in manufacturing have been lower than in the whole economy. Wage differentials have increased. The difference between the highest and lowest wages was DM1,300 by October 1992. In 1995 the gap increased to almost DM2,200. Male wages were around DM3,810, DM500 above female wages. Firms up to 50 workers paid DM650 per month less than medium-sized and bigger firms. Thus, all important indicators of wage differentials have adjusted to the west.

The speed of adjustment may be seen from the official figures for gross monthly wages/salaries in 1991 and 1995 (table 6.11). In 1995 wages paid in the east were about 72 per cent of western gross wages. However, most recent collective bargaining agreements have slowed down the speed of adjustment. Due to gaps in competitiveness and productivity, further adjustment of wages and salaries will take more time than had been expected during the unification years.

Wages in THA firms have increased, and the combination of collective bargaining with privatization has led to large wage differentials between industries. Table 6.12 shows the level and structure of wages in March 1993 and table 6.13 gives more details by industry. Gross monthly wages/salaries increased by 86 per cent in two years. In March 1993 male workers' salaries were DM450 per month higher than female wages in THA firms, while in privatized firms men got over DM500 more than women. Firms employing more than 80 per cent female workers pay only 72 per cent of average wages in THA firms, and only 74 per cent in privatized ones.

Wage increases varied between industries, from 41 per cent in stone, glass and ceramic industries to 143 per cent in the very low-paying leather and shoe industries, indicating large differentials in pay rises during 1991-93. Wages for women were below average in all industries. In 14 out of 24 industries, wages in privatized firms were lower than the wages in comparable THA firms. It was not possible to control for employment structures,

Table 6.12. Wages and salaries in THA firms and privatized firms

	THA firms		Privatized firms	
	DM	Index (March 1993 = 100)	DM	Index (March 1993 = 100)
March 1991	1 530	53.8	n.a.	n.a.
September 1991	2 083	73.2	1 991	70.8
March 1992	2 237	78.6	2 299	81.8
September 1992	2 593	91.1	2 679	95.3
March 1993	2 845	100.0	2 811	100.0
Selected industries:				
Agriculture	2 373	83.4	2 164	77.0
Energy, water	3 517	123.6	3 306	117.6
Mining	3 344	117.5	3 348	119.1
Manufacturing	2 562	90.0	2 547	90.6
Construction	3 538	124.4	3 202	113.9
Female share in workforce:				
Less than 20%	2 659	93.5	2 880	102.5
More than 20%	2 040	71.7	2 073	73.7

Source: Survey of firms (see Appendix).

qualification levels, short-timers and firm size. Even within single industries, wage differentials between firms were high and increasing. In September 1992, for example, THA construction firms paid workers DM3,311 gross per month on average, with a dispersion of DM365. The lowest-paying firms offered DM2,106, while the highest-paying gave DM4,170. Privatized construction firms paid DM3,154 gross per month on average, with a dispersion of DM359. The lowest wage was DM1,500, the highest wage DM4,562. In 16 out of 24 industries the lowest wages in privatized firms were below those in THA firms. The highest wages in privatized firms were higher than those paid in THA firms only in six industries. While wage increases in privatized firms were higher than in THA firms in all industries in 1992, there was a slowdown in this wage dynamic during 1993/94. Mainly owing to collective bargaining, comparable wage increases began to prevail in THA firms and in privatized firms.

Privatization has had a significant impact on the productivity of firms. Because it was not possible to ask for production figures in the surveys, sales per worker are used as a proxy for productivity. Table 6.14 again compares the two groups of firms and indicates great but declining differences in productivity between eastern and western Germany.

Privatized firms expected DM143,000 sales per worker in 1993, a little over half the figure for western Germany, but well above that for THA companies. Although there are some indications of progress towards more stable productivity gains, it should not be forgotten that both THA firms and privatized firms reduced their workforce during 1991-93, which was to some extent responsible for productivity gains. In 1995 sales per worker climbed to DM235,000, or 83 per cent of western manufacturing industries. The annual increase in productivity is well above 20 per cent.

Workforce reductions apart, the most important sources of productivity gains were innovations both in products and in production processes, investments and firm-specific training measures. Modernization of capital equipment, adequate supplies of materials, smaller production units and a more efficient organization of production also contributed to increased productivity. Whereas many old firms produced a considerable range of goods and services, the privatized firms tend to concentrate their production on a very limited range.

Table 6.13. Monthly gross wages/salary per full-time worker in THA firms, March 1993

Industry	Level DM	Change from previous year (%)	Index (April 1991 = 100)	Female wages as % of level	THA wages as % of wages in privatized firms
Agriculture	2 373	26.6	173.8	92.5	109.7
Energy, water	3 517	21.3	171.7	88.7	106.4
Mining	3 344	37.4	195.7	94.1	99.9
Chemicals	2 817	19.8	173.2	91.7	98.3
Synthetics	2 444	20.9	184.6	91.9	104.0
Stone, glass, ceramics	2 497	27.4	141.1	87.5	95.7
Iron, non-ferrous metals	2 603	23.0	181.3	93.4	107.6
Steel, light metals	2 563	19.4	171.1	97.2	99.9
Machinery	2 626	24.7	190.2	91.7	102.3
Vehicles, auto industries	2 376	17.6	174.6	94.9	96.0
Electrical, electronic	2 468	18.5	188.4	88.7	97.8
Precision machinery, optics	2 528	22.2	188.8	93.5	108.0
Metal goods, sport, toys	2 167	15.0	201.6	88.1	94.3
Wood	2 489	25.5	176.9	84.9	107.7
Paper, printing	2 619	15.6	187.2	88.4	95.8
Leather, shoes	2 096	15.7	243.4	94.5	110.3
Clothing, textiles	2 081	26.2	201.5	93.0	102.2
Food, drink	2 436	28.5	181.8	85.0	101.9
Construction	3 538	24.2	161.8	90.2	110.5
Other building industries	2 650	16.2	146.5	93.9	93.4
Trade (wholesale, retail)	2 776	25.8	148.9	86.3	104.1
Transport and communications	3 178	39.0	186.7	71.5	109.4
Services	2 661	21.1	160.6	89.7	95.3
Unknown	3 048	28.1	202.5	83.4	109.1
Total	2 845	27.2	185.9	89.0	101.2

Source: Survey of firms (see Appendix).

Table 6.14. Sales per worker in manufacturing industries, 1991-94 (DM 000s)

Industry	THA firms			Privatized firms					Western Germany		
	1991	1992	1993	1991	1992	1993	1994	1995	1991	1993	1994
Basic products	61	94	143	86	131	149	184	299	329	329	364
Investment goods	46	82	114	81	97	126	179	195	206	203	201
Consumer goods	27	53	78	63	81	97	118	144	177	181	189
Food and drink	120	82	189	206	267	289	355	492	400	403	415
Manufacturing	49	82	118	94	123	143	185	235	237	237	2 541

[1] The figure for 1995 is 283.

Source: Surveys of firms (see Appendix).

Investment is crucial for economic reconstruction, although the primary impact on employment differs according to individual firms' capacity for rationalization. The level of investment in THA firms was well below that in privatized firms (see table 6.15). In 1992 one-third of all THA firms did not invest at all, and the majority of firms invested only DM3.1 million per firm, that is DM20,000 per worker, mostly to repair machinery, to replace those machines most urgently in need of replacement, and to improve the general working environment. Seen against the needs of modern production, the level of investment in THA firms was too low and its structure did not favour reconstruction. In contrast, investment in privatized firms expanded very rapidly to remarkable levels per firm/worker/unit of sales. If, however, we compare actual investment to the DM150 billion worth of investment promised in the near future by privatized firms at the beginning of 1993, we see that actual investment fell far below both promises and medium-term needs. It is also worth noting that more than two-thirds of all investment orders went to manufacturers in western Germany.

Table 6.15. Investments in THA firms and privatized firms, 1992-93 (DM billion)

Industry	THA firms		Privatized firms		Private investments in eastern Germany
	1992	1993	1992	1993	1993
Agriculture	n.a.	0.0	n.a.	0.1	2.0
Manufacturing	n.a.	4.9	n.a.	26.6	46.4
Wholesale and retail trade	n.a.	0.2	n.a.	2.0	6.5
Transport and communications	n.a.	0.3	n.a.	2.7	24.0
Total	n.a.	5.5	n.a.	35.4	113.2
Investment per firm (DM m)	3.1	3.9	4.2	5.6	n.a.
Investment per worker (DM 000)	20.0	19.0	28.0	38.0	n.a.
Investment per unit of sales (%)	12.0	16.0	19.0	22.0	n.a.

Sources: See Appendix; total private investments, IFO Institute.

Table 6.16 shows the development of investment in privatized firms in the manufacturing industries in comparison to eastern and western Germany's investments total. After an investment maximum of DM14.1 billion (i.e. 75 per cent of all eastern Germany's investments in manufacturing) was reached in 1993, both the level and the share of investments fell in privatized firms. Investments per worker remained stable during 1992-95 and showed more than double the ratio observed in the west. Investments are heavily subsidized and concentrated on four industries: energy/water, 38 per cent; chemicals, 9 per cent; transport/communication, 8 per cent; and mining, 7 per cent. While west German firms invested 5 per cent of their turnover/sales, privatized firms spent 11 per cent on investments. Nevertheless, much remains to be done in order to keep up with western Germany.

Table 6.16. Investments in privatized firms and in eastern Germany, manufacturing industries, 1991-95 (DM billion)

Year	Investments			Investments per worker	
	Privatized firms	Eastern Germany	Share of privatized firms (%)	Privatized firms (DM 000)	Western Germany (DM 000)
1991	4.8	12.9	37	18	14
1992	12.5	17.5	71	29	13
1993	14.1	18.8	75	31	11
1994	11.5	18.8	61	28	11
1995	11.0	20.0	55	29	13

Source: Surveys in privatized firms and *ifo-Schnelldienst*, No. 2411995, pp. 3 and 6.

Taking all economic indicators together, the privatized firms performed quite well over time in terms of wages, sales and investment. Firms privatized in 1990/91 performed better than those privatized later. In recent years all firms have suffered from the recession in western Germany and the fight for jobs between east and west, from the loss of markets in Central and Eastern Europe, from losses in total employment and purchasing power, and from shortcomings in the way the reconstruction of Germany has been tackled.

8. Deindustrialization in eastern Germany

Total employment in the German Democratic Republic in 1989/90 was 9.8 million. This figure fell below 6.2 million on average in 1993, including 250,000 in job creation programmes and a further 200,000 in short-time working schemes. The workforce (those who pay social security contributions) was down to 5.3 million by the end of March 1993. Employment in agriculture, manufacturing, transport/communications and public services was still declining, while construction, trade, finance and private services showed some increases in the number of jobs. Increasing numbers of young people are unable to get an apprenticeship training place. Manufacturing production was down to 59 per cent by May 1993 (index: second half 1990 = 100), and manufacturing employment was down to one-quarter of the late 1989 level (756,000 workers in April 1993). Industrial production contributes just 15 per cent to GDP, half the figure achieved in western Germany. Sales of industrial products per 1 million inhabitants were only one-fifth of the western figure. Since 1994-95, total employment grew slowly, mainly due to transfers, subsidies and active labour market policies.

Small and medium-sized firms in eastern Germany remain economically weak; they invest too little and do not make sufficient use of the huge range of public subsidies and promotion programmes available. Nor do they offer enough training places. The structure of new enterprises does not favour reindustrialization; the rate of new firms starting up is declining; the rate of closedowns is increasing. Only one-third of training and retraining is aimed at industrial occupations. Trade unions are losing members, and they are afraid of having more unemployed than employed members. Firms are leaving employers' organizations, and new firms are not joining them. Massive investment subsidies have not succeeded in stabilizing the manufacturing sector so far. Industrial research and development has almost ceased. Privatized firms in the mid-1990s retained just one-quarter of the jobs offered by THA firms in 1990, and employment continued to decline after firms were privatized. It is hard to believe that manufacturing production and/or employment will ever again reach the levels formerly prevailing in the German Democratic Republic.

Nevertheless, privatized firms number about 1 million employees, and sales, investments, productivity and unit labour costs are all improving steadily. Almost half of all privatizations transferred only parts of firms — the more successful parts — to the new owners. But there was no concept of reindustrialization: the THA and the BA spent almost one-third of eastern GDP, but they had no legal basis for pursuing industrial and regional policies. Their instruments, budgets and personnel were not suited to such activities. The states are responsible for structural policies, but they have neither the means nor the ideas needed to formulate and implement them. The THA ceased privatization operations in 1994, and left the public budget with a total debt of DM270 billion.

9. Conclusions

Rapid privatization by the THA transferred 1 million out of 4 million jobs into the private sector. THA official indicators for jobs and investments promised in the sales contracts, and for gross revenues, were quite impressive. But the labour market effects have been severe: 3 million workers had to leave THA companies, mainly for unemployment, retirement or participation in active labour market policy measures, including employment companies.

Spending more than DM200 billion from 1991 to 1995, the Federal Employment Office has faced increasing expenditures to deal with the employment consequences of THA activities. THA expenditures were DM166 billion between 1991 and 1995, but only a small part of that money was spent on reconstructing firms. The THA's and BA's expenditure combined made up almost one-third of GDP in eastern Germany, but neither institution had any explicit targets relating to the reconstruction of the country or regional/industrial policies. An efficient, high-budget labour market policy is nevertheless a precondition for rapid privatization. The same is true of employment companies, which take over redundant workers from firms that are downsizing in order to make them sufficiently attractive for private investors to buy, even at negative prices.

The economic performance of privatized firms in terms of sales, investment, productivity and wages was far better than that of THA firms. Wage differentials between firms, between industrial sectors and in the whole economy increased in the process of privatization, mainly owing to collective bargaining.

Instead of reconstructing firms before privatization, the THA strategy contributed to a rapid deindustrialization in all industrial sectors and in almost all regions. The THA argued that as a public institution it had no responsibility for regional and industrial policies, which are the responsibility of the five new states. Reconstruction and reindustrialization may cost more than DM1,000 billion in the end.

Given the low number of jobs offered by the privatized firms, the huge deficits left by the THA at the end of its operations, and rapid deindustrialization, there are some doubts whether the German model of privatization should be exported to the other countries of Central and Eastern Europe. Even the THA President Breuel does not recommend this solution.

The THA philosophy of rapid *economic* privatization within four and a half years, i.e. mid-1990 until 1994, up to a debt limit of DM270 billion, aimed at an almost complete withdrawal of state agencies and central planning from the core industries and state-owned companies. A federal headquarters and 15 regional agencies brought about the fastest privatization in the world. Policy-makers hoped to restructure the productive capacity of eastern Germany by private ownership and investments, new products and markets, self-sustained growth, rising real wages and comparable standards of living that prevail in the west. Neither approaches of *political* privatization, i.e. providing all citizens with shares or vouchers of the state enterprises regardless of their economic future, their modernization and their management, nor *fiscal* privatization, i.e. selling firms to anybody who pays the highest price in order to increase public revenues regardless of economic effects, were pursued in eastern Germany.

By the end of 1994 the THA ceased to exist. The follow-up institution is the *Bundesanstalt für Vereinigungsbedingte Sonderaufgaben* (BVS), which spent DM17 to 18 billion in 1995 compared to revenues of DM13 to 14 billion, pushing the annual deficit to DM4.2 billion. By the end of 1994 the new owners of ex-THA-companies still had to pay DM4.5 billion.

The official THA success story is quite impressive (*Jahreswirtschaftsbericht* 1995):

— The reorganization of THA companies by splitting them up, MBOs, mergers and so on brought about a total portfolio of 12,356 firms. More than half of them, 6,546, have been completely privatized. In addition, more than 7,600 parts of firms and 25,030 small-scale units (retail trades, restaurants and the like) have been sold to private owners. 1,588 firms have been reprivatized and 2,670 parts of firms were given back to their former owners. Local public authorities took over 265 companies. 3,712 firms were closed down because of bankruptcy. Just 192 firms remained at the end of 1994 and 65 were still for sale.

— The new owners promised a total of DM207 billion for investments between mid-1990 and the near future compared to annual investments of DM53 billion in physical capital and DM103 billion in construction in 1994 (total private and public investment, constant 1991 prices). The THA reported that in 1993 investment was 23 per cent higher than promised. There were large subsidies to private investments, of up to 5 per cent.

—   The new owners promised a total of 1.5 million jobs out of a yearly average of 6.3 million jobs in 1994, or more than 4 million jobs which existed in 1989-90 in all companies which came under THA supervision in spring 1990. The THA reported for 1993 that on average 15 per cent more jobs than promised were filled in that year. 7,300 firms altogether employed 30 per cent more workers/employees than had been fixed in the contracts; 1,500 firms did not fulfil their contracts, but most of them did not have to pay the fines agreed upon. At the beginning of privatization no jobs were promised to be kept; later on, some firms were easily able to employ more staff than the low levels promised. It is difficult to fix the period jobs had to be kept. Some have promises already expired, some only hold good for future years or under favourable economic conditions. While *per saldo* of all completely or partly privatized firms' jobs promises were close to reality, one out of four jobs promised were to be created in agricultural or industrial areas sold to private owners. Even if we believe in half of the number of jobs promised, the question remains why so few jobs were secured by sales contracts.

The vast majority of firms was sold to big companies in the west, some to foreigners; just 6-7 per cent of the new owners stem from eastern Germany. Although the estimates of total THA assets, real estate, etc., declined from several hundred billion DM down to a total loss of DM270 billion, domestic buyers had too little capital or credit to buy firms and property from the THA. Leading west German and foreign firms took over almost everything of economic worth. Until November 1994, just 840 enterprises have been sold to foreigners who paid DM6.2 billion and promised to invest DM19.8 billion, i.e. 11 per cent of all investments, in order to create or secure 148,000 jobs.

Deindustrialization in the east and "transition by transfers" from the west lead to the effect that since unification final demand in east Germany exceeds domestic production by 40 to 50 per cent. Despite rapid economic growth, around 9 per cent per year, a self-sustained development is still to be achieved: the level of GDR production will not be reached again during 1996, while the level of employment may never again be close to 9.7 million. Although the share of industrial production in total GNP is lower than in post-industrial societies, the remaining structure of production is far away from competitive structures of the future. R & D has been lost to a great extent; training and retraining in private firms and with private money is very small.

The record of the THA on privatization is quite impressive, but the effects on restructuring are judged controversial (Priewe, 1993; Rider, 1994). THA operations were very expensive and left huge deficits. Large parts of BA expenditure, around DM40 billion, have their origin in THA operations. The German model of broad consensus between interest groups once again operated successfully: the supervisory board of the THA consisted of all *Ministerpräsidenten* of the new states, high-ranking employers and union leaders, two representatives from federal ministries and one from the central bank.

The THA operation is a unique solution to privatization. Unification of the two German states, the financial, legal, institutional and social framework of the west, and the hard currency, the huge net transfers[5] and political support show that the THA model may not be an ideal approach for other Central and Eastern European countries in transition (Balasubramanyam 1994).

Appendix: Database

Most data stem from surveys of all THA firms and all privatized (ex-THA) firms carried out twice a year since 1991 by a panel on firms in eastern Germany. The following table shows the representativeness of the surveys, which were all carried out by the Institute for Social, Economic and Structural Analysis (SOESTRA, Berlin) at the request of the Institute for Employment Research (IAB). Surveys were continued twice in 1994, and the last survey was taken in October 1995. Out of 8,532 completely privatized firms 2,249 firms (26.4 per cent) answered. They employed 362,000 workers, 38.1 per cent of all workers in privatized firms.

Table 6.17. Representativeness of surveys carried out by the Institute for Social, Economic and Structural Analysis (SOESTRA), 1991-93

Survey date	Contacted		Answers of firms		Usable answers			
	Firms	Employment	No.	%	Firms		Employment	
	No.	000s			No.	%	000s	%
THA firms								
4.91	8 468	2 653	5 657	67	5 269	62	2 025	76
10.91	8 047	2 000	5 192	65	4 894	61	1 384	69
4.92	6 688	1 235	n.a.	n.a.	3 838	57	783	63
10.92	5 187	626	3 473	67	3 044	59	474	76
4.93	3 390	382	n.a.	n.a.	2 290	68	317	83
10.93	2 808	251	n.a.	n.a.	1 855	66	205	82
Privatized firms								
10.91	2 039	285	1 003	49	909	45	191	67
4.92	4 100	553	n.a.	n.a.	1 595	39	246	44
10.92	5 820	885	2 406	41	2 114	36	346	39
4.93	6 988	1 047	2 473	35	2 385	34	387	37
10.93	7 603	999	2 515	33	2 515	33	351	35

n.a. = Figures not available.

Source: The reports are published by the IAB: *Beiträge zur Arbeitsmarkt- und Berufsforschung* in 1991-93, Vols. 152, 160, Nos. 1-4.

References

Balasubramanyam, V. N. 1994. "The Treuhandanstalt, FDI and employment in Germany", in *International Journal of Manpower*, Vol. 15, No. 6, pp. 72-84.

Carlin, W.; Mayer, C. 1992. "Enterprise restructuring", in *Economic Policy*, Oct., pp. 311-352.

Fritzsche, H.; Gross, J.; Voelkel, B. 1993. *Counselling in the area of employment promotion — State-of-the-art and preliminary evaluations.* IAB-Workshop Report, No. 12, 1 July 1993.

Kaiser, M.; Otto, M. 1993. What job creation schemes have done; *Results of an empirical analysis of institutional frameworks so far.* IAB-Workshop Report, No. 13, 21 July 1993.

Priewe, J. 1994. "The price of rapid privatization — A preliminary concluding balance sheet for the Treuhandanstalt", in *Employment Observatory East Germany*, No. 11, May, pp. 3-6.

Rider, C. 1994. "Privatization in the transition economies: A critique", in *Journal of Post-Keynesian Economies*, Vol. 16, No. 4, summer, pp. 589-603.

Notes

[1] By May 1993, foreign investors had bought 657 firms (or parts of firms), paying DM4.6 billion. They guaranteed 132,200 jobs and promised to invest DM18 billion, which is 10 per cent of all investment promised by all new owners over the period 1990-94.

[2] The data stem from internal THA sources; more recent figures are not available.

[3] On survey method, database and representativeness, see Appendix.

[4] By and large no new instruments were introduced by policy-makers, but those already existing in western Germany were adapted to the new problems arising from the process of transition. In addition to migration to the west and commuters working in the west, four major measures dealt with the rapid decline in employment:

(a)   Support for workers taking early retirement at 57 years until regular pension schemes step in.

(b)   Public job creation schemes (ABM) offering wage-cost subsidies of differing extents, project costs, large-scale measures (Mega-ABM) and recently a wage-cost subsidy of DM15,200 per annum per worker. In general the subsidies offered by job creation schemes have decreased over time.

(c)   Short-time working allowances down to zero hours worked in order to finance the wages of redundant but so far not dismissed workers.

(d)   Training and retraining measures offering wage substitutes to workers, such as costs of full-time or part-time training courses. The possibility of combining "zero hours" short-time working schemes with training was not successful because the incentives for participation were too low.

Most of these measures were financed under the Labour Promotion Act (AFG), which produced large deficits in the east. They were financed by surpluses from the contributions of workers and firms in western Germany and by public deficits of the Federal Government.

[5] Transfers 1991-95 in DM billion.

	1991	1992	1993	1994	1995
Gross transfers	75	88	114	128	151
Net transfers	42	51	75	86	106

Source: *Bundestagdrs.* 13/160, 30.12.1994, p. 26.

7. Privatization and employment in the Czech Republic

Liba Paukert*

1. Introduction

Prior to 1989, there were few private enterprises in Czechoslovakia. State and cooperative property were the only ownership forms recognized by the constitution. Nationalization in the late 1940s and early 1950s had left less room for private enterprise than in Hungary, Poland or the former German Democratic Republic. The "velvet revolution" of November 1989 brought a democratic government to power and President "Havel to the Castle", as chanted the millions of demonstrators filling the streets of Prague. The velvet revolution gave the signal for far-reaching changes, both political and economic. The separation of Czechoslovakia into two independent states, the Czech Republic and Slovakia, on 1 January 1993, had a traumatic effect on large sections of the population in both parts of the country, as well as a negative impact on economic growth. At the time it occurred, however, the separation could no longer hold back the sweeping wave of economic reform, particularly on the Czech side of the new border.

In the period 1990-94, many small and medium-sized private enterprises were successfully developed. The number of private entrepreneurs and small business owners increased from an estimated 70,000 in mid-1989 to about 600,000 in mid-1994 in the Czech Republic alone.[1] The number of companies in Czechoslovakia — limited liability, joint stock and public limited companies, etc. — went up rapidly during 1991 and 1992. In the Czech Republic the number is estimated to have doubled between January 1993 and July 1994. At the same time, the number of state enterprises declined. The pace of decline was relatively moderate at the beginning of the reform process, but it gathered momentum as the so-called large-scale privatization started to show its effects. By now, most assets are in private hands.

This chapter first looks at the progress of privatization and the corresponding shifts of labour from the public to the private sector, setting these changes against the background of a general decline in output and employment. It then examines the impact of the different methods of privatization on employment restructuring. It presents various scenarios of enterprise privatization and illustrates the ways in which workers have been affected by them and have reacted to them.

*International Labour Office.

2. The restructuring of employment

2.1 Trends in output and employment

During the first four years of transition, GDP declined by 21.1 per cent. Table 7.1 shows that GDP had already started to decline in 1990, although this was only a year of preparation for reform, which was launched "in earnest" on 1 January 1991. During 1991, the first year of intensive reform, when most of the reform measures were introduced, GDP fell by 14.2 per cent. In 1992, it fell again by 6.6 per cent. In 1993, many commentators expected a reversal of this trend, but it failed to materialize. A major reason for this was the separation of Czechoslovakia into two independent states on 1 January 1993. Domestic demand increased considerably in the Czech Republic in 1993, but exports to Slovakia declined by almost one-third. In 1994, an increase in GDP was registered for the first time since the start of the reform process. In the first half of 1994, GDP increased by 2.2 per cent. Official forecasts put the growth rate for the whole year at 2.5 per cent.[2] The upturn in the first half of 1994 was due to growth in services and construction; output in construction increased by as much as 6.7 per cent. Industrial output increased by 2 per cent in the first eight months of the year, but agriculture more or less stagnated (CSO, 1994, No. 9).

The sizeable decline in GDP between 1989 and 1993 was due, to a large extent, to an abrupt fall in industrial production. The decline in industrial production during the initial phase of transition was a general phenomenon in the countries of the region. It was largely related to the disintegration of the CMEA and the collapse of intra-regional trade. The decrease in trade between the Czech Republic and Slovakia after the split of Czechoslovakia in 1993 further aggravated the decline. In the Czech Republic, mining was particularly hard

Table 7.1. Main economic indicators, annual rates of change, Czech Republic, 1990-94

Indicator	1990	1991	1992	1993	1994
GDP	−1.2	−14.2	−6.6	−0.3	2.5 (P)
Industrial output[1]	−3.4	−16.6	−10.6	−5.3	2.0[2]
Employment A	−1.0	−5.5	−2.6	−1.5	−5.0 (P)[3]
Employment B	−4.8	−3.1	−3.7	−0.5	−
Total labour productivity	−0.2	−9.2	−4.1	1.2	7.6 (P)[3]
Industrial employment	−4.2	−3.8	−7.7	−4.9	−
Industrial labour productivity	0.8	−13.3	−3.1	−0.4	−

[1] All enterprises. [2] January-August 1994. [3] January-June 1994.

Employment A: calculated from annual averages; includes second job holders; excludes workers on maternity and child-care leave.

Employment B: calculated from end of year data; one or main job holders; includes workers on maternity and child-care leave.

P = Provisional.

Source: Czech Statistical Office (CSO); *Statistical Yearbook of the Czech Republic, 1994*; *Monthly Statistics of the Czech Republic, 1994*, No. 11. Prague. 1994.

hit by the transition process, although it had already started to decline in 1989. Manufacturing output began to fall in 1990. The decline affected all branches of manufacturing without exception, but to different degrees. Basic metals and heavy engineering were particularly badly hit, whereas in some branches of light industry, such as glass and ceramics, a timid upturn had already started in 1992. The ultimate result was a relative weakening of heavy industry and strengthening of light industry. The increase in total industrial production in the first part of 1994, shown in table 7.1, was due entirely to growth in light industry, whereas most heavy industry continued to decline.[3]

Since the start of the transition process, almost half of male workers and over 40 per cent of female workers have changed their job at least once.[4] The final effect of this vast reshuffling was a far-reaching transformation of the structure of employment. The change in the distribution of employment by form of ownership is illustrated in table 7.2. The share of the cooperative sector decreased but its nature changed. Until 1989 cooperatives were usually assimilated with the state sector to form one large public sector, since they had a similar system of decision-making and management, but in 1993 the new Labour Force Sample Survey began to equate employment in the cooperative sector with self-employment. On the basis of this change of methodology, it may be concluded that the share of private sector employment grew from about 1 per cent in 1989 to 60 per cent four years later.

Table 7.2. Structure of employment by sector of ownership, 1989-93 [1] (per cent)

Sector	1989	1990	1991	1992	1993
State	84.3	79.6	70.5	60.2	40.2
Cooperative	12.9	12.3	9.6	7.5	5.7
Private[2]	1.3	7.0	19.1	31.4	53.5
Ownership of public associations	1.5	1.1	0.8	0.9	0.6
Total	100.0	100.0	100.0	100.0	100.0

[1] End-of-year data. [2] Including the mixed sector with joint public and private ownership.

Source: CSO, data communicated to the ILO.

The rapidity of the shift of labour from the public to the private sector is illustrated further in table 7.3. It can be seen from the data presented in the table that state sector employment declined by 58.1 per cent between 1989 and 1993, an average of 20 per cent a year. At the same time, private (including mixed) sector employment increased 37-fold. Over the four-year period, there was a net loss of employment in the state sector of 2,662,000 and a net gain in the private sector of 2,487,000. As a result the private sector had a larger share in employment than the public sector — a position that was accentuated by the loss of employment in the cooperative sector and in public associations. Total employment declined by 656,000 (12 per cent). About one-third of this decline was accounted for by the growth of unemployment, which at the end of 1993 represented 206,000 (ILO definition), corresponding to an unemployment rate of 3.9 per cent. The remainder can be explained, in part, by the decline in secondary occupations, as the data in table 7.3 include second job holders. The most significant factor contributing to the decline was, however, a fall in labour force participation, which was about twice as great as the increase in

Table 7.3. Employment level by sector of ownership, 1989-93[1] (000s)

Sector	1989			1990			1991			1992			1993		
	Total	Female	% F	Total	Female	% F	Total	Female	% F	Total	Female	% F	Total	Female	% F
State sector[2]	4 581	2 111	46.1	4 289	1 988	46.4	3 499	1 604	45.8	2 870	1 387	48.3	1 919	987	51.4
Cooperative sector	703	328	46.7	662	305	46.1	470	216	46.0	357	173	48.5	273	135	49.5
Private sector	69	13	18.8	376	62	16.5	917	323	35.2	1 483	532	35.9	2 250	858	38.1
Mixed sector[3]	—	—		—	—		17	5	29.4	15	6	40.0	306	125	40.8
Ownership of public associations and organizations	80	38	47.5	60	29	48.3	36	18	50.0	41	23	56.1	29	14	48.3
Total	5 433	2 490	45.8	5 387	2 384	44.3	4 889	2 166	44.3	4 766	2 116	44.4	4 777	2 119	44.4

[1] End-of-year data; includes second job holders. [2] Includes local government ownership. [3] Joint public and private ownership; category not applicable before 1991.

Source: Federal/Czech Statistical Office, Prague, published statistical series and direct communications to the ILO.

unemployment. Thus, the growth of private sector employment, while appearing extremely rapid (starting from a low base), was nevertheless insufficient to absorb the labour made redundant in the public sector by the privatization process. This did not lead to the dramatic growth in unemployment predicted by a number of commentators at the start of the reform, but instead resulted in a significant reduction in the labour force, amounting to about 8 per cent.

A notable development revealed in table 7.3 concerns gender differences in the shifts of labour from the public to the private sector. Male labour has moved to the private sector much more rapidly than female labour. At the end of 1993, 59 per cent of male workers were employed in the private sector, compared to only 46 per cent of female workers. Women have tended to remain in the declining state sector. To what extent this is due to a lack of initiative and drive, to gender-biased recruitment in the private sector, or to the occupational and skill profile of the female workforce, is a matter of debate. The largest gender gap — and the highest degree of male over-representation in private sector employment — can be found in the first years of reform, when real personal initiative was needed to find a private sector job and when considerable risks were involved in launching a private business. Once the stage is reached when most of the economy is privatized, the share of women in private sector employment will automatically increase. But women's concentration in the public sector is likely to continue, as women represent the large majority of employees in budget-financed activities which will remain in government hands, namely education, social services, public administration, etc.

Between 1989 and 1993, total employment declined by 10 per cent, when annual average data on employment are used, and by about 12 per cent when end-of-year data are used. Employment trends differed widely according to economic sector, as shown in table 7.4. These vast differences provide additional evidence of the large amount of restructuring achieved during the four years of reform. The total decline in industrial employment was 19 per cent but, owing to the large size of the industrial sector, the number of jobs lost in industry was much greater than the number lost in agriculture. The average annual rate of decrease in industrial employment was 5.2 per cent. In industrial enterprises with more than 25 workers the rate of decrease was much faster, declining by about 30 per cent, as against 19 per cent in all industrial enterprises between 1989 and 1993. Employment thus increased in enterprises with less than 25 workers, including newly created small industrial

Table 7.4. Annual percentage change in employment by economic sector, 1990-93 [1]

Sector	1990	1991	1992	1993	1989-93
Agriculture[2]	0.3	−19.6	−16.2	−22.1	−47.4
Industry[3]	−4.2	−3.8	−7.7	4.9	−19.1
Construction	2.8	0.4	1.0	11.0	15.6
Services	1.0	−4.1	4.4	2.7	4.0
Total	0.9	−5.5	−2.6	−1.5	−10.2

[1] Based on annual average data, including second job holders and excluding workers on maternity and child care leave. [2] Agriculture, forestry, hunting and fishing. [3] Mining and quarrying, manufacturing and public utilities. All enterprises.

Sources: CSO Statistical Yearbook of the Czech Republic, 1994; data communicated by the CSO.

establishments and workshops, mostly belonging to the private sector. However, precise information on employment trends in small private industrial establishments is not available.

The overall declining trend of industrial employment covers a number of opposite tendencies. For example, many new private enterprises experienced setbacks, and their relatively high rate of failure resulted in frequent employment cuts. Some state enterprises, on the other hand, did sufficiently well to hire extra labour, particularly those that were able to work for the export market,[5] as illustrated in table 7.5.

Table 7.4 also reveals that employment in construction continued to grow throughout the transition period. Construction was thus the only sector of the economy where employment did not decline under the impact of reform. And if members of farming cooperatives were classified according to their real activities, the growth in construction employment would be even higher than indicated in table 7.4 (about 20 per cent over the four-year period), as cooperatives were often engaged in construction work.

Table 7.5. **Distribution of industrial establishments by changes in the workforce between 1990 and 1993** (%)

	Increase	Decrease	No change	Other answers[1]	Total
Total	23.8	56.7	17.7	1.7	100.0
Heavy engineering	2.2	95.6	2.2	0.0	100.0
Light industries	30.8	54.9	11.0	3.3	100.0
Food industries	28.3	38.0	32.6	1.1	100.0
Ownership					
Public	6.5	86.0	7.5	0.0	100.0
Private	35.5	37.0	24.6	2.9	100.0
Size of establishment					
Up to 25 employees	44.6	18.5	33.8	3.1	100.0
26-500 employees	22.3	61.2	15.5	1.0	100.0
501+ employees	4.8	88.9	4.7	1.6	100.0

[1] Mostly referring to establishments created after 1990.

Source: ILO survey data, April 1993. See Paukert, forthcoming.

Employment in services rose slowly. It increased every year during the transition period with the exception of the "shock therapy" year of 1991.[6] However, the total increase over the four-year period was only 4 per cent, too low to compensate for the dramatic decline in employment in industry and agriculture or the overall decline in employment.

2.2 Labour productivity

From the beginning of the transition process until 1993, the decline in employment, although substantial, lagged behind the slump in output. The result was a fall in labour productivity. Between 1989 and 1992, overall labour productivity fell by about 13 per cent. Labour productivity started to rise again in 1993, as GDP stagnated and total employment continued to decrease. In the first four years of transition, labour productivity fell by about

12 per cent. According to preliminary data for the first half of 1994, overall labour productivity continued to rise. It is reported to have increased by more than 7 per cent.

The overall decline in labour productivity during the first years of reform suggests that enterprises continued to hoard labour. However, given the fall in real wages since the start of transition (both consumer and producer wages), a temporary increase in the labour intensity of production cannot be interpreted as a sign of irrational behaviour on the part of firms, despite the likely slowdown effect on the general restructuring process. After the launching of the reform process, labour became cheaper in relation to capital and other inputs. Real consumer wages (i.e. nominal wages deflated by the consumer price index) declined by almost 25 per cent in the "shock therapy" year of 1991. Despite increases in 1992 and 1993, at the end of 1993 real consumer wages were still 19 per cent below their 1989 level. Real producer wages (nominal wages deflated by the producer price index) were about 18 per cent below their 1989 level. As a result, the often criticized labour hoarding by state enterprises may be considered as normal profit-maximizing behaviour, whatever its consequences at the macro level (Dyba and Svejnar, 1994).[7]

The available information on labour productivity in industry, differentiated by sector of ownership (table 7.6) reveals that it is the cooperative sector and the private sector — largely small or medium-sized enterprises — which have a particularly low level of labour productivity, not the enterprises of the declining state sector. Employment in the cooperative sector is now taken to mean self-employment by the Czech Statistical Office, so the very low level of labour productivity shown for the cooperative sector in table 7.6 can also be taken to refer to small-scale private sector undertakings. Private enterprises now account for almost 60 per cent of industrial enterprises and employ more than one-third of the industrial workforce. While the average size of enterprise is relatively small, the overall weight of this sector in terms of enterprise numbers is therefore considerable. Moreover, the share of this sector in the total number of industrial enterprises has been growing.

The low level of labour productivity in private enterprises indicates that labour-intensive technologies have been chosen mostly by the small and medium-sized private firms set up since the start of reform. Given the shortage of capital and the high cost of credit, this represented a rational decision for the new private entrepreneurs — indeed, they rarely had any other option. Companies with foreign ownership or participation, on the other hand, have had levels of labour productivity much above the average. This is largely related to their incomparably greater opportunities to invest in high-level technology.

The differences in labour productivity between the sectors of ownership have been reflected in relative levels of earnings. In August 1994, for example, private sector industrial earnings were 6 per cent below the overall average, earnings in the cooperative sector were 26 per cent below average, while earnings in foreign-owned enterprises were 18 per cent above average. State sector earnings were 2.8 per cent above average (CSO, 1994, No. 11).[8] The relatively high earnings in foreign-owned enterprises represent an important "pull factor" encouraging workers to quit state sector employment and join the newly created foreign firms. However, the relatively small number of these firms, combined with limited geographical labour mobility and a long-standing housing problem, has limited the size of such employment shifts. But the possibility of substantially increased earnings in the private sector has had a psychological effect on the workforce, and has no doubt influenced the number of voluntary worker departures from state enterprises to the private sector.

Table 7.6. Distribution of enterprises, output and employment in industry[1] by sector of ownership, 1993-94 (%)

Date	Sector	No. of enterprises	Production of goods	Employment	Index of labour productivity
Feb. 1993	Total	100.0	100.0	100.0	1.00
	1. Private[2]	30.8	8.2	9.3	0.88
	2. Cooperative	9.2	1.5	3.4	0.44
	3. State[3]	54.4	84.5	84.0	1.01
	4. Property of public associations	0.4	0.1	0.2	0.50
	5. Foreign ownership or participation	4.4	5.5	2.8	1.96
	6. Mixed (1-4)	0.8	0.2	0.3	0.67
Nov. 1993	Total	100.0	100.0	100.0	1.00
	1. Private[2]	49.8	22.2	27.3	0.81
	2. Cooperative	8.1	1.5	3.4	0.44
	3. State[3]	28.7	45.3	49.5	0.92
	4. Property of public associations	0.1	0.0	0.0	—
	5. Foreign ownership or participation	6.6	9.8	5.5	1.78
	6. Mixed (1-4)	6.6	21.2	14.3	1.48
June 1994	Total	100.0	100.0	100.0	1.00
	1. Private[2]	57.0	27.2	34.4	0.79
	2. Cooperative	6.7	1.3	3.2	0.41
	3. State[3]	22.2	41.5	42.4	0.98
	4. Property of public associations	0.1	0.0	0.0	—
	5. Foreign ownership or participation	8.2	12.0	6.7	1.79
	6. Mixed (1-4)	5.8	18.0	13.3	1.35

[1] Mining, manufacturing and public utilities; enterprises with 25 or more workers. [2] Private domestic sector, mainly small and medium-sized enterprises. [3] Includes local government ownership.

Source: CSO, *Monthly Statistics of the Czech Republic*, various issues.

2.3 Unemployment

Voluntary departures of workers to the private sector, whether to become employees of a new firm or to launch their own business, have been an important factor in keeping down the level of unemployment, which has rarely exceeded 4 per cent, whatever definition of unemployment is used (tables 7.7 and 7.8). Other factors that have helped keep unemployment at a low level are the labour-intensive methods used by new small enterprises and the continued labour hoarding by large enterprises — both state-owned and privatized — related to the decline in real wages and low unit labour costs.

Table 7.7. Monthly rates of registered unemployment, 1990-94

Month	1990	1991	1992	1993	1994
January	0.1	1.1	4.4	3.0	3.8
February	0.1	1.4	4.1	3.0	3.7
March	0.1	1.7	3.7	2.9	3.5
April	0.1	2.0	3.2	2.7	3.3
May	0.1	2.2	2.9	2.6	3.1
June	0.1	2.6	2.7	2.6	3.1
July	0.2	3.1	2.7	2.8	3.2
August	0.3	3.4	2.7	3.0	3.2
September	0.5	3.8	2.6	3.2	3.2
October	0.6	3.9	2.5	3.2	3.1
November	0.7	4.1	2.5	3.3	3.1
December	0.8	4.2	2.6	3.5	3.3

Source: CSO, *Monthly Statistics of the Czech Republic.*

Table 7.8. Unemployment rates based on Labour Force Sample Surveys and on registered unemployment

Date	LFSS[1]	Registered unemployment [2]
Spring 1993	3.9	2.8
Summer 1993	3.8	2.7
Autumn 1993	3.7	3.2
Winter 1993-94	3.9	3.6
Spring 1994	3.7	3.4
Summer 1994	3.9	3.2

[1] ILO definition of unemployment. [2] Moving averages corresponding to the respective LFSS periods.
Source: CSO, Labour Force Sample Survey.

Another important reason why unemployment has remained low is the decline in the labour supply, referred to earlier. This is due mostly to the withdrawal from the labour force of older workers, particularly those above pension age, and to the liberal granting of pensions to older or disabled citizens willing to take early retirement. Although the policy of pushing workers entitled to a pension into retirement as soon as possible was reversed in 1993, it was nevertheless responsible for a reduction in the labour force of almost 5 per cent. The proximity of the Western border, and the possibility of migrating or commuting for (undeclared) work to Germany and Austria, has also led some younger workers to retire from the official labour force. The lure of undeclared profits in the grey economy has had a similar effect. The withdrawal of workers below pension age has reduced the official labour force by about 3 per cent, the total decline being 8 per cent. A certain proportion of the withdrawals from the official labour force have corresponded to worker discouragement and to hidden unemployment, the exact amount of which is so far unknown.

A final factor contributing to the low level of unemployment has been the high standard of employment services. Almost half of the workforce have changed jobs at least once since the reform started, so a relatively large share of the workforce have experienced some unemployment. However, this has mostly been of a relatively short duration or of a purely frictional character. About one-fifth of the workforce have registered at some time with the employment offices, which manage to place about two-thirds of applicants. The high rate of outflow from unemployment has been a major factor keeping down the level of unemployment.

The conclusions that can be drawn from this section concern, first, the large amount of structural change achieved during the four years following the velvet revolution. Employment shifts between sectors of ownership, between industries and between industrial branches reached impressive proportions. The final outcome, however, was an overall decline in employment of 10-12 per cent, since the growth of demand in the expanding sectors (in services and construction) was insufficient to compensate for the large-scale job losses in industry and agriculture. Second, the progress of privatization has been extremely rapid. The share of private sector employment increased from 1 per cent in 1989 to 60 per cent at the end of 1993 and to over 80 per cent at the end of 1995. Third, the transition reform was accompanied by a significant decline in labour productivity and an 18-19 per cent fall in real wages over the four-year period. Real unit labour costs went down significantly. In industry, the lowest level of labour productivity was found not in the declining state sector but in the private, accounting for about two-thirds of all industrial enterprises in mid-1994. Low wages acted as an incentive for large enterprises to continue hoarding labour, even when output was declining. At the same time it encouraged new industrial establishments, particularly the small and medium-sized ones, to rely on labour-intensive technologies, thus keeping down investment. Transition restructuring thus resulted in considerable shifts in employment to labour-intensive production and services. This, together with a substantial reduction in the labour supply, helped keep the unemployment rate among the lowest in Europe. Direct foreign investment — the level of which is lower than in Hungary but about the same as in Poland — has played a leading role in the development of relatively efficient, well-managed private sector firms, with above-average labour productivity and high wages.

3. Policies and management practices affecting labour transfers from the public to the private sector

The decision to launch the reform programme initiated a long and arduous process of building the legal and institutional framework for a functioning market economy. Many existing laws had to be revised, new laws and statutes had to be introduced, countless government decrees had to be drafted. All this represented a tremendous amount of work for the Government, for the administration and for Parliament. Although public opinion polls have revealed certain signs of discontent with the work of Parliament, the capacity of which was sometimes overstretched, at least the transformation policies could be implemented on the basis of a body of laws. This was a considerable advantage, since the lack of legal framework has represented a serious hindrance in some other transition economies.

The transformation of institutions was equally important. In particular, a banking system corresponding to the requirements of a market economy had to be set up, replacing the previous monobank system, and the necessary institutions for privatization had to be created (Dyba and Svejnar, 1994). The institutional changes were among the basic prerequisites without which reform could not have been successfully implemented.

3.1 Methods of privatization and their impact on labour

One of the guiding principles of privatization in the Czech Republic was to privatize enterprises as quickly as possible and leave it to the new owners — rather than the Government — to take on the task of restructuring (Lastovicka et al., 1994). As a result, large-scale retrenchments by state enterprises before privatization were relatively rare.

Restitution and small-scale privatization

Privatization has taken a number of forms. Chronologically, the first was the restitution of property to previous owners or their heirs. This was followed shortly afterwards by the so-called "small-scale" privatization in which small units were sold by public auction to prospective entrepreneurs. About 100,000 property restitution claims were settled in the Czech Republic and Slovakia in the years following the velvet revolution, and about 30,000 small firms were auctioned in the small privatization (Lastovicka et al., 1994).

The impact of these two privatization methods, in terms of the value of property changing hands, was relatively limited compared to that of the "large-scale" privatization. From the point of view of structural change, however, it was very important. The restitutions and the "small-scale" privatization paved the way for the development of the small enterprise/small business sector. About 600,000 entrepreneurial jobs have been created in this sector, so far (table 7.9). If family helpers and members of producer cooperatives are included, the total number of self-employed people engaged in small private businesses/enterprises amounts to 760,000. In addition, it is estimated that about 500,000 employee jobs have been created. Together these represent one-fifth to one-quarter of total employment.[9]

In addition to the overall employment-creating effect of small business development in the wake of the restitutions and small-scale privatization, the fact that small businesses could take off right at the beginning of transition meant that job opportunities were provided for those whose employment became threatened in the public sector. The legislative framework for small business development was created in spring 1990. Although many amendments were made later, small businesses started to develop only a few months after the velvet revolution.

However, restitutions could also lead to job losses. Typical examples were service establishments (hairdressers, cleaners, etc.), formerly part of public sector service networks, which had to be closed down after the premises they occupied had been restored to their

Table 7.9. Entrepreneurs, business owners and other self-employed people active in the production/business sector, summer 1994 (000s)

Category	Total	Main or only occupation	Secondary occupation
Entrepreneurs/business owners	597.4	490.3	107.1
Without employees	437.0	338.5	98.5
With employees	160.4	151.8	8.6
Family helpers	23.4	20.0	3.4
Members of producer cooperatives	138.6	137.2	1.4
Total	759.4	647.5	111.9

Source: CSO, Labour Force Sample Survey, summer 1994.

original owners. The new owners usually decided to put the restored property to a different personal or business use, and/or started to charge market-determined rents. As a result, the service enterprises had to look for new premises, which they were mostly unable to find, and in the end many had to close down. The workers were made redundant and were left to their own devices to find a new job or to launch their own business.

Large-scale privatization

The bulk of state enterprises were privatized in the so-called "large-scale" privatization. This involved a range of different privatization methods — auctions, tenders, direct sales to domestic and foreign buyers, and above all the much-publicized "voucher privatization method".

The basic principle of the voucher method is as follows: state enterprises are transferred into the ownership of private citizens not for money but in exchange for investment vouchers. Every citizen over the age of 18 can buy investment vouchers, in the form of a voucher booklet, containing 1,000 investment points, a form of "investment money", for a registration fee of Kc.1,000 (US$35 — originally one-quarter of the average monthly wage). These vouchers entitle all citizens to bid for ownership of shares in any company included in the voucher privatization scheme, or to entrust their investment points to an investment fund, making investment decisions centrally and holding a diversified portfolio (Lastovicka et al., 1994).

The voucher privatization had two waves. The first wave took place in 1992-93. It involved 1,500 enterprises and 8.5 million citizens participated in it. The second wave started in autumn 1993 and was completed in 1995. The voucher method represents an attempt to solve the problem of the insufficient level of resources of the population, which could not otherwise have bought up state enterprises with their savings, certainly not in a short period of time. However, speed was considered important for the success of the privatization operation — and of reform in general. The voucher method is considered fair to all participating individuals, and each individual is able to take decisions about capital investment according to his/her own preferences. Moreover, the investment funds have been able to behave like private investment funds rather than state-administered institutions.

Finally, the high number of new investors, both individual and institutional, has created new constituencies in favour of a market economy. The psychological and political impact of this last factor has been considerable (ibid.).

Effects of large-scale privatization on employment: Main scenarios

In the large-scale privatization process, whole enterprises and institutions have often passed from the public to the private sector as a result of an administrative and legal decision, while the workers remain in their jobs and experience no immediate changes to their daily routine. However, this is not always the case.

When a state enterprise is transferred to the private sector as a whole by a straight procedure of ownership change (sale, auction or voucher privatization), which has happened in about half the cases so far (Kotrba, 1994), employment restructuring most often follows the privatization decision and is carried out by the new management. After taking over the newly privatized company, the management has to decide which plants or units to keep/develop, which parts to sell and which parts to close down as irretrievable "junk". Its decisions will result in more or less significant lay-offs, internal labour transfers, and sometimes even recruitments.

In the case of those state enterprises not privatized as a single unit, the enterprises are split up and reorganized before the process of privatization starts, and lay-offs are sometimes carried out by state enterprise managements. Such lay-offs are often motivated by the wish to make the enterprise more attractive to potential private buyers; they can be selective or on a mass scale. If they are selective, they are likely to focus on the categories of worker considered to be easy to rehire, for example administrative and clerical workers or unskilled operatives. The best qualified technicians and skilled operatives will then be mostly kept on the payroll, even if the enterprise is in financial difficulties. Managers are reluctant to break up teams that work well together, and many of them continue to fear a shortage of qualified technicians. Many managers intend to acquire a stake in the company and/or to keep their post after privatization. Their staffing decisions therefore tend to be influenced by a desire to strengthen their own position in the company. This they can do easily since before privatization they usually operated under very soft budget constraints.

The scenario just described goes some way towards explaining the substantially higher rate of job loss and unemployment for women than for men in the Czech Republic. The ILO survey of Czech manufacturing establishments carried out in 1993 revealed that, in contrast to other countries of the region, a significant proportion of establishment managers admit to using gender criteria for lay-offs.

In other cases, whole units or plants of state enterprises may be closed down before privatization because they are considered unattractive or "irretrievable" for various technical or economic reasons, and the managers want to keep the best and get rid of the "junk". This might lead to the retrenchment of all the workers in the units concerned.

The strategies of managers in state enterprises put up for privatization have had a significant effect on the privatization process. Most managers are highly concerned about their own prospects, about the possibilities of acquiring property in the company and/or of keeping their managerial post. At the same time, their freedom of action is considerable. It is their role to prepare and submit the basic privatization project. In the enterprises that are not involved in the voucher scheme, they are free to suggest any eligible method of privatization (direct sale, division of the enterprise into two or more units each to be privatized separately, etc.). Even in firms involved in voucher privatization, the management can suggest the division of the firm into several units and the privatization of some units by other methods. The managers can try to acquire the new company, or part of its stock. They can, on occasion, privatize the most attractive parts of the enterprise on their own account and leave the rest. They can also submit the privatization project in such a way as to maximize their chances of keeping their managerial position, though without getting a share of the property. This has apparently happened quite often. Finally, some managements try to make the privatization process as lengthy as possible, with the aim of taking advantage of the lack of ownership control to further their private activities. In these firms privatization can take three years or more. Generally speaking, managers, both at the top and at the middle levels, are the group which profits most from the privatization process. However, it would be wrong to conclude that they are the only group to benefit. The rules of large-scale privatization are specially framed to ensure that the game remains open to other players (foreign and domestic investors) (Kotrba, 1994).

Managerial behaviour during privatization has had a sometimes positive and sometimes negative impact on the workforce. The basic guiding principle, however, has been to avoid mass lay-offs as far as possible. When they become unavoidable, firms frequently assist workers to find alternative solutions.

3.2 Worker initiative during the privatization process

Workers have not remained passive during the privatization process. As soon as privatization started, many workers began to consider the possibility of leaving their public sector jobs voluntarily. They gauged their chances of being kept on and their pay prospects, and many workers, particularly the most dynamic, began to look for private sector employment. Many took the step of leaving on their own initiative, taking advantage of the new functioning of the labour market and of its services (government-run or private). Workers often left enterprises put up for privatization long before the privatization process was completed and/or lay-offs had started. A good many workers were even prepared to change their occupation and pay for retraining courses, which started to be run on a commercial basis throughout the country (including evening and weekend courses). The result was that when the time came for the privatized establishments to make employment cuts, the need for retrenchments was usually relatively limited. The option of early retirement for older workers has of course been useful in reducing employment. But it is only one possible solution, the importance of which should not be exaggerated.

Workers considering quitting a public enterprise in advance of privatization have to weigh the advantages and disadvantages. Among the chief advantages is the possibility of choosing a new job according to their personal preferences and of joining an expanding branch of activity at an early stage when many openings are available (e.g. banking, business services, tourism or construction). But workers who leave voluntarily are not entitled to severance pay, which, in the case of establishments closed as a result of the reform programme, amounts to a full five months' salary at the height of the transition process. Experience has shown that sometimes workers who decide to wait for the severance pay lose out in the end: for the five months when they are receiving severance pay, they are not allowed to have another job. During this time they often "lose their place in the queue for the best new jobs", as well as the opportunity of earning a higher income. This is true particularly of the better qualified, more dynamic workers. For less qualified, less dynamic workers, on the other hand, it is more advantageous to stay on in the public sector establishments that are about to be privatized and to collect the severance pay.[10] The second option has been taken by women more than by men.

Many workers have left their public sector job in order to launch a small business. A common practice is to launch the business before leaving the public sector job and to run the business as a secondary occupation for some time, so as to be reasonably sure that the business has a good chance of lasting. Surveys carried out for the ILO in the Czech Republic have established that it is much more common for prospective business owners to leave a state sector job voluntarily because they have a business plan than for unemployed workers to start a small private business as a way out of unemployment.

3.3 The speed of privatization and its impact on employment

While the methods adopted for large-scale privatization — and particularly the voucher scheme — were intended to privatize a maximum of property in a minimum of time, the results have not fully met these intentions, especially with respect to the speed factor. When complications start to emerge in individual privatization projects, speed and simplicity tend to be sacrificed in favour of such criteria as flexibility and space for competition. The latter, in particular, is considered more important than the speed with which the property transfer takes place. This has led to the wide variety of privatization outcomes referred to earlier, and has resulted in large delays.

One advantage of the rather slow progress of privatization is that it prevented mass retrenchments, with their destabilizing effects, in the initial phase of reform. Moreover, the long lapse of time that usually occurs between the decision to privatize an enterprise (the basic lists were made quite early in the reform period) and actual implementation of restructuring measures gives both managers and workers ample time to look for solutions. As already mentioned, many workers did not wait to be laid off, but tried to find jobs in the private sector or to launch a business as soon as the new economic legislation allowed them to do so. The significant time-lags involved in the privatization process have thus softened its impact on labour. Combined with the unexpected amount of initiative, imagination and entrepreneurial spirit shown by workers, they represent yet another factor that has contributed to keeping unemployment levels down.

3.4 Bankruptcies

One scenario which has played a less important role than was hoped for by some commentators is that of enterprise bankruptcy. The bankruptcy law was enacted in October 1991 and amended in spring 1993 (Law No. 122/93 Sb., amending Law No. 328/91 Sb.). In fact bankruptcy seems to have affected newly established private firms more than the large state enterprises. Data available for the period 8 October 1992 to 30 November 1994 show that during those 25 months 3,051 new proposals for starting bankruptcy proceedings were made, but of these only 319 led to bankruptcy being declared. In 32 cases the six months' "protection delay" foreseen by the law was ordered. The large majority of cases (1,760) were awaiting decision at the end of 1994, and 940 cases had been settled by other means. The 319 bankruptcies that have been declared have involved mostly new private enterprises.[11]

Many enterprises, state-owned and privatized, have had problems of insolvency and have been trapped in the chain reaction of non-payment of bills. At the time of writing, inter-company indebtedness is variously estimated at Kc.150-400 billion (US$5-15 billion).[12] In addition, many firms owe considerable sums in social security contributions to the social security administration.[13] A number of firms are also in arrears with tax payments.

In some cases, companies have been bailed out by the Government, particularly large companies of national or regional importance. Some have received emergency bridging credits guaranteed by the Government and some have had their debts just written off by government decision. There are three main reasons why the Government adopted this surprisingly anti-liberal attitude. First, the cost of lost output, added to the cost of lost tax revenue and the cost of unemployment benefits (and of other social payments resulting from the closure of large enterprises), seemed to offset the cost of enterprise support. Second, mass retrenchments might have had a negative impact on social stability. Third, the Government would have risked losing political credit for keeping unemployment at a low level.

But there are other reasons why the number of bankruptcies has remained limited. First, bankruptcy has to be decided by a court of law. The Czech judicial system has been so overburdened since 1989 that it may take months, even years, for a case to be heard and settled. The number of pending bankruptcy cases has been high. Starting bankruptcy proceedings is not, therefore, likely to have an effect in the short run and creditors may prefer other (directly negotiated) solutions. Second, the banks, which are usually the main creditors, and which often initiate bankruptcy proceedings and subsequently play an important role in enterprise liquidation and resale or restructuring, have felt ill-equipped and ill at ease in dealing with these cases. In the end, however, if the market economy system is to start working properly, firms that are unable to pay their debts will have to be declared bankrupt.[14] The present practice not only perpetuates past distortions, but is also unfair to small and medium-sized enterprises, which do not benefit from similar protection. Organizations of small and medium employers have started to raise protests against such governmental practices, which they consider to be discriminatory.[15] Continued government intervention to save large firms from bankruptcy suggests that the transition process is far from complete and that much remains to be accomplished before the enterprise sector can be considered to be operating as a real market economy.

4. Summary and conclusions

This chapter has attempted to illustrate the scope and depth of structural change achieved in the Czech Republic during the four years since the 1989 velvet revolution. It has shown that employment shifts between sectors of ownership, industries and industrial branches have reached impressive proportions. The share of private sector employment increased from 1 per cent in 1989 to 60 per cent at the end of 1993 and over 80 per cent by the end of 1995. More than 1 million jobs have been created in the small private enterprise/business sector, which was almost non-existent five years ago. The final outcome of this rapid restructuring during the first four years of transition is, however, an overall decline in employment of 10-12 per cent: the growth of demand for labour in services (amounting to 4 per cent) and in construction (16 per cent) has been insufficient to compensate for large-scale job losses in industry and agriculture, amounting to one-fifth and one-half, respectively, over the four-year period.

The decline in employment has not been matched by a corresponding growth of unemployment. On the contrary, unemployment has remained at a very low level, whatever definition is used, rarely exceeding 4 per cent. The unemployment rate has been one of the lowest in Europe. But the labour supply has declined sharply. In the initial phase of reform, workers past retirement age were strongly encouraged to withdraw from the labour force, which very many of them did. During the first four years of transition, the labour force was reduced by 8 per cent; about 5 per cent was accounted for by the departure of post-retirement age workers and 3 per cent by the departure of people of working age. Many of the latter — but also many who were past retirement age — became engaged in the black economy. Some workers decided to migrate or to start commuting across the border, often on their own initiative and without waiting to lose their jobs. The proximity of the Western border has facilitated migration movements, both registered and unregistered.

The transition process was accompanied by a significant decline in labour productivity (of about 12-13 per cent) and by an 18-19 per cent fall in real wages (both producers' and consumers' wages) over the first four years of reform. In industry, the lowest level of labour productivity has been found not in the declining state sector but in the private sector, accounting for about two-thirds of enterprises in mid-1994. Low wage levels have acted as an incentive for large (state or privatized) enterprises to continue hoarding labour, while inducing the new industrial enterprises, particularly the small and medium-sized ones, to rely on labour-intensive technologies, thus keeping down investment. Restructuring in the transition period has thus resulted in considerable shifts in employment to labour-intensive production and labour-intensive services, with enterprises relying on low wages to survive. The decline in net fixed investment has gradually become a cause for concern, although the ratio of fixed investment to GDP has remained higher than in most countries of the region. Direct foreign investment has played a leading role in the development of relatively efficient, well-managed private sector firms, with above average labour productivity and wages.

This chapter also examined the policies and practices affecting labour transfers from the public to the private sector, surveying the different methods of privatization and their impact on employment. It showed how the the restitutions and "small-scale" privatization, involving a relatively limited transfer of property, paved the way for the development of the small business (enterprise) sector, where over 1 million new jobs have been created. "Large-scale" privatization, on the other hand, can result in vast transfers of property and labour from the public to the private sector "by the stroke of a pen", while the workers concerned experience no change in their daily routine, at least in the short run. This has happened in about half of the cases of voucher privatization. Where regroupings, split-ups, closures and similar forms of enterprise reorganization have taken place, the long delays usually involved have given workers time to look for other employment. Workers have shown a remarkable amount of initiative and resourcefulness in finding jobs during the transition process. As a result, the number of retrenchments directly associated with transition reforms has been lower than expected. The number of bankruptcies has also been low, compared to the high number of firms in serious financial difficulties. This is because the Government has preferred to give support to certain firms of national importance rather than risk their being closed, with the widespread economic and social consequences this would entail.

References

Benacek, Vladimir. 1994. *Small business and private entrepreneurship during transition: The case of the Czech Republic*. Prague, CERGE, Charles University, April.

Czech Statistical Office (CSO). Various years. *Statisticka Rocenka Ceské Republiky* [Statistical Yearbook of the Czech Republic]. Prague.

———. Various years. Labour Force Sample Surveys. Prague.

———. 1994. *Statistické prehledy* [Monthly Statistics of the Czech Republic]. Prague.

Dyba, K.; Svejnar, J. 1994. *An overview of recent economic development in the Czech Republic*, Working Paper No. 61. Prague, CERGE, Charles University, April.

Kotrba, J. 1994. *Czech privatization: Players and winners.* Prague, CERGE, Charles University, April.

Lastovicka, R.; Marcincin, A.; Mejstrik, M. 1994. *Privatization and opening the capital markets in the Czech and Slovak Republics*. Prague, CERGE, Charles University, April.

Lidové Noviny. Various issues. Prague.

Paukert, L. Forthcoming. *Women's employment in Central and Eastern European countries during the period of transition to a market economy system*. Geneva, ILO.

Notes

[1] Czech Statistical Office (CSO), Labour Force Sample Survey, June-Aug., 1994.

[2] Statement by I. Kocarnik, Minister of Finance, *Lidové Noviny*, 8 Oct. 1994.

[3] In June 1994, for example, a growth rate of 17 per cent was registered in paper, printing and publishing. Output also increased in leather and footwear (by 15 per cent), rubber and plastics (8 per cent), electrical and optical instruments (6 per cent) and glass and ceramics (5 per cent). The spectacular rates of growth in certain light industries — which were matched by equally high rates of decline in heavy industries — have been quoted here mainly to illustrate the extent of industrial restructuring and of employment shifts that have taken place.

[4] CSO, *Labour Force Sample Surveys*, Spring 1993-94.

[5] A survey carried out for the ILO in Czech manufacturing in April 1993 established that 6.5 per cent of state sector industrial establishments increased their workforce between 1990 and the first quarter of 1993. Admittedly, the overwhelming majority (86 per cent) of state enterprises made personnel cuts. In the private sector, 35.5 per cent of establishments increased their personnel, while a slightly larger proportion — 37 per cent — had to make cuts. In the heavy engineering branch, where public ownership was still predominant at the time of the survey, establishments that had made employment cuts greatly outnumbered those that had increased

employment. The same was true of large establishments with more than 500 employees; 4.8 per cent of these, however, managed to increase their workforce.

[6] The 1991 decline in service employment was due mainly to significant job losses in public administration, in government-financed service activities, such as research and development (–24 per cent), in public cultural institutions (–31 per cent), in municipal services (–35 per cent) and in the trading institutions characteristic of a planned economy, i.e. in material-technical supplies, in agricultural procurement and in state monopoly enterprises engaged in foreign trade (–23 per cent). Employment in health and education declined by about 4 per cent in 1991, but the trend was reversed in 1992. However, employment growth in the newly developing service branches (wholesale and retail trade, banking, business services, tourism, etc.) was insufficient to offset these reductions in 1991, either because growth was too slow, as in the large domestic trade sector (4 per cent increase), or because the branch of activity accounted for too small a proportion of total employment; this was true, for example, of business services, despite a 109 per cent employment increase in 1991.

[7] The Czech Republic has been an exception among the countries of the region in that real consumer and real producer wages moved more or less in parallel during the first transition years.

[8] Information available for the construction industry shows that labour productivity in the state sector is well below average (30 per cent), whereas labour productivity in the private sector (now accounting for 70 per cent of total construction output) is slightly above average. Labour productivity in foreign and mixed enterprises is considerably (24 per cent) above the average. In the construction industry, differences in labour productivity have also been reflected in the relative levels of earnings, which are higher in the private sector than in the now much reduced state sector.

[9] After the start of reform, many licences to run small businesses, to act as entrepreneurial agents, or to be otherwise self-employed in business started to be issued. At the end of 1993, 1,262,264 such licences had been registered. However, several licences can be issued for the same entrepreneur, often to action a part-time basis, or the same business entity can have on its staff more than one entrepreneur. Some businesses can also become dormant (see Benacek, 1994). The real number of small businesses operating, and the real number of entrepreneurs, was revealed for the first time only when Labour Force Sample Surveys started to be published, in spring 1993.

[10] Information derived from case-study material collected for the ILO in the Czech Republic.

[11] Only 37 state enterprises (so-called rest or hard-core state enterprises) have been declared bankrupt. The rest were limited companies (148), individual entrepreneurs (82), public limited companies (27), cooperatives (22) and public trading companies (3) ("I statni podniky bankrotuji", in *Lidové Noviny, Koruna* (economic supplement), 7 Jan. 1995, Prague).

[12] With government approval, the banks have been allowed to organize rounds of computer-assisted debt compensation and cancellation. Enterprise participation in the debt compensation rounds has been voluntary.

[13] "Pad velkych podniku je risk", in *Lidové Noviny*, 5 Oct. 1994.

[14] "The new Bohemians", in *The Economist*, 22-28 Oct. 1994, London.

[15] *Lidové Noviny*, 15 Oct. 1994.

8. Privatization of telecommunications in Hungary

László Neumann*

1: Introduction

The main issues investigated in this chapter are the special features of privatization policy in the field of infrastructure; workplace industrial relations in the process of changing ownership; and the consequences of the change in terms of the reshaping of working conditions and industrial relations in private (or partly privatized) companies. In order to judge the actual possibilities for employees' interests being represented, we will look at not only the claims of the trade unions but also the behaviour of those who are selling the enterprises (state administration, enterprise management, etc.). Is labour completely excluded from decision-making in relation to privatization, or is its role confined to being kept informed and voicing opinions according to valid legal regulations, or are the unions really able to influence the terms of privatization? Employees and/or managers can acquire a proportion of the shares, so in theory they may be able to exercise an actual influence on the privatized companies' decision-making as partial owners.

This chapter thus aims to evaluate the impact of privatization on employment, industrial relations and wages. In this context, it first analyses the effect of privatization on the level and structure of employment, including changes in job security, employment practices and methods of reducing employment. It then describes the evolving patterns of industrial relations in privatized firms, including union density and recognition and enterprise-level collective bargaining. Finally, it examines changes in wage differentials, remuneration, and the link between wages and productivity. Special attention is paid to the emerging labour practices of multinational corporations and the transformation of those elements of the former "second" economy that used to play an important role within state enterprises.[1]

The empirical phase of this research was focused exclusively on telecommunications. The reasons for singling out this field were practical: telecommunications is the sector in which privatization has proceeded furthest so far; in addition, its strong ties with the privatized manufacturing base and with development projects involving private finance foreshadow the wide variety of options to be used in other fields of public infrastructure. The applied research methods relied heavily on a series of case studies, complemented by

*Labour Research Institute, Budapest

secondary analysis of media accounts and official state administration and company documents. The case studies cannot be considered representative; the aim is simply to illustrate organizational forms typical of the telecommunications sector. Naturally, the most substantial report deals with the huge Hungarian Telecommunications Company (HTC) itself. One other company was selected from among the small and medium-sized companies in the orbit of HTC; it is a typical result of decentralization of a former HTC department (EMTEL). Finally, two equipment manufacturers were selected, each representing a different stage of privatization: one company that has been "commercialized" but not yet sold (MW) and a former state enterprise that has been entirely bought out by a giant multinational enterprise (MNE).

2. The main features of privatization in Hungary

Privatization-oriented reorganizations of state-owned enterprises date back from before the political changes of 1989-90. The 1988 Act on Economic Association made it possible for state-owned enterprises to found limited liability and joint stock companies and to contribute part of their assets to these newly established business organizations pending the decision of enterprise councils (the self-governing bodies of state enterprises consisting of managers and employee representatives, formed in the mid-1980s to curb the scope of direct ministerial intervention in enterprises). Although this so-called "spontaneous privatization" process was not proper privatization in the sense of a change of ownership, organizational changes and decentralization did take place (table 8.1).[2] The most significant lasting outcome of this process was the creation of many joint ventures. In this early phase of privatization almost every case of joint venture creation meant an inflow of additional funds over and above the original equity (table 8.2). So far, Hungary has attracted the biggest per capita foreign direct investment (FDI) in the region. The 1989 Transformation Act

Table 8.1. Changes in the legal structure of organizations, Hungary

Type of organization	1988	1989	1990	1991	1992	1993	1994	1995
State enterprise	2 378	2 400	2 363	2 233	1 733	1 130	821	761
Limited liability company	450	4 484	18 317	41 206	57 262	72 897	87 957	102 697
Joint stock company	116	307	646	1 072	1 712	2 375	2 896	3 186
Cooperative	7 414	7 546	7 641	7 764	8 229	–	–	–
Private partnerships	29 657	24 143	34 095	52 136	70 597	69 973	92 393	106 245
One-person business (self-employed)	290 877	320 619	393 450	500 000	606 207	68 843	778 036	791 496

Source: Central Statistical Office, 1993.

Table 8.2. Number of enterprises with foreign direct investment and capital paid in

	1989	1990	1991	1992	1993	1994
Number of organizations	1 350	5 693	9 117	17 182	20 999	23 557
— of which firms only with foreign capital	25	231	1 190	4 653	7 377	9 372
Foreign capital paid in (billion forint)	30.0	93.2	215.0	401.8	662.9	833.5
— of which firms only with foreign capital	0.4	5.5	38.3	118.3	202.9	n.a.
Total foreign investment, stock (US$ million)*	550	1 450	3 150	4 850	7 400	8 700

n.a. = not available. * Hunya (1996); estimates for 1995: 12,700.
Source: Central Statistical Office (KSH), Statistical yearbooks 1994 and 1996.

provided for the transformation ("commercialization") of entire state enterprises into limited liability or joint stock companies. In this case the shares are made over to the State. Ownership rights are exercised by the State Property Agency (SPA), an organization set up specifically for this purpose.

Enterprise managements (or even the "nomenclature" once assigned on political grounds) were thus the initiators and the beneficiaries of this so-called "spontaneous privatization" process, which put them beyond the effective control of either the State or the general public. The ostensible "sale price" acquisitions of companies, "salvaging" managerial seats, were the targets of political attacks, especially before the general election in 1990.

The first freely elected government, coming into power in May 1990, extended the SPA's authority over state property and thus expanded the scope of state intervention. The legal status of the SPA has been revised (it now reports to the Government and not to Parliament) and it has been assigned the task of safeguarding state assets through central control and direct management of the privatization process. The responsibility of the SPA has been extended to include terminating enterprise councils, which means that it can act directly as the seller of a firm. Although the SPA is part of the state administration, its decisions and resolutions taken as "owner" cannot be appealed against.

A study of the underlying assumptions and aims of the Government's privatization policy was published in autumn 1990 (Government of Hungary, 1990). The draft report suggests that the Government wants privatization to take place fairly rapidly. It plans to transfer 50 per cent of state property to private owners or various institutions (churches, social security boards, local governments, foundations, etc.) over a period of four years. It defines the basic goal of privatization as the sale of assets at competitive prices — and not their return to former owners or their free distribution among citizens. (The only exception is arable land, which former owners may reclaim. The former owners of other property can expect only symbolic compensation.) The proceeds of privatization are intended to pay off state debts. Reiterating a promise made by the Hungarian Democratic Forum, the biggest government party in its electoral campaign, it is suggested that the employees of state-owned enterprises may acquire shares in their enterprises on favourable terms. Management initiatives in state-owned enterprises and offers from international investors may also trigger privatization.

The privatization process seemed to accelerate from 1990 onward. First, the SPA itself initiated the privatization of 20 large enterprises. The sale of several thousand small shops and restaurants was also started.[3] Privatization initiated by enterprises themselves also continued at a higher rate, although most of these were simple transformations into joint stock companies and the shares have yet to be sold (table 8.3).[4]

Table 8.3. Proceeding of privatization

	Number of companies	State assets book value (billion forint)
State assets prior to privatization:		
SPA	1 841	1 098
SAT (State Asset Trust)	171	1 477
Others	86	200
Total	2 098 (100%)	2 775 (100%)
Initiated by SPA until end of 1994:		
Liquidation	523	322
100 per cent of shares sold	653	206
Partially sold	248	147
Total	1 424	675
Initiated by SAT until end of 1994:		
Liquidation	13	15
100 per cent of shares sold	–	–
Partially sold	23	138
Total	36	153
Other deals approved by SPA	–	168
Total privatized until end of 1994	1 460 (70%)	996 (36%)
State-owned assets, end of 1994	823	1 578

Note: Shares of 10 banks (60 billion forint book value) excluded.
Sources: SPA and SAT data.

Procrastination has been a typical feature of the direct sale of state-owned companies by the SPA (by 1993 the State still owned half of the 20 companies covered by the First Privatization Project of 1990). During the lengthy administrative process companies are typically "wrecked", assets are devoured and debts surge. Another typical feature is the priority given to maximizing state revenues and the relative neglect of other issues such as employment prospects, anti-monopoly regulations and additional investment. Negotiations between company management and the SPA over the terms of sale often end up in compromise. The task of representing "company interests" is normally referred to the top management. The company's bargaining position depends on the knowledge and expertise of its professionals and managers, as the central bureaucracy cannot complete the process of sale without their active assistance in the technical preparations. Several huge enterprises, including some near monopolies, have been privatized in accordance with a strategy of transformation virtually developed by the management alone, with the rather formal assistance of the SPA.

By the end of 1990 the approach to the "spontaneous" process was beginning to change. Realizing its own limits, the SPA was assigning an increasing role to enterprise management initiatives in the search for potential investors. At the same time, the Government's privatization practice emphasized the importance of personnel matters in an effort to establish loyal cadres of the governing parties in key positions, especially the top managerial positions in big companies.

In 1991 the Government attempted to accelerate the process of privatization through the "self-privatization" programme, under which most of the administrative functions of the SPA were transferred to consulting firms. The managers of small and middle-sized state enterprises were advised by the Government to select one of the listed firms operating as consultants.[5]

In the majority of cases employees have bought shares in privatized companies, at discount prices, with the permission of the SPA. However, until Parliament passed the Employee Share Ownership Programme (ESOP) law in June 1992, in most cases employees' shareholdings remained too small to influence companies' strategic decisions. The new legislation sets out in detail the preconditions for launching ESOP projects (40 per cent of the employees' vote, the consent of the owners, a feasibility study accepted by a commercial bank, etc.), the terms of credit available to employees, and the tax exemption to be enjoyed by the company subsidizing the deal as well as by employees investing their money in shares. It was assumed that employee ownership, perhaps along with other new methods of employee participation, would provide new scope for cooperation and eventually ensure higher profitability for the company. In fact, the completed deals have not so far justified these expectations. In the vast majority of cases management dominates the ESOP organization (Trust) by holding a decisive share in the property. Rank and file employees as partial owners have not been able to prevent the implementation of tougher labour policies either. Given the lack of attractive schemes for management buy-outs, it is understandable that managers preferred ESOP schemes and the favourable tax and credit conditions they offer.

In 1992, in order to speed up the process and meet the political preference for the creation of a new "class of domestic owners", the Government decided to introduce new privatization instruments (more preferential credit lines, the issue of cheap bonds at the stock exchange, the launch of a "voucher privatization" project following the Czech model, etc.). Apart from improving citizens' and employees' purchasing power, a more deliberate policy of decentralization would attempt to make the market supply more attractive by offering smaller business units separated from large enterprises.

As in other East European countries, privatization inevitably takes place alongside industrial restructuring because of the backwardness in products and technology and the loss of previous markets. The Government has gradually had to recognize that the crisis in the economy would be deeper and more enduring than policy-makers had expected. Threatened industries (mining, metallurgy, heavy engineering, some branches of the food industry, chemicals, etc.) would collapse and unemployment would rise steeply unless the Government gave up its entirely market-led privatization principle, which left no room for the assertion of any industrial policy. There is thus a growing awareness on the part of the Government of the need to reassess the objectives of privatization (for example, to identify those enterprises to be excluded from privatization, and to establish industrial policy guidelines).

In mid-1992, new privatization legislation accordingly identified enterprises that were to remain partly or wholly state property in the long term. At the same time the Ministry of Industry and Trade highlighted 13 manufacturing enterprises that were to be safeguarded, mainly large "flagships" of the state sector.

Emerging industrial policy objectives also meant curtailing the power of the SPA. A new state holding, the State Asset Trust (SAT), was created to exercise ownership rights in the case of enterprises that were to remain the property of the State in the long term, and ministries were assigned an increased role in the privatization process. All in all, a new phase of restoring the role of the State has begun.

As a result of the 1994 general election, the Hungarian Socialist Party and the Free Democrats formed the new governing coalition which brought about substantial changes in the privatization policy. Firstly, the new government merged the two privatization agencies (SPA, SAT), and the organizational changes caused serious delay in the decision-making process of almost all pending cases until mid-1995. Secondly, state revenue became the number one aim of privatization, and this meant the preference of cash-paying buyers. The new government abandoned its predecessors policy which wanted to help "domestic buyers" by providing them with preferential loans. Instead of restitution and employee ownership, the new policy focused on managers and private business owners who are able to pay cash for the property, even if the sales price of the shares must be fairly depressed in order to accelerate the pace of privatization. Since the profitable part of the companies in manufacturing and food processing have already been privatized, the rest of the small and medium-sized companies are offered to managers in the framework of the new "simplified privatization" project. Thirdly, the new government agency in charge of privatization focused its attention on the huge public utility companies (such as power stations, different energy suppliers, telecommunication) and the remaining national companies in monopoly position (the characteristic example is the Hungarian Oil and Gas Company operating oil refineries, pipelines and gas stations throughout the country.) This shift in the policy is quite understandable, if the primary goal of the Government is to increase budget revenue and raise moneys to pay off the state debt. By the end of 1995 the privatization agency managed to privatize regional gas suppliers and completed privatization of telephone operations so successfully that the actual revenue exceeds the planned figures by 192 billion forint (US$1.4 billion).

3. Special features of public infrastructure privatization

It is generally agreed that services and infrastructure were systematically neglected in the former state socialist countries. Historically, development decisions in the centrally planned economies favoured investment in the primary and secondary sectors; the growing backwardness of services and infrastructure can be clearly demonstrated by comparative statistical data.[6] Apart from physical output (length of highways, telephone penetration rate, etc.), basic macroeconomic data (on the share of services and infrastructure in assets, investment and employment) also reflect this lagging behind. Despite the recent impressive growth in the share of services in employment in East European countries, they still lag behind Western countries by 20-30 percentage points. Moreover, a large part of the increase in employment in service industries is a result of the need to counterbalance the lack of capital stock and backward technology (Major, 1991).

In Hungary telecommunications is probably the only infrastructure sector where, abandoning the tradition of preceding decades, development has been contemplated since the mid-1980s. In the recent decade, modernization of the telephone system has become a political issue. The promise to improve the low penetration rate and to reduce the time new applicants for telephones have to wait was seen as a matter of winning popular support both by the last communist administration and by the newly elected governments. Decisions were also influenced by the obvious fact that infrastructure investment, particularly in telecommunications, is an essential part of creating a business environment, and a pre-condition for a thriving economy.

The 1989 ten-year development programme envisaged a 10.8 per cent annual increase in telephone lines; this would have meant a 37.6 per cent penetration rate by the year 2000. Investment requirements for the first three years would have amounted to 160 billion forint (US$2 billion, based on 1990 prices and exchange rate). The lack of available capital is the key obstacle to development, because the profit generated from operating the current telephone network is not sufficient to finance a modernization programme. It is not a new practice in Hungary to seek private funds for infrastructure development. In the 1980s the holders of debentures issued by the Hungarian Post were entitled to preferential treatment ahead of other people waiting for telephones. Recently, development/investment companies have been set up to raise funds from applicants for telephones to help finance local network development. A more substantial amount has come from a World Bank loan (US$150 million in 1990) and from the EBRD (80 million ECU in 1991 and DM185 million in 1992) for the specific purpose of funding the technological requirements of telephone development. However, privatization seemed the most promising approach to raising funds.

Privatization of the telecommunications sector covers several more or less segmented areas such as telephone service provider units, base telephone network investment and development, local network building, value-added services and manufacture and installation of switches and terminal equipment. The separation of these functions also means decentralization of the telecommunications sector. Moreover, owing to the specific problems of the infrastructure sector, privatization has also required some general government decisions and revisions of law. Parallel to privatization and deregulation, the legislature has the new task of creating efficient regulatory bodies to replace existing government bureaucracy. (In theory, this implies a clear distinction between different functions of the State, as the owner of public property and as the regulator of the economy.)

First of all, in early 1990, the Hungarian Post was restructured to form three organizations, dividing the functions of postal services, broadcasting and telephone services. In mid-1992 the Hungarian Telecommunications Enterprise (HTE) was transformed into a state-owned joint stock company (Hungarian Telecommunications Company — HTC), in preparation for privatization. Discussions at this stage focused on the problem of how to identify areas to be privatized from the operations of this state-owned service company, and at the same time to retain full state ownership of the base network, which forms a natural monopoly. Reform economists, however, put forward the view that even a private monopoly should be more capable of bringing about change than a state-owned monopoly. It was finally agreed that privatization of the HTC as a provider of services was inevitable. However, the really radical idea concerned the privatization of the telecommunications market itself. According to this approach, market shares are sold under the recently passed Concession Act, which means that the State deliberately endorses private firms' monopoly or oligopoly position on the market in return for a concession fee settled in a bidding process.

Naturally the objectives of privatization change somewhat according to the influence of different pressure groups on the actual decision-makers. Around 1990, the key objective was considered to be the attraction of development finance. At the same time the HTC management has always been interested in preserving its monopoly position.

Some of these questions are resolved by the Telecommunications Act, passed in 1992. The first version of the Bill was tailored to the HTC monopoly, allowing competition only in the area of so-called value added services — which are, by the way, completely dependent on the HTC-controlled base network. This version was not approved by the opposition parties or the governing parties' advisers. According to them, the HTC should be deprived of its exclusive right to use the base network without a concession, and competition should be more or less liberalized. Despite the consensus among the parties in Parliament, the final version of the Act reflects the Government's original proposal, in that it partly preserves the privileged position of the HTC. The most important objective of the privatization of the HTC became to raise revenue for the Government.[7] There are few other saleable monopolies of this size and nature. Another important consideration was the political preference of Hungarian small shareholders; thus 10 per cent of the shares was planned to sell for compensation notes issued under the Restitution Act. According to the 1992 decision of Parliament, 51 per cent of HTC shares would have been retained by the State. Allegedly, potential international buyers were willing to pay for a minority but still controlling share (30-35 per cent) only if the monopoly of the HTC continues.

A number of different pressure groups were at work in this field. The HTC experts seemed to be more competent than the officers of the Ministry of Transport, Telecommunications and Water Management or the SAT; consequently the company itself was unusually well placed to control its destiny. The lobbies acting in Parliament, with their apparent preference for greater liberalization, clearly yielded to local government interests. The Government itself was interested in raising money — although the final decision made by the SAT necessarily was a compromise between the demands of raising revenue and involving development finance. A number of legal regulations and governmental decisions were needed for privatization. Otherwise the risk taken by investors would have become so untenably high that it could jeopardize the large amount of revenue expected by the Government. Further directives were needed to implement the Telecommunications Act and the Concession Act, for example to govern the tariff system (the different call rates and interconnection fees) and the sharing of revenue between different service providers using each other's networks.

As soon as the legislation institutionalized the concession granting process, the Government allowed localities to put their networks for sale to the best bidder in tenders for local monopoly operations (LTOs); and in this way it successfully attracted foreign investment and expertise. On the other hand, SAT invited tenders for partial ownership and operational management of the HTC which included exclusive concessions rights for international and long-distance services for a period of eight years as well as local telecommunication operation for certain districts. A consortium formed by equal stakes of Deutsche Telekom and Ameritech International won the bidding and purchased 30.29 per cent of the shares at the end of 1993. The sales price was $875 million, but only a minority of that was actually invested into the company, while the majority was treated as state revenue.

In May 1995 with the new privatization law, the Parliament changed the provision for the minimum threshold of the State's stake in HTC. Now, it is 25 per cent plus one share, so the SPA could offer for sale the rest of its property. As a result of the second phase of privatization the above-mentioned consortium became the owner of 67.35 per cent of the shares by the end of 1995. When the bidding process for LTOs completed by 1996, HTC had won concession rights for 36 districts, so altogether HTC has 80 per cent market share in local telephone services.

No doubt, the achievements of the telecommunications reform and industry development over the last five years were impressive. They included the establishment of legal and regulatory framework, licensing of operators in some local areas, introduction of two competing operators to provide state-of-art cellular phone (GSM) service and attraction of large-scale foreign investment into the sector. The rate of network expansion accelerated .to above 10 per cent, and the main line penetration rate reached 21.72 per cent in 1995. (This compares well with growth rates in those OECD Member countries where network expansion is fastest, i.e. Portugal and Turkey.) However, a lot of old and new problems remained unsolved. As a recent OECD study claims, government actions should be taken in the field of telecommunications policy, developing market structures and improving regulations. For instance, the reassessing of the distribution of responsibilities between the Ministry and the Telecommunication Inspectorate, the introduction of a fully competitive market-place especially in long-distance services and enforcement of the price-cap, i.e. adjustments to bring the current price control arrangements in line with the effect intended when they were formulated (OECD, 1996). Some of these problems stem from global changes in the industry and Hungary's urge to join the European Union, but others are obvious consequences of a privatization policy which has reserved areas for monopoly service providers in order to attract foreign investors hoping for a rapid return and to increase instant state revenue through different channels.

Involving foreign finance in the manufacture of telecommunications equipment seemed an easier task. The so-called "system selection tender" for the supply of exchanges for the national overlay digitized backbone network was issued by the Government at the end of 1990. It was specified as a condition of tender that a joint venture should be formed between a foreign partner contributing the know-how and a Hungarian manufacturer. The tender was won jointly by Siemens-Telefongyár (Telephone Works) and Ericsson-Müszertechnika (Instrument Engineering). A five-year frame agreement was signed. However, they had to bid against each other every year for the quota of shipments (35 per cent to 65 per cent in a given year). It is a widely held view that this decision on the part of the Government was driven by political rather than technical or business considerations. As a consequence of this decision one of the losers of the tender, the Budapest Telecommunications Equipment Works (BHG), more or less collapsed. Whereas it used to employ 10,000 people manufacturing telephone exchanges, it now has only 3,000 employees and manufactures other items apart from exchanges. The same happened to Videoton (bidding with SEL-Alcatel of France), the other big loser, which was forced to lay off most of its staff. The Hungarian telecommunications manufacturing sector, which employed about 60,000 people at the beginning of 1990, has been destroyed.[8] The list of state-owned companies to be safeguarded and maintained by the Ministry of Trade and Industry includes only the BHG. The other companies have been written off.

4. Privatization and its impact on labour relations

4.1 Hungarian Telecommunications Company (HTC)

The telephone service, with its staff of about 22,000, was separated from the Hungarian Post on 1 January 1990, and HTC is now one of the biggest enterprises in Hungary. The process of separation did not itself entail any employment problems as the operations had already been separate at the level of facilities and post offices. Considering its existing telecommunications monopoly and the Government's (regulatory) pricing policy, it is not surprising that the HTC has always been a sound, profitable business.

Since 1990 employment in the HTC has diminished slightly, mainly owing to decentralization in the form of creating new spin-off companies. The first limited liability companies thus created mainly involved departments engaged in other than basic operations. Later companies were formed with the purpose of seeking trade investors for specialized services. (The best example of this process is the cellular radio telephone company WESTEL, a US-Hungarian joint venture set up with US-WEST.) The first spin-off companies, created through simply separating off former departments, inherited from the HTC several obstacles to thriving business such as excess staff and an outdated organization structure. It is by now accepted among HTC management that a profound transformation of the old, established organizational structure should have been more strongly encouraged. The largest of the HTC spin-off companies include EMTEL Ltd. (a network-building organization, with almost 2,000 staff initially), TÁVISZ Ltd. (repair and maintenance operations with 300-400 employees) and rural network-building organizations. The HTC has in fact remained the exclusive owner — as well as the key customer — of all these organizations. EMTEL is the only exception, as it has small shareholders other than the HTC. This early decentralization wave occurred in 1990-91, but new spin-off companies based on the regional units of HTC were formed when the company won exclusive concession rights for local services and set up legally independent companies for network development in 1994-95. Nowadays, HTC has a major share in three joint stock companies and 15 limited liability companies, while it holds minority but controlling shares (between 25 and 50 per cent) in six joint stock companies and three limited liability companies.

The HTC's double role as owner and customer has led to quite a schizophrenic situation. At the time of transformation, the parent company promised a certain level of orders, but this did not really materialize. The HTC does not interfere directly with employment matters, but it does have an indirect influence as owner in that it has to approve the annual business plans. Staff reductions are included, for example, in the requirements for profit generation or in efficiency plans. The apparent autonomy of these organizations is illusory.

Compared to other large companies, wage levels in the HTC are relatively high. Direct wage costs are in the range of 15 per cent of total costs; the rate is growing steadily, but is still low compared to the figure of 40 per cent which is usual in telecommunications sectors in the West. The general view of experts is that the overall efficiency of the HTC has been very low by international standards and it was inevitable to reduce its 1993 staffing level of 22,000 after privatization.

The company's overall labour productivity has recently improved, but this is hardly attributable to any success of the "staff efficiency programme" implemented in the HTC.

Even absolutely minimal staff reductions can record spectacular achievements when the size of the network is growing by 13-15 per cent a year. According to estimates based on this trend, by 1996 HTC staffing levels should correspond to 60-70 per cent of accepted Western efficiency standards. This growth in efficiency must naturally be supported by the replacement of old equipment by new generations of switchboards and networks which require much less maintenance per unit. The new control and information systems can also be managed by a reduced number of administrative staff.

As to the productivity figures, over the time period 1990-94 HTC has shown a steady increase; the ratio of main lines per employee grew from about 45 to nearly 80 (OECD, 1996). HTC increased this ratio mainly by its rapid addition of main lines, but also by an initial reduction in the labour force. Employment at HTC has decreased by about 5,500 within the last five-year period, but it was due mainly to decentralization measures in which former HTC employees were simply displaced into the new spin-off companies. According to experts' estimates the real shrinkage was about 1,500. There was little change in workforce during 1994, because of the provision in the agreement of privatization which requires that the current staff must remain for a period of at least one year. As of 1995, after the expiration of the agreement, no significant reduction was made (OECD, 1996). However, in the beginning of 1996, HTC top management presented an annual business plan including massive lay-offs (1,500 people, i.e. near to 10 per cent of the actual employment). Details of the implementation were not announced until April 1996.

A national company obviously cannot have a homogeneous labour market. Regional variations in wages have historically followed local wage levels. Wages are typically higher in Budapest. Moreover, qualified labour is most easily available near training centres, whereas it is difficult to hire qualified staff in remote areas because of the lack of housing mobility.

The decentralization of the HTC and its progress towards privatization was being accompanied by the emergence of competitors in the labour market. This occurred first in the areas of network building and extension switchboards assembly. Really fierce labour market competition will emerge only after the entry into the arena of non-HTC service providers. These competitors will try to attract qualified HTC staff, as will the broader sector of electronics and information technology, which is likely to represent powerful competition after economic recovery. However, the HTC's best qualified staff are already tempted by wage competition. In an effort to protect its labour market, the HTC launched a "key employee project". About 1,000 rank and file employees were identified as "people with drive" and given wage increases of as much as 70-100 per cent.

Formerly integrated in the old HTC organization, training, holidays and welfare facilities have become competitive services offered to spin-off companies. But the HTC has preserved a closer relationship with its affiliates in respect of vocational training. The HTC continues to maintain training centres and offers their services not only to daughter companies but also to its subcontractors and even to its emerging competitors (with different fees for each category). Most investment or development projects (such as World Bank projects) include a human resources development component. Both management training and further training for skilled workers have also improved. Vocational training is rather asset-intensive in this sector. For example, dedicated training bases have been established for familiarization with the new Ericsson and Siemens systems at a capital expenditure of US$1 million each. The HTC also contributes to the costs of relevant professional education in public secondary and high schools. The share of training costs in HTC total costs is growing much faster than that of wage costs. A traditional scholarship system still exists but its importance has lessened. As a result of changes in the labour market, the HTC no longer has difficulties in recruiting secondary school leavers, so it has largely ceased to grant scholarships at secondary level.

The 1990 separation of the HTC from the postal services also entailed separation from the old Postal Workers' Trade Union. Moreover, the trade union structure has been further fragmented along with the decentralization of the HTC. Independent trade unions (Workers' Council and LIGA unions emerged in Hungary during the political changes of 1988-90) have appeared at a few rural HTC organizations, although their membership is limited. The scope of their activity covers only the relevant organization; they have no say in company-wide issues, such as the collective agreement. Union density in the HTC is decreasing: it is currently estimated to be in the range of 50-60 per cent.

Trade unions have little influence on major government decisions concerning organizational changes, privatization or tenders. When the HTC was transformed into a joint stock company, the trade union tried to contact the SPA in order to conclude an "agreement on cooperation". This request was rejected on the grounds that this phase only included exercises of "spontaneous privatization"; the managements of the concerned companies were named as competent partners. The union's right to voice its opinion about the "transformation plan" was also confined to consultation with the HTC management. However, the latter could discuss only their own ideas. Company managers were not in a position to negotiate on the standpoints of the real decision-makers in the SPA and the Ministry of Transport, Telecommunications and Water Management.

Consultations were held between the union and Ministry officers in the drafting phase of the Telecommunications Act. There was no conflict between the parties. The idea of maintaining the HTC's monopolies as fully as possible received enthusiastic support from the trade unions, who felt that this would mean indirect job protection as the key areas of services employed most of the staff. In agreement with the company management, the trade union's basic aim was to ensure that capital would be raised in the course of privatization, as it was assumed that this would bring new development projects and create jobs, or at least preserve the current level of employment. The trade union failed to see the dilemma that insisting on HTC's monopoly may have contradicted the crucial objective of attracting additional finance for development: preserving the monopoly inevitably inflated share prices and concession fees (the sum to be paid by foreign buyers), and growing revenues eventually were channelled mainly for budgetary purposes. As a result, there are probably less resources left for further investment.

Although the trade union did not envisage any appreciable employment shock resulting from the privatization process either, it is fairly content with the provisions in the contracts about privatization of HTC and concession for local telephone services. In both cases there are clauses in the contracts about maintaining employment level and observing existing collective agreements for the period of at least one year. Union leaders are aware of the temporary job-preserving effect of development project and well in advance worrying about lay-offs due at the time of finishing the ongoing projects.

Wages are relatively high at HTC by Hungarian standards. In 1995 the monthly average wages were 60,000 forint (US$430); only the "banking and finance services" industry could afford higher average wages in Hungary. Wage costs are low compared to OECD countries, and that is why the company could maintain its favourable expenditure and wages per main line figure (US$400-US$500 and US$490-US$570 respectively)

(OECD, 1996) once development is completed, as some of the network-building staff will become redundant. This is already a problem area because of tasks being assigned to subcontractors. Whether or not to subcontract work is now considered a purely operational business decision, to be taken by management without any say on the part of the trade unions.

The relevant units' trade union representatives were involved in decisions to create limited liability companies. They were particularly concerned about the future financial position of the new business (looking for sufficient equity, quality of business plan, and inclusion of welfare costs). In fact all the employees were passed on to the limited liability companies when they were established in 1990, or in the years thereafter. The old collective agreements remained in force for a year or until new ones came into effect in the spin-off companies. This was a reasonable arrangement from the employer's point of view also, as it solved many problems of the transition period.

The three successor companies of the Hungarian Post, and even the smaller limited liability companies, all made their own collective agreements — provided that a trade union organization existed at the given unit. There are no unions in companies created for new operations that recruited staff subsequently (WESTEL is a typical example). The HTC collective agreement is used by the daughter organizations as a basis for local negotiations, always taking into account the financial position of the particular company. Employers insist on the strict legal default interpretation, namely that each organization must have its own collective agreement, with the powers of HTC headquarters and its trade union limited to moderation. The competence of the company managing director with respect to collective bargaining is claimed to be absolute, and not limited by interventions on the part of the owners. Partly inspired by this problem, the company level union organizations recently formed the Telecommunications Branch Union in order to conclude an industry level agreement which would cover both successor organizations of the former "Greater HTC" and newly set-up companies. Their major obstacle is similar to that of other branch unions in Hungary: there are no appropriate employer organizations in place to sit on the other side of the negotiation table, therefore the only hope of the branch union organization is to convince the Ministry of Labour to extend the collective agreement concluded at HTC as the decisive employer in the industry to the entire telecommunications industry which is, at least in theory, an option in the Hungarian Labour Code.

Collective agreements at the HTC and their limited liability companies do not include provisions relating to staff reductions. At the HTC the provisions on wage increases are renegotiated every year. In 1992 no agreement was reached about the "company minimum wage" (12,000 forint was demanded and 10,000 forint offered). While it was agreed that the annual wage bill would be increased by 16 per cent during 1993, the system of allocation between different units in the organization followed the old pattern of central wage control, with each unit's wage bill calculated on the basis of the performance and efficiency index of the unit. Similar agreements and implementation were concluded in the subsequent years. As the company trade union and local trade union officers both advocate a flexible wage negotiation system, bargaining has started again at local level. In practice, what was at stake in these local negotiations was the allocation of wages between different groups of employees. At the shop-floor level, adjustment in wage rates virtually means negotiation by individuals.

A compulsory wage bracket system to be applied to all jobs is practically ruled out by this system of wage determination. The impact of a local labour market and the old development priorities are strongly reflected in wage differences. In principle, the trade union stands for improving the position of the lower strata, reducing wage differentials, and moving towards a more homogeneous wage system. The new wage tariff system included into the 1995 collective agreement may help to meet this requirement. In fact, the HTC does not have any effective job ladder or promotion system. The old bureaucratic wage bracket system had already been abolished in the Hungarian Post. It is no more than a generalization that working for HTC means job security.

Trade unions are consulted about further training, but the collective agreements do not address issues such as the funds available for training, the targeted skill structure or the conditions for individuals attending courses. Collective agreements contain provisions only on reduced working time, consequences of in-house transfer, and exemption from the liability to pay for damage caused by workers in some special cases.

The privatization strategy was criticized by the trade union because of the lack of a well-developed employee ownership system. Considering the high asset value of the company, even a small share could be quite significant and even the management admit that this would encourage popular acceptance of privatization. (Owing to the magnitude of the equity, there is nothing to fear from the acquisition of substantial amounts of shares by management.) "Property notes" were issued on two occasions in the amount of 300 million forint and involving 20-25 per cent of the staff. (Details are treated as confidential information in the HTC!)

For the time being, HTC has not developed a detailed plan for issuing employee shares. However, the Government promised to sell the employees shares at preferential price and terms from the state-owned stock exceeding the expected level of 25 per cent plus one share, but this eventually will be only 2.5 per cent, far less than what the employees could have been eligible for according to the privatization law which was valid during the first phase of privatization in 1993.

4.2 First Hungarian Telephone Cable Ltd. (EMTEL)

The network-building department of the Hungarian Post built 50-60 per cent of Hungary's telecommunications network over several decades. As part of the Hungarian Post its network-building department used to enjoy a monopoly position. Apart from its monopoly position, labour shortages were another typical feature of the Hungarian Post in the 1980s. In addition to 700-800 full-time employees, the telephone cable department regularly hired a construction battalion of the Hungarian Army; this represented a labour supply of 400-700 people, used flexibly according to the amount of work available. Teams were also borrowed from cooperative farms, and a significant number of intra-enterprise teams (VGMK) were employed, especially at weekends. (At the busiest times eight VGMK organizations with a total membership of about 200 were active, mainly in basic construction operations. The two surviving such organizations include a team of surveyors and a team manufacturing customized products, both highly specialized and skilled.)

Since 1990 the telephone cable department has been operating as a separate business unit — the First Hungarian Telephone Cable Ltd. (EMTEL) — but it is practically fully owned by the HTC. Although 0.9 per cent of the shares are held by the top 50 people in the organization, their stakes, ranging from 20,000 to 100,000 forint, do not represent any actual rights, given the total equity value of 320 million forint. At the time of establishment, the new organization had to keep all the existing staff on their original employment contracts (which meant that everybody with a long period of service was eligible for a severance payment amounting to six months' salary) and to take over all the fixed assets.

In the first two years EMTEL performed quite well. In the meantime, however, the network-building market began to change. Construction firms that were losing their original markets made bids in the hope of gaining big development projects. The market is dominated by personal contacts rather than tangible criteria such as costs or technical capabilities, so it can happen that a project is finally implemented by EMTEL as a subcontractor of the winner of a tender. At the same time many contractors work as subcontractors of EMTEL. (These subcontracting relations go back to the 1980s when the Hungarian Post had a "supply liability" and it trained employees of third parties in the skills of network building.) The smaller private competitors have gradually been replaced by bigger ones such as the FÅZIS Co., formed by 96 private individuals with sufficient connections with bankers to finance projects costing billions of forint.

The HTC has remained the number one customer. The roles of shareholder and customer are separate here. At the time of forming EMTEL, the HTC promised orders to the value of 700 million forint a year; however, it has actually placed orders only to the value of 250 million forint. The HTC department that places orders refers to the law of fair market competition and refuses any request to give preference to HTC subsidiaries. Lately EMTEL has accepted contracts to install emergency phone boxes on motorways and it has won more than one international network-building tender. When local telephone operators won their concessions and started network development, HTC tried to limit EMTEL to take up other than HTC orders. This limitation was somewhat relaxed later and the share of local telephone operators' orders in the revenue of EMTEL reached 40 per cent by 1995.

EMTEL's revenue dropped from 2.7 billion forint in 1990 to 1.1 billion forint in 1992. Eighty per cent of its income was earned by network construction, 10 per cent from planning and 10 per cent from the sale of precast concrete units in 1990. An absolute drop in output was recorded in 1992. In the first half of the year EMTEL did practically no work — everybody was on cold weather leave — but rent payments had to be continued. This was reflected in the company profits: EMTEL ended up with a loss of 360 million forint in 1992. Help finally arrived from the HTC in autumn 1992 in the form of a loan of 120 million forint. At the same time the HTC does not fail to charge substantial rents for its property. (It was agreed that rents should be increased each year, and, in line with the agreement, it actually reached the market level in 1993.)

In April 1992 EMTEL initiated bankruptcy proceedings. Despite its serious cash-flow problems it managed to pay all its debtors before the court decision, so it finally escaped bankruptcy. Upon the request of the shareholders a recovery programme was drafted and approved after several rounds of discussions. The company's financial position seems to have stabilized. EMTEL hopes to repay the loans without any problem. In 1994-95 the business operation was fairly profitable, so that the company could compensate the majority of the losses hoarded in the previous years.

The staff at EMTEL was reduced from 1,100 at the end of 1991 to 750 by the end of 1992. The number of staff actually working on network installation was reduced from 640 to 380 (40 per cent of these were unskilled manual ditch diggers). In the first half of 1992 the method of slow and steady "headcount sinking" was used, followed by mass lay-offs in the summer and early autumn. Blue-collar and white-collar groups were affected equally, although many of the latter left voluntarily. The initial plan was to dismiss people who commuted from a distance of more than 50 kilometres in order to save travel costs, but in the end a system of selection on quality grounds was implemented. The permanent staff of the company had decreased to 500 people by the end of 1994, and it seemed to be stabilized at this level. However, this core workforce is more and more supplemented (perhaps sometimes replaced) by temporary workers, so the actual workforce was between 700 and 750 during 1994 and 1995. The company introduced "fixed-term contracts" and even "contracts for specified tasks", i.e. it prefers hiring casual workers for each construction project. As the construction sites are scattered across the country, it is cheaper to hire local unskilled workers for digging ditches and for conventional construction tasks. Moreover, the company can get rid of them without paying any severance pay when the project is finished.

Redundant employees received severance payments according to their legal entitlements; some people (30 altogether) were to receive a pension through an early retirement scheme under which three years' costs were covered by the company. The "lay-off committee" assisted in drafting guidelines and administering grievances, but it was not responsible for selecting the employees to be dismissed.

The relatively low number of grievances taken out by redundant workers may be due to the fact that many people have second jobs. The more enterprising ones set up independent businesses and made some investment while working in VGMK organizations or formal second jobs. Working for a VGMK team used to be a good way of making extra money. Many people still work for small businesses organized outside the company. Other people kept their full-time jobs and obtained licences to work as designers or network assemblers. In 1992, when it became obligatory to report any second job, 92 people — in fact all the key technical staff — declared that they had a second job. They actually do the same work as in their main job and for the same customer, that is, HTC Investment Department. Naturally the small businesses get the small tasks. This area, too, is dominated by personal relationships established while working for the company. All strata of the labour force are involved in these businesses. This is obviously detrimental to the company; it is "known to everybody" but there is no way of preventing it, frequent scandals notwithstanding. EMTEL, as the main employer, naturally tries to control second jobs with its competitors and abuses (typically theft of materials), but its efforts are fairly futile. The company chose an unusual way to discipline their moonlighting workers. Terms and conditions of taking up second jobs were regulated in the 1995 collective agreement. It introduces procedures for registration of such side jobs and appropriate penalties (including firing) in case of abuses.

The new competitor organizations are naturally interested in recruiting EMTEL employees, either as full-timers or for a second job, because their skills, information and contacts are needed if these organizations are to be able to undertake activities associated with the HTC. (The same is true in respect of technicians working on the installation of telephone exchanges. COMEX, the limited liability company formed for this purpose, has a monopoly in vain as most of the competition comes from its own employees.) Small firms are typically formed by people from the HTC. Tender processes turn out to be meetings of old friends and acquaintances.

Wage competition has developed to a certain extent between competitors seeking qualified professionals, and EMTEL must adapt to the new labour market conditions. In 1992, a wage increase was specifically aimed at paying the "market value" to the best 50 experts. In 1995, foremen and chief engineering staff in this category were paid 80,000 to

130,000 forint a month, and prominent skilled workers (such as fibre optic cable layers) were paid at the range of 80,000 forint for a month. Otherwise the average blue-collar wage was a modest 40,000 forint per month in 1992.

Trade union membership has shrunk to 240 paying members. The EMTEL trade union complains that the HTC trade union and the sectoral federation have neglected them. They pay 40 per cent of their membership fees to these union centres but do not receive any commensurate services in return. There has been a fierce debate between the HTC and the EMTEL trade union about access to one of the former corporate holiday places since the formation of EMTEL. For two years the local union has been trying to prove in law that it was built using money from trade union members now employed by the new limited liability company.

Trade union representatives are informed about the financial position of the company through informal channels. There is no formal participation, nor was there at the time the crisis management programme was drafted. The trade union has no chance to comment on subcontracting agreements.

The EMTEL collective agreement largely follows the pattern of the HTC agreement. Annual negotiations on wage increases or about other changes, for example tariff systems, are taking place when the HTC collective agreement is already stricken. Both managers and union officers are keen to take over as many paragraphs as possible of the HTC contract, because the management wants to avoid wage competition between companies, and on the other hand, the union tries to capitalize on the advantages of the better bargaining position and expertise of HTC union officers. The trade union was present at the talks on staff reductions, but the employees in fact made few claims. Many of the best workers left voluntarily, and the principle of selection by quality was actually agreed by the trade union. In particular, it agreed to the dismissal of "undisciplined" or unskilled staff. People who are laid off cease to be trade union members and have no relations with the union.

In recent years, when wages have been increased, foremen and more highly qualified workers have received larger amounts with the consent of the trade union. This principle of distribution has not been an issue at the official wage negotiations. The passive attitude of the trade union with respect to individual wages may partly be explained by the Hungarian labour law, and partly by the fact that earnings have always been determined by incomes from second jobs.

4.3 Mechanical Works

The huge facility of Mechanical Works (MW), located outside the administrative borders of Budapest, was an ammunition manufacturer before 1956. Its activities were gradually diversified to include different "civil" product lines. Oil stoves were the big hit of the 1960s (500,000 units a year). Licences were bought and enormous batches of Wagner painting equipment, telephone sets and condensers were produced for the safe Soviet market.

The collapse of the Soviet market was a disaster for all these operations. At the same time MW has lost its old monopoly on the domestic market for traditional telephone sets. This segment of the market has been invaded by the highest number of small importers and even local manufacturers. Most of the staff employed in these operations were dismissed and only some key people have been retained. In 1993, the current staff was in the range of 1,000 as against 2,500 in the mid-1980s. MW used to have two rural plants; one of them was closed and the other had reduced its staff complement from 1,000 to 300 employees by 1993. The workforce was also reduced steadily in the subsequent years, so at the end of 1995 only 550 people were employed altogether.

Telephone set production is perhaps the best surviving operation. Moreover, the different new areas of telephone development offer the only prospect for future development. In 1992, MW, together with MONÉTEL of France, won an HTC tender for public payphones and card-operated equipment. The initial order included 20,000 sets to be delivered in about a year as well as electronic control systems, again to be supplied with an international partner. MW is making other tenders in conjunction with ASCOM, the Swiss parent company of the French MONÉTEL. They have recently won tenders in Latin American countries, and now the Hungarian factory produces a large amount of components of payphones for this new market. The company is also a permanent supplier of payphones for the Hungarian telecommunication service providers.

In preparation for privatization, MW was broken up into four divisions according to product lines. The first step was to transform the whole company into a joint stock company. The SPA engaged a British consultant for the privatization process. The consultant proposed to find different investors for the different operations. (Predictably, the joint stock company as a holding organization will create smaller limited liability companies for each operation; it will then withdraw from its role as owner by gradually liquidating itself and eventually taking away the debts and dead stocks.) The tenders for investment were issued but it was closed without any results. The future of this privatization project is still insecure, the current government's plan, for example, would provide minority but controlling shares to the Hungarian Army.

The potential buyers of the telephone set manufacturing division include the company's existing French and Swiss partners in bidding for HTC orders. Consequently the managers, who are acquainted with the prospective investors, try to influence the privatization discussions that take place at the SPA. This is not simply a matter of selling out the State's share and raising capital for development. Also at stake is whether ASCOM headquarters itself or its French affiliate MONÉTEL will be the controlling shareholder. This point is considered to be irrelevant by the SPA staff (as are the company's requests concerning employment guarantees and technology transfer following privatization); they care only about the amount and timing of the SPA's income.

Investors have shown little interest in other than the telephone operations. There may be some British and Japanese interest in condenser production, but in contract work rather than its acquisition. The painting equipment manufacturing is a hopeless case, while a Swedish manufacturer may be interested in the production of commercial explosives. Company managers' expectation is high, because the Swedish defence industry wants to ship aircraft to Hungary, and in this case, in return, the Hungarian Government requires some subcontracting or joint venture agreements with Hungarian companies.

Considering this lack of interest, it may seem surprising that the Employee Share Ownership Programme (ESOP), organized at MW, was aimed at preserving the unity of the organization and acquiring it as a whole. The ESOP team was backed by the trade union (and ostensibly by the former party secretary). The management naturally resisted this scheme interfering with its privatization plans, as it could deter international buyers even if it rapidly proves to be a failure. The management evaluated the ESOP business plan as an unrealistic one, which simply ignores the small size and limited purchasing power of the market and makes unfounded promises in order to keep the jobs of all the staff. In any case, the ESOP loan, however favourable the terms, would absorb the company's profits for the next ten years and deprive it of any funds for development, for improving its cash-flow position or, indirectly, for employment growth. The ESOP proposal was not rejected by the SPA but it recommended that the organizers should discuss with investors the possibility of some sort of joint buy-out. The actual implementation of ESOP has been postponed together with the actual privatization of the whole company.

Though indirectly, the problem of employment was raised in the tender for card phone boxes. This tender was subject to the World Bank's standard selection process. This was actually intended to offer a 15 per cent price advantage to any bid proposing to retain 20 per cent of the production in Hungary. Owing to the high-tech specifications, only international bidders in partnership with a Hungarian company have the potential to participate. The basically labour-intensive production phases, which require a relatively highly skilled workforce, are to be performed in Hungary. (The Hungarian partner, with its backward research and development facilities, will not have any real chance of contributing its engineering products.) The Hungarian management is likely to be interested in long-term cooperation, and to try to make itself indispensable and to persuade the potential privatization partner to avail itself of the opportunities for low-cost, high-quality, reliable production in Hungary. There is absolutely no assurance, however, that the operations of a multinational will long remain in Hungary. The true objective of the assistance and investment of Western partners is naturally to have access not only to the Hungarian market but ultimately to the former Soviet market through their Hungarian subsidiaries.

In the Budapest agglomeration area MW is an average wage-payer. The monthly wage for semi-skilled work was between 13,000 and 16,000 forint in 1993. Middle-aged electrical engineers were hired for salaries of 30,000-40,000 forint. Wage levels at the one remaining rural location are fairly low. The availability of relatively cheap labour, well trained in assembly, is considered by the management as a comparative advantage.

The situation with lay-offs following the collapse of MW's market was not bad. Selection on grounds of quality was the declared principle for the implementation of staff reductions. Most of those who were made redundant came from the less qualified, less experienced, so-called "undisciplined" labour force. At first the staff was streamlined by people leaving voluntarily. Deliberate employment reductions began only in summer 1991. At that time 150 people were transferred to other jobs and about 100 actually left. Later another 100 employees left gradually in groups of not more than ten. Of the roughly 300 people who left MW from 1991 until mid-1993, 50 were of pension age and 80 left under the early retirement scheme; only 100 were actually given notice.

Since about summer 1991 the collective agreement has provided for severance pay, using more or less the same brackets and values as were later included in the Labour Code. As an additional benefit, those who are dismissed are free from work for the complete period of notice. (The law provides for only half of this period, but at times when there are no orders this does not involve any sacrifice for the company.) The pace of staff reduction slowed down in 1992, mainly because of the financial burdens imposed by notice periods and severance pay, especially as the remaining staff, with higher qualifications and longer service, would be more expensive to lay off. The trade union did not make any strong stand over staff reductions.

The really important question was in 1993 whether the continuity of service of people who are transferred to smaller limited liability companies will be recognized legally, that is, whether they would be entitled to severance pay. The MW management tried to include in the collective agreement a provision that no severance is payable to employees who have refused the offer of another job. But even the company's own legal consultants admitted that this provision would be unlawful, so the trade union was able to fend it off.

Staff reductions have not yet come to an end, however. It is estimated that the Budapest facility must shed another 100 employees. The rural facility also faces problems as it will not in the long term need more than 100 people. Naturally all this depends on further discussions on privatization.

4.4 A multinational telecommunications equipment manufacturer (MNE)[9]

In the years 1987-88, the predecessor factory, then celebrated as an "outstanding state enterprise", sold most of its output on the Soviet market. It supplied mainly telecommunications equipment and control equipment for gas and oil pipelines. In 1989 the management decided to divide the enterprise up into several small companies. The objective was to force the rural facilities to improve their efficiency and adopt a more autonomous business management. The privatization story thus began with the creation of entirely enterprise-owned limited liability companies. Then a company was formed with nominal equity for the machine tool-making shop; however, it went bankrupt and was liquidated rapidly. The 100 employees transferred there were taken back by the parent company. Another limited liability company formed with a staff of about 100 for equipment installation and repair services was more successful.

Discussions about financial involvement with foreign partners went on for some time. The process accelerated towards privatization when a tender for delivering exchanges to the HTC was won by the joint bid of the enterprise and the present owner in 1990. The sale of the company was finally negotiated by the SPA. As the price was pushed down by the investor so the equity share to be sold climbed; finally the multinational enterprise acquired the entire company. The actual sale was postponed until September 1991 and the registration of the limited liability company to April 1992. This delay was partly due to the fact that the assets were valued several times because of disagreements over the selling price. The issue of employees buying shares was not considered in the privatization process; neither the managers nor the trade unions raised it seriously. (In fact, the multinational enterprise would probably have accepted it. In its other Hungarian subsidiary the welfare component of the company assets was paid into a separate foundation and an ESOP scheme was implemented.)

During the preparatory negotiations, the enterprise management and the representatives of the buyer agreed to divest the rural facilities prior to the takeover. One facility manufacturing electromechanical equipment with 450-500 employees was closed before the end of 1990. Employees were compensated by 3-4 month periods of notice in lieu of severance pay. In April and May 1991 a similar facility with 400-450 employees was transferred to another local factory. The new owner did not pay a penny but agreed to take over the entire staff.

It was only at this point that an agreement on redundancies and compensation was reached with the trade unions. The terms were quite favourable, and severance pay could be as much as 12 months' average pay. This revision of the collective agreement was in anticipation of the takeover by the multinational enterprise (originally scheduled for June

1991). Basically, the management wished to present the new owner with a *fait accompli* and to sell the high severance pay as a company tradition, which naturally covered managers as well. (Compulsory severance pay was enacted only six months later in the Labour Code.) The move was successful: though this provision of the collective agreement formally expired by the end of 1993, it remained in effect for the so-called reorganization period. The management was instructed by the international headquarters to return to the six-month minimum provided by law after the reorganization period, and the re-negotiation of the contract took place in 1995.

A further rural factory was divested in May 1991. This one simply continued to supply coils for new products to the parent company as a subcontractor. It was transformed into an independent state-owned company and retained all its 700 employees. Finally, in June 1991, the last rural facility, with a staff of 450, ceased production.

The change of ownership entailed profound changes in management. At the beginning there were four managing directors (two Austrians and two Hungarians) and several Austrian middle managers. Each Austrian was assigned to a corresponding Hungarian manager, and the Austrian member of each pair had the final say. "Assistants" of other managers were nominated from Vienna. Personnel decisions about senior managers were initially made in Vienna, but this is now the responsibility of the board of directors or the supervisory committee. (This is a supervisory committee in the German sense, with actual powers; it includes trade union representatives.) The Hungarian managers are embarrassed by the uncertainty. They have no reliable information about headquarters' intentions, for example about the range and pace of future staff reductions. A business plan is available but it changes frequently.

In the central factory, employment had been reduced from 1,900 to 1,200 by 1992. Staff reductions started with voluntary leavers. The costs of early retirement for 300 employees were borne by the SPA, on the insistence of the multinational enterprise. At the point of takeover the company still employed 1,650 people. The SPA then met the costs of severance pay or early retirement for a further 450 employees to bring the total staff complement down to 1,200.

The SPA agreed to do this because of a specific employment provision in the purchase and sale agreement, which the management of the company insisted upon. Excluding the trade union from talks did not present the SPA with any difficulty: any substantial discussion was refused on the ground of confidentiality. The management was successful in persuading the multinational enterprise to accept the remaining 1,200 employees on their existing contract. The SPA might have been persuaded to back this employment requirement because it provided some sort of satisfaction (and some defence against future political attacks) to the SPA officers, who were selling the company for a heavily reduced price. Later there were discussions about how this provision was to be construed. The foreign managers included in the total of 1,200 registered inactive staff employees (women on maternity or child-care leave and soldiers). This made a substantial difference (initially 250 people), especially as following rural lay-offs the central factory had to take over more such inactive registered employees.

The employment provision in the contract was strictly applicable only at the date of takeover. At the same time the company's business plan is drawn up for five years. For the first years, losses are planned because the company will be spending a great deal on renewal of buildings, training and new equipment. Thereafter, the company must be profitable, and this will require a still smaller staff. Despite this, the staff complement is still over 1,200.

Although more than 2,000 employees had been shed without difficulty, the scale and rate of further lay-offs was an issue between the new foreign managers and the old Hungarian ones, regarding whether to keep the old production line or remove it, as the Austrians wanted to do. Maintenance of the staffing levels depended on the survival of the old technology. According to a headquarters decision, it had to be phased out by the end of 1993. The whole operation, including equipment, markets and staff, was transferred to another firm in 1995. This meant a sizeable drop in employment — more than 150 people were laid off at the time of divesting the old production unit. However, most of them were actually hired by the small firm which took over the manufacturing.

The new digital technology came on-stream in mid-1994. The HTC represents the key market, as the multinational enterprise already has subsidiaries in former Czechoslovakia and the former USSR and it wants to avoid any competition between its own companies. However, this advanced technology has incomparably lower staffing require-ments than the old production process. Apart from manufacturing, the multinational enterprise may put some software adaptation activities out to its Hungarian affiliated company. It is not specified in the HTC telephone tender exactly what percentage of the output value should be produced in Hungary; in any case, a multinational can easily circumvent such a regulation. As the same switchboards are manufactured in Vienna or Berlin, importing some components may still make better economic sense, despite the higher wage costs, than installing all production capacities in Hungary. The five-year period of the tender seems too short because production will take five years to come on-stream. However, the second tender invited in 1995 was also won by the same companies (both of them are multinational enterprises with production facilities in Hungary), so the next five-year period seems to be more secure than the first epoch was. It is also a remarkable new development in 1995, which is fairly promising in terms of employment, that the multinational company employs more and more people in its software development unit. Similarly to other multinationals in manufacturing, this company also realized that relatively cheap but well trained engineers are abundant in the country, so the content of the required "domestic contribution" has gradually shifted towards research and development projects, especially towards the field of computer software production.

The new-generation manufacturing, the expanded commercial departments, and the software development activities altogether need a staff of 300 people. However, it has been estimated that only 200 of these can be employed on the long run from the existing staff. The others, with new skills, will have to be recruited. The employees of the present central factory already include about 110 newcomers (software engineers, sales agents, solderers). The hiring policy of the foreign management actually states that only university or high school graduates who speak other languages and are not over 40 years of age will be considered. This has naturally triggered objections on the part of the Hungarian managers, as the core staff of the factory consists of people between 40 and 50 years of age. There has been a real fight to prevent the dismissal of people over 40 if they are capable of doing the work.

Attempts have also been made at retraining. Thirty Hungarian software developers received training in Vienna for almost a year. Training, both in languages and in professional skills, is a substantial investment item. As neither languages nor software skills are specific to the company, the company is vulnerable to people leaving with their new skills. As employees actually undertake training for the sake of the company, they cannot be forced to accept any modification of their personal employment contract. In the case of disagreements, the courts have already decided in favour of the employees.

The wages system has been simplified; only the base rate and two or three types of compulsory supplement are now paid. In 1993, top managers received bonuses regulated by separate contracts. Middle managers and heads of department were paid between 100,000 and 110,000 forint monthly but usually did not receive bonuses. The wages paid to blue-collar employees are not high. Young female solderers were hired for a near-minimum hourly rate of 70-74 forint. At the time the lowest monthly wage paid in the company was 11,000 forint per month. The main objective is to cut back on wage costs. The old value system has been reversed, and production workers are now clearly at the bottom of the pile. As the traditional production process is discontinued, these people are the most vulnerable to redundancy; consequently their positions are undefended. In any case, the company is a fairly average payer for Budapest, with an average wage of 29,000 forint monthly (20,000-21,000 forint for blue-collar workers and around 40,000 forint for white-collar categories) in 1953. Since then wages of blue-collar workers and salaries of white-collar employees kept in pace with the consumer price inflation and the gap between managers and employees has widened further. The company is keen to preserve its relatively good position in the local labour market, therefore on 1995 it started up a company pension fund in which the company's regular contribution on behalf of each employee amounts to 5 per cent of the actual wages and salaries.

Two trade unions are active in the company. The Iron Workers Union's membership is about 40 per cent, while the independent trade union may have no more than a dozen members. Cooperation between the two unions is smooth, and they always harmonize their views before presenting them to the management. The management has not attempted to pit one against the other. A joint committee was set up for works council elections, as required by law. However, all seats were won by the candidates of the old union.

All in all, the trade unions are satisfied with the way redundancies have been handled in the company. A staff reduction team has been set up, with members assigned by both trade unions. It has achieved considerable results with respect to early retirement and in-house displacement arrangements.

The trade unions received no proper information about the negotiations that took place before privatization. They learned that the SPA had accepted the management demand that 1,200 people should remain employed by the company, but did not receive a copy of the agreement, which was said to be confidential. If the new owner had been unwilling to comply with this provision, the unions would thus have been unable to enforce it.

Privatization has not interfered with the continuity of trade union rights nor with the validity of the collective agreement. Although the management tried to use the falling union density as an excuse for not negotiating with the trade unions, it was forced to do so because the unions collected the signatures of non-union workers in support of the union negotiating team.

In the trade unions' opinion the agreement of a company minimum wage (11,200 forint in 1992) is their greatest collective bargaining success. The annual increase (15 per cent in 1992, said to follow the inflation rate) was adjusted to the recommendations of the Iron Workers' sectoral collective agreement. The scope of trade union involvement in wage determination is limited to enterprise average wage levels and the general outlines of wages policy. In practice, however, actual changes have not followed this pattern because of the simultaneous discontinuation of extra payments. In 1992, at a time when the company had absolutely no orders, VGMKs were wound up; the total earnings of the once most privileged workers thus dropped despite the rise in gross wages. At the same time the trade unions complain that remuneration and fringe benefits for managers (such as company cars) are escalating.

5.   Conclusion: Changing labour relations

Most of the lessons of our case studies are in line with experience gained from other sectors of the national economy. The fortunes of telecommunications equipment manu-facturers, in particular, are more or less typical of engineering firms in general, because the reasons for their poor economic situation are similar: loss of previous markets, lack of finance, poor management, backward technology, overstaffing, etc. If they can avoid total economic collapse, however, recovery could stem from their involvement in telecom- munications development. Their economic prospects are even better as providers of telecommunications services. Rather than declining, they in fact face the problems of growth and new technology. Capital investment and development in telecommunications pose different questions in the field of human resources too, such as criteria for recruitment, further training, improvement of remuneration systems, and performance policy.

The case studies also reinforce earlier research findings. Enterprise managers usually try to avoid immediate dramatic reductions in employment in order to ensure a smooth transition during the legal and financial process of transformation and privatization. As far as the unions are concerned, their primary interest is to preserve as much as possible from the "achievements" of the "old" system of industrial relations. There is certainly some continuity in respect of industrial relations between state enterprises and newly privatized firms. However, the union claims are not confined to the transition period. They also attempt to resolve major issues for the longer term: to preserve jobs, welfare facilities and other employee benefits; to extend employee ownership; to secure the continuity of contractual relations between employer and employee. Owing to the tendency to overstaffing among state-owned enterprises, safeguarding the previous level of employment (or, more reasonably, "fair" treatment for people who are laid off) seems to be the least successful area of union activity.

Although the established legal framework ensures that the basic issues regarding employees' prospects after privatization (level of employment, wages, training, access to welfare facilities, and other provisions contained in collective agreements) can be dis-cussed, the possibilities for real participation seem fairly limited, depending on the actual bargaining strength of local trade unions. It is obviously in the workers' interest to transform these talks ("consultations") into negotiations, and finally to conclude a written (collective) agreement, but the sellers of the firm (managers and state officers) usually refuse to strike any binding agreement. The general economic position of the new firm (details of contracts, equity structure, business plan, production mix, further investments, subcontractors, etc.), which would generally be the subject of discussion, is not on the consultation agenda. Company managers tend to refuse to disclose such information on the ground of business confidentiality, while state officers, in the role of vendors, are more interested in securing the maximum income for the State than in industrial policy and employment considerations (HTC, MW).

From 1992, with the steep growth in unemployment, a gradual shift in emphasis towards employment issues can be detected. Such issues were stressed in the 1992 Property

Policy Guidelines (the parliamentary resolution governing the activities of the SPA). The new laws on privatization stipulated that an "employment plan" should be considered. These legislative changes were obviously stimulated by the trade unions; however, their implementation in the everyday practice of the SPA is rather contradictory. Nowadays, the SPA generally accepts valid collective agreements as part of a company's attributes, but rejects union requests to renegotiate them.

What is generally offered to employees is a minority shareholding in their company at a discount price. However, despite major union efforts devoted to making the terms of employee shareholder projects more favourable, workers' shareholdings have generally remained negligible — much less than would be needed either to exercise any influence over company affairs or to introduce a real incentive element into pay systems (HTC, EMTEL). Moreover, management prerogatives relating to the internal distribution of the gains of such projects may cause new conflicts within the company. The evolving role of the new ESOP law is also contradictory. Initiatives for employee buy-outs are sometimes based on unrealistic economic forecasts. Moreover, they may jeopardize the viability of a firm that is in a precarious financial position (MW).

In fact, most former state-owned companies have to face massive lay-offs. Newly privatized companies often take over all the employees from the predecessor organization, so the necessary dismissals or restructuring usually take place in the period succeeding the takeover. These long-postponed lay-offs and organizational changes (for instance divestment, hiving off or closure of underutilized internal service units and remote rural production facilities) are necessarily the first steps to be taken by the incoming foreign management. It rarely happens that a prospective buyer insists on employment reductions or closure of unnecessary establishments as a precondition of the takeover (MNE).

It seems to be a special feature of the telecommunications sector that agreements between the Government and buyers or equipment suppliers often include a clause about employment levels or the share of production to take place in Hungary. However, the effectiveness of such provisions is dubious, because the Hungarian parties concerned are in no position to enforce them (MNE, MW, HTC).

While the unions are usually content with the provisions for severance pay and extended notice periods, collective agreements rarely contain stipulations with regard to the procedure for lay-offs or company obligations in relation to retraining (MW, HTC, MNE). Nor can the unions cope with the situation of organizational changes that result in reduced job security (EMTEL). Employers' attempts to evade the severance pay regulations contained in the Labour Code or in the collective agreement have led them to adopt various strategies, both at the time of privatization and during the actual lay-offs (MW). At the same time the unions' position is sometimes quite ambiguous: they tend to accept the managerial argument that employment reductions should be achieved by first phasing out unskilled, less experienced, and allegedly less disciplined workers (MW, EMTEL).

The dramatic change in the labour market, namely the threat of unemployment plus trade union weakness, has undermined workers' previous bargaining position and reshaped almost all dimensions of workplace industrial relations. Wages and terms of employment correspond fairly directly to labour market conditions. The single nationwide labour market is confined to the highest strata of managers and professionals; job mobility elsewhere is quite restricted by housing costs and inflexible systems of housing tenure. Privatized firms, as a rule, pay their employees the standard local wages. It is usually in the foreign owner's interest to utilize cheap labour.

Surprisingly, changes in wages systems have tended to involve replacing systems of payment by results with payment by fixed hourly wages. In fact, the threat of unemployment is itself a disciplining force. A change in wage levels is often accompanied by a thorough reshaping of the wages system, termination of the complicated system of brackets, and removal of the means by which extra income can be earned — such as bonuses, overtime and VGMKs (MNE). The once-typical juxtaposition of the official work organization and the "second" economy is now fairly rare (EMTEL).

The retreat from binding contracts is a general problem of workplace industrial relations, not confined to newly privatized firms or small businesses. While the revised Labour Code envisages a greater use of contractual ties rather than statutory regulations, employers are unwilling to enter collective agreements. When the collective agreement inherited from the state-owned enterprise expires, the new owners often want to withdraw all the previous concessions. The employers' preference for relying exclusively on personal employment contracts is supported by a fresh ideological surge in favour of market freedom. The new Labour Code abolishes the union right to be informed about individual wages and to veto individual basic wage settlements (MNE, HTC).

Legislative changes apart, the weak bargaining position of the trade unions is also a factor in determining the emerging pattern of industrial relations. The weakness of the unions is mainly a result of the labour market environment and of their own organizational structure. At present union density is significantly lower than it used to be, regardless of whether or not enterprises have been privatized. Non-unionized plants are typically emerging in the case of "greenfield" investments by multinational enterprises and joint ventures with newly hired staff. Another reason for the "wearing down" of unions may be that many privatized companies come into existence as a result of the decentralization of large enterprises. In these small and medium-sized units unions face new problems; it is more difficult to continue collective bargaining relations with management, and sometimes even the recognition of the union is questioned by managers (HTC).

References

Central Statistical Office (KSH). 1992, 1993, 1994, 1995. Statistical Yearbook 1991, 1992, 1993, 1994.

———. 1993. Economic trends 1989-92. Employment, economic growth, investments. Mar.

———. Monthly Bulletin of Statistics, No. 1.

Government of the Republic of Hungary. 1990. Property and privatization. Aug.

Hunya, Gábor. 1996. Foreign direct investment and its employment effects in the Czech Republic, Hungary and Poland (mimeo), the Vienna Institute for Comparative Economic Studies.

HVG. 1992. "Supplement on telecommunication". 10 Oct.

Major, Iván. 1991. "Private and public infrastructure in Eastern Europe", in Oxford Review of Economic Policy, Vol. 7, No. 4 (Oxford).

OECD (1996): Review of Telecommunications Policy: Hungary Examiner's Report (29th Session of the Committee for Information, Computer and Communications Policy, 29 March 1996).

PRIVINFO. 1993. Facts about privatization in Hungary, 1990-92, No. 14.

Notes

[1] Of all the different forms of small private business introduced in Hungary since 1982, the Enterprise Work Partnership (VGMK, according to its Hungarian abbreviation) was the most widespread. In 1986, more than a quarter of a million employees of state enterprises worked overtime in these intra-enterprise "businesses", in most cases for their own organizations, to earn considerable additional income. Because of the widespread labour shortages at that time, it was in the interests of enterprises to seek additional labour sources and to evade the state-imposed restrictions on their own employees' wage increases.

[2] Statistics do not properly demonstrate changes in ownership structure. Firm registration data collected according to different legal forms of business organization show a mushrooming of limited liability companies, but these can equally be "commercialized" former state enterprises, pure private businesses or any combination of different owners, including foreigners.

[3] In 1991 privatization of 3,133 outlets worth 5 billion forint was completed. The following year 4,504 units were sold within the framework of the "pre-privatization" programme, and the state revenue was doubled (PRIVINFO, 1993).

[4] However, government officers regard state revenue as the main "success indicator" of privatization. No data are available on the progress of privatization in different sectors. Some subsectors of food processing (tobacco, sweet factories, sugar refineries, beer breweries, alcohol distillers), road construction, the printing industry, construction materials, insurance and commerce seem to be the most privatized sectors (PRIVINFO, 1993).

[5] This programme included 80 consulting firms and 700 state-owned companies, of which 30 per cent had been privatized by the end of 1992. The state revenue amounted to 3 billion forint (PRIVINFO, 1993).

[6] For example, the average telephone penetration rate (lines per 100 inhabitants) of the 24 OECD countries is 4.1 times higher than that in Hungary. Even among East European countries, Hungary ranked low in relation to telephone density. In the early 1990s: 8.7 lines per 100 inhabitants in Hungary, 9.4 in Romania, 14.2 in Czechoslovakia and 22.2 in Bulgaria (HVG, 1992).

[7] This objective was clearly evidenced during the scandalous tender process for the GSM (Global System for Mobile Telecommunications) in summer 1993. After inviting bids, the Ministry of Transport, Telecommunications and Water Management changed the conditions of the tender and abused its own rules in order to increase the minimum concession fee to be paid to the Government from US$12 million to about US$45 million. The winners, WESTEL and Pannon-GSM (including several Scandinavian telecommunications companies), are entitled to make a contract with the Government to develop and operate a new generation of cellular phones. (The loser, Deutsche Telekom, is one of the candidates for acquiring a 30 per cent stake in the HTC, so it reconsidered its initial plans in protest against the Government's decision.) For details of the story see *HVG*, 7 Aug. 1993; *Budapest Sun*, 2-8 Sep. 1993.

[8] The contraction of the telecommunications equipment manufacturing and repair subsectors is clearly shown by the data on output and employment. In 1990-91 output and employment declined by 47 and 36 per cent respectively (HVG, 1992). Although a slight recovery occurred in 1994-95 (when the annual increase of the output was 16.4 and 8.2 per cent respectively), employment steadily decreased by 10-12 per cent in each year (KSH, 1995; KSH, 1996).

[9] The company permitted publication of the research findings only if the name of the firm was not mentioned.